Solving Am
Health-
Crisis

Solving America's Health-Care Crisis

A Guide to Understanding
the Greatest Threat to
Your Family's
Economic Security

BY THE STAFF OF

The New York Times

EDITED BY

Erik Eckholm

TIMES T BOOKS

RANDOM HOUSE

Portions of this work were originally published
in *The New York Times*.

ISBN: 8129-2279-4

Manufactured in the United States of America

9 8 7 6 5 4 3 2

ACKNOWLEDGMENTS

Nearly three years ago—just ahead of the curve of public concern, which is not a bad place for a newspaper to be—*The New York Times* began an unusually aggressive and sustained effort to cover the mounting afflictions of American health care. This book includes a sampling of the fruits of that effort, which has involved contributions from nearly every section of the newsroom and every region of the country as well as from correspondents abroad—articles about technology and ethics and business and politics and, above all, on how individuals are affected.

The initial searching questions came from Max Frankel, the executive editor, and his inspired prodding has never stopped. Joe Lelyveld, managing editor, John Lee, former assistant managing editor and Soma Golden, for most of this period the national editor and now an assistant managing editor, have also been especially influential in shaping the paper's coverage of health care. Among other editors, Gerald Boyd, assistant managing editor; Linda Mathews, Phil Taubman, and Carl Lavin on the national desk; Nicholas Wade and Katherine Bouton on the science desk; Bill Stockton, Karen Arenson, and Glenn Kramon on the business desk; Mike Oreskes and Suzanne Daley on the metro desk, and Johnny Apple, Andy Rosenthal, Cory Dean, and Jon Landman in the Washington bureau have all made important contributions—and the list could go on.

In my own nontraditional role as a "player-manager," I have collaborated with all these editors in planning strategy and assignments and have also had the pleasure of editing dozens of outstanding reporters, many of whom are contributors to this book. I will let their work, identified by the author's initials at the end of each chapter, speak for itself.

Steve Wasserman, editorial director of Times Books, had the idea for the book, sped along its production, and gave useful advice throughout on the contents.

CONTRIBUTORS

Lisa Belkin [LB]
Adam Clymer [AC]
Erik Eckholm [EE]
Timothy Egan [TE]
Milt Freudenheim [MF]
Daniel Goleman [DG]
Steven Greenhouse [SG]
Peter Kerr [PK]
Peter T. Kilborn [PTK]
Gina Kolata [GK]
Glenn P. Kramon [GPK]
Tamar Lewin [TL]
Barry Meier [BM]
Peter Passell [PP]
Robert Pear [RP]
Andrew Pollack [AP]
Robert Reinhold [RR]
Elisabeth Rosenthal [ER]
James Sterngold [JS]
Mary B. W. Tabor [MBWT]
Robin Toner [RT]
Louis Uchitelle [LU]
Craig R. Whitney [CRW]

CONTENTS

Ethics and Economics

How Others Do It

States and Cities Experiment

Coping With Change

The Politics of Reform

The Clinton Proposals

INTRODUCTION
By Erik Eckholm

President Clinton's proposal for revamping health care has been compared to the New Deal and the Great Society, with vast potential to reach into many corners of American life, from the intimate relations of doctor and patient to the ability of American industry to compete. But has any debate over a major social initiative ever been argued over more tortuous and unfamiliar terrain?

Nothing is more personal and vital than how we get our medical care, and its quality. Yet, paradoxically, the discussion of how to protect all families from financial calamity, how to extend better care to everyone and how to tame the soaring costs of American medicine tends to be convoluted, confusing, and arcane. As experts debate the merits of managed competition and single-payer systems, the structure of health boards and health alliances, the ins and outs of cost-shifting and premium caps, consumers are more apt to wonder about their own fates: will I pay more for care, will I be able to use doctors I trust, will I face longer lines and scrimping on costly treatments?

The outlines, if not the ultimate consequences, of the Clinton proposal are easy enough to sketch. He wants to take the historic, long overdue step of guaranteeing health insurance for everyone by requiring all employers to contribute to coverage of their workers, and all individuals and families to pay a share, with government subsidies for hardship cases. This, the White House argues, would help not only the poor but also everyone else, providing cradle-to-grave security of coverage.

Clinton also wants to halt the rampant growth in medical costs, which is bleeding the rest of the economy, driving up the federal deficit and pushing more people into the ranks of the uninsured, by reorganizing the way care is paid for and delivered. In drawing up his plan he rejected liberal proposals for a complete government takeover of health payments as beyond the political pale, and rejected conservative proposals to simply foster a more competitive marketplace in health insurance as inadequate to the challenge at hand. Instead—characteristically for a president who scrambles so intently for the middle ground —he combined elements of both approaches, proposing a blend of market competition and strong government oversight and regulation.

Speeding up a transition toward "managed care" that is already underway, the plan would make most doctors and hospitals join together in groups, such as health maintenance organizations, that would offer everyone the same standard package of benefits. Buying their coverage through large regional brokers, or "health alliances," consumers would be steered by financial incentives to join such groups, choosing among them on the basis of service and price. Hoping to quell public concerns over the freedom to choose doctors, the President would give people the option of joining a more traditional plan allowing unrestricted choice—but by paying extra, an amount meant to reflect the true extra cost of open-ended medicine.

The theory is that competition among health plans for customers within each region would force the plans to become ever more efficient by, for example, bargaining down the prices of their specialists and drugs and avoiding excess hospitalization, surgery, and tests. In case that does not suppress costs enough, the White House wants also to establish mandatory ceilings on the growth in medical spending, keeping it in line with growth of the national economy. Giving flesh to this broad structure are a thousand intricate details, each with important consequences for one interest group or another.

As Clinton unveiled his proposal in September 1993, debate was already flaring over four aspects in particular. First was the practical matter of financing the government subsidies needed to extend generous benefits to all. With broad new taxes seen as politically impossible, Clinton discussed new taxes on cigarettes and on large corporations that stay out of the public insurance alliances, and said that much of the rest of the needed money would be carved out of future growth in federal medical programs. This was widely seen as unrealistic and officials were scrambling for other politically feasible sources of funds.

Second, and a more direct political threat, was the ire of small business owners who said a requirement that they help cover their workers, even with subsidies, would cause bankruptcies and layoffs. Yet without such a mandate, the government would have to raise all the more money to achieve universal coverage. Third was the charge that the proposal would thrust government too directly into medical care and would require costly new bureaucracies in Washington and each state. Fourth, and perhaps the most emotion-laden issue of all, was the charge that the proposed spending limits demanded too much progress too soon, and could cause an erosion of the quality of care if not outright rationing.

Through it all, many consumers wondered if they would end up paying little more than they already do for care that was as good or better than they already had, as the White House argued, or would pay more for fewer choices and lower quality, as critics charged. The White House was not lacking in powerful arguments. The promise of lifetime security of coverage had strong appeal among middle-class Americans in an increasingly unsettled job market who worry about the possibility of being written off by insurers or priced out of the insurance market. And the White House from the beginning signaled a willingness to compromise. Hillary Rodham Clinton, who supervised the writing of the plan, said the goal was to begin "a great national discussion."

Such a discussion is badly needed, but it needs informed participants. This book, drawn from the best of recent writing in *The New York Times* on the crisis in health care, closes with a section analyzing the proposal Clinton presented to the nation in September 1993—its reasoning, its vulnerable points, its potential social impacts and political prospects. But lurking behind public debate over the specifics of this plan are deeper, enduring questions that are taken up more fully in the book's eight preceding sections.

These start with an overview of the growing crisis, its causes and effects on people and business. Next is a detailed look at how the security blanket of health insurance has begun unraveling. Two sections, on the technological and economic roots of medical inflation and on medical ethics and economics, explore some of the most fundamental and divisive issues in American medicine, from the seemingly thoughtless proliferation of costly new technologies to doctors' conflicts of interests, from the wrenching decision of when to put a minuscule newborn or a critically ill ninety-year-old on a breathing machine to the fight over when insurance should pay for a promising new treatment. Though one would hardly know it from the dry jargon that usually characterizes the debate, it is answers to divisive, 3:00 A.M. questions like these that are at stake as the country reshapes its medical system.

Following sections look at how some other countries provide medical care to all for much less money, but with problems of their own; at some intriguing experiments around the United States in reshaping health care; at the striking changes already occurring in the worlds of medicine and health insurance, the base on which Clinton wants to build, and on the political and ideological landscape he faced as he put together his proposals.

Though they all first appeared, with minor differences, in a newspaper, the articles in this book were not chosen to provide a snapshot of what the press said at a particular moment. Rather, each examines issues of lasting importance, providing information and insights that should remain pertinent whatever the vicissitudes of specific proposals in Washington. Where feasible, statistics have been updated. But personal stories of patients or other individuals—included in the original article because they brought to life a relevant point—have not been altered.

Readers will not find a simple diagnosis of the country's health-care problems, nor a simple answer. What the reader can gain is the knowledge and confidence to cut through the tangled, numbing debate and ask questions that matter, the first step toward making up one's own mind.

Signs of Distress

THE SPREADING INSECURITY

LONG a gnawing worry of the poor, medical expenses and health insurance are now sources of mounting anxiety for millions of middle-class Americans—healthy or sick, insured or not. For a growing number of people, insurance status has become the pivotal factor in important personal decisions, trapping some people in jobs they do not want and forcing others to forgo needed medical care.

One spreading phenomenon is known as "job-lock": fear of changing jobs because of a medical history that, in today's more stringent insurance market, would probably prevent a worker's acceptance by a new health plan. Cancer patients or those with chronic diseases are most vulnerable. Anna Wu Work, a thirty-six-year-old molecular biologist, says it is only her health coverage that keeps her working full-time as a researcher at the City of Hope National Medical Center in Duarte, California, when she would rather spend more time with her daughters, Elizabeth, four, and Kelsey, almost one. She is afraid to leave her job or ask for part-time work because she was treated for an early stage of breast cancer three years ago and needs health insurance in the unlikely event of a recurrence. "It's a special time," Dr. Work said, "and I want to be with my children, especially since I know I might not be there forever. But the one thing I can't do now is quit, because I have insurance here, and I'm uninsurable if I leave."

As the nation's medical costs soar, more and more people are being squeezed financially or abandoned altogether by insurers. Their fears, and the vaguer disquiet of many well-insured people who see awesomely high bills for common medical procedures, are becoming important new forces for change in the nation's health system. "We've gotten to the point where everybody is scared," said Robert J. Blendon, a professor at the Harvard School of Public Health and an expert on public opinion and health policy. "Everyone has heard these terrible stories about some middle-class working person they can identify with who had no insurance and got into an awful situation."

If concerns about health insurance are an emerging obsession for America's middle class, it is stories like Brent McRae's that shape the worst nightmares. McRae was twenty-seven years old and only two months into the new sales job that made him move to California from Texas in 1988 when he began to lose weight and feel ill. After five weeks of testing and finally surgery, he was diagnosed with colon cancer. The bills were more than $100,000. But after his release from the hospital, he found out that the insurance he was still paying for through his former employer in Texas had been canceled because the employer had not sent his premiums to the insurer.

"To this day, I have no idea who kept the premiums," McRae said, "but that was just the beginning." During his time in the hospital, McRae passed his new employer's ninety-day waiting period and under the company's insurance became eligible for coverage of the six months of chemotherapy that he faced, at $700 a week—or so he thought.

"Five weeks into the chemotherapy," McRae recalled, "with a catheter imbedded in my chest, I walk into my oncologist's office, and he sits me down, puts his hand on my knee, and tells me there's been no payment because John Hancock is denying coverage, saying the cancer was a preexisting condition, even though it hadn't been diagnosed when the coverage began.

Then he said he could no longer bankroll my treatment." McRae went without chemotherapy until he got new insurance, and in 1990 had further surgery because the cancer had spread to a new part of the colon. "At one point in the middle of the whole thing, I hit bottom, between having cancer and being told I had no insurance, and I tried to commit suicide," he said. But his story has a happy ending: In March 1991, in an out-of-court settlement, the former employer and the two insurance companies paid his medical debts and legal fees. McRae had been cancer-free for a year.

Most Americans still have health-insurance coverage, either through their jobs or, if they are elderly or poor, through Medicare or Medicaid. But some thirty-seven million Americans, one in seven, most of them lower-income workers or their families, live without this basic necessity of modern American life. And tens of millions more have such limited policies that they are at risk of financial devastation. Even those numbers underestimate how many people are at risk and the scale of public insecurity. In a twenty-eight-month period beginning in the late 1980s, a Census Bureau study found that more than one in four Americans went at least a month without coverage. The proportion was higher still among black and Hispanic Americans.

Dr. Blendon pointed out that several polls have shown that most Americans worry about their insurance coverage, especially in the future. "If you ask people about their coverage, thirty percent say they're not sure their current insurance would cover a major bill, but if you ask about the future, sixty percent say they're not confident about their insurance." And, he adds, "Insurance costs are doubling every seven years, and what employers are doing to contain costs, principally, is cutting back benefits. Working people are already paying more for less coverage, and they know that in the next negotiation the company will take back more benefits."

The American health-insurance system is based primarily on

group coverage provided by employers. But as the costs of insurance policies have risen to keep pace with medical bills, employers have tried to shift more of the burden to employees, forcing them to pay larger deductibles, higher copayments, and in many cases an ever-larger portion of their own premiums. And an increasing number of working families work for companies that offer no health insurance at all. Small businesses and service businesses are especially likely not to provide insurance, and even large companies are hiring more part-time and per-day workers who are not eligible for benefits like insurance.

"Our health-insurance system is based on the idea that employers provide insurance, but more than three out of four uninsured Americans are either workers or dependents of workers," observed Nancy Barrand, a senior program officer at the Robert Wood Johnson Foundation in Princeton, New Jersey. Insurers, faced with the ever-higher costs of medical technology, are trying to limit their risks by seeking to exclude people most likely to need expensive medical care. In the process they are undermining the very notion of insurance as a strategy for spreading risk.

Insurance fears press especially hard on those who have already suffered a serious health problem such as cancer or a heart attack and find themselves unable to get any insurance to cover the condition. Cancer patients, even those who have long been free of the disease, may face waiting periods as long as twenty years after applying before their insurance will cover a recurrence. Other people who are deemed health risks may be forced to consider policies with deductibles as high as $20,000.

The rising number of uninsured families sends ripples through the health-care system. "As the number of uninsured people goes up," Barrand noted, "it affects everybody else because people without coverage still need health care. So they go to the hospital and end up getting uncompensated care, which forces the hospital to shift those costs onto those who have coverage."

Maintaining adequate health insurance has become a worry even for many workers who have never spent a day in a hospital and have always taken for granted that health insurance would be there, free, as a fringe benefit of their employment. Hope Chasin, forty-four, says she never thought twice about insurance in all the years it came with her job, but now that she works on a per-day basis at a New York record company and has no employer-paid benefits, she is obsessed with the topic. "Not a day goes by that I don't worry about insurance. When I start thinking about it in any way, shape, or form, I get too scared. It seems very bleak. I'm saving my money for a mammogram, and this sounds ridiculous, but I'm praying, please, let me not need root-canal work right now."

Chasin, who earns less than $25,000 a year, said she researched every possible insurance policy for which she was eligible when her former job at Time-Life Inc. was moved to Cincinnati. But the comprehensive coverage she wanted cost about $2,500 a year, more than she could afford, so she bought only a Blue Cross/Blue Shield hospitalization plan, for which she pays $250 a quarter and which does not pay any of her regular doctor bills.

That was the approach most families used to take, until the advent of employer-paid health insurance in the 1950s. But the affordable hospitalization insurance that used to provide genuine protection to so many families is not much of a buffer against the price of medical care these days, when bills for one visit to a specialist's office, together with fees for tests and procedures, can be many hundreds of dollars.

Even as the insurance system's gaps widen, the medical system's prices all but assume that an insurer is paying bills. And Chasin, who says she cannot afford to see a specialist about a pain in her arm that has bothered her for months, knows it. "As you get older, you realize all the things that can happen; that tomorrow morning you could wake up with some serious illness and enormous medical bills. I never thought I'd be in this situation, and now that I am, I'm noticing how many of the people around me have no insurance at all. I'm also noticing that whenever I talk about it, people get all heated up."

Dr. Blendon and most other experts believe that the number of uninsured workers is likely to continue rising. "The small businesses that are the fastest growing part of the economy universally don't offer fringe benefits," he said. "So you leave your job at Apple and go work for Apple Lookalike, and you lose your insurance." Medicaid provides insurance for the poorest families, but covers less than half of those below the poverty line nationwide. In all but a handful of states, a family of three must have a yearly income of less than $7,000 to qualify for the state-federal program. (Pregnant women, infants, and those with special medical needs can often qualify for Medicaid with a somewhat higher income.)

Children are especially likely to be uninsured. Indeed, about half of all uninsured Americans are under twenty-five, and about a third are under eighteen. "In the same period that the number of uninsured overall rose twenty-four percent, it was forty percent for kids, almost all among working families," Dr. Blendon said.

Dana Van Putten, a New York theatrical wardrobe worker, is insured through her union. But her month-old son, David, and her five-year-old daughter, Dina, have no coverage at all because Van Putten, a single mother, cannot afford the extra $400 a month it would cost to convert to a family policy. Van Putten, thirty, who is diabetic and had a difficult pregnancy, has recently been living on a $280-a-week unemployment check. She said she has been worried about insurance ever since she found out that her union coverage would not pay for the baby's hospital costs. David's bills turned out to be particularly steep because he was in intensive care for five days. "I just got the bill, which was $16,195, and I clutched my hand on my heart when I saw it," Van Putten recalled. "I'll never get that paid off, and I'll never be able to save money to buy a house. What are you supposed to do, go bankrupt?"

*   *   *

In a telephone poll of 1,368 adults nationwide in March 1993, more than 30 percent of those contacted said they or a family member had taken one job rather than another or remained in a job they wanted to leave because of health benefits. (The poll, conducted by *The New York Times* and CBS News, had a margin of sampling error of plus or minus three percentage points.) Workers with a history of cancer, diabetes, or heart disease, or those whose spouses or children need expensive long-term treatment, often find themselves locked into the job and insurance they had when the medical condition began, because any new insurer will reject coverage for a preexisting condition, either for several years or indefinitely.

Counselors at cancer-support groups tell of a Hollywood executive who turned down a tantalizing job at another studio without telling his wife, who had cancer, after he realized that the insurance at the new job would not cover her treatment. Similarly, a New York social worker recounts the story of an unhappy corporate vice president who raised capital for a new venture of his own, but gave it up after realizing that he could not get insurance to cover his four-year-old son's treatment for a heart defect.

And Dr. Work, the California researcher afraid to leave her job at the City of Hope, originally thought she could get around the insurance issue by obtaining coverage under the policy covering her husband, a cardiologist who joined a private group practice after her cancer treatment. When he joined the practice, the group policy would cover cancer-recurrence costs only after two years had passed since the end of the original cancer treatment. But when the two years were up, and they applied, Dr. Work and her husband found that the exclusion period had been extended to five years. "I did everything right, I found the lump early, I had it taken care of, but I'm still being penalized," Dr. Work said. "Insurance is supposed to be about sharing the risk, but nobody wants to share with the people who need sharing with."

Others with a history of medical problems find that insurance concerns make it difficult to find employment. Betty Moore, sixty, of Alpharetta, Georgia, said she was unable to find a job in 1970 after her first round of heart surgery to replace a valve weakened years earlier by rheumatic fever. "Everybody said they couldn't put me on their insurance because of my record, and they said I couldn't work without insurance, so I finally got a small-business loan and bought a florist shop."

At the time, Moore was still covered under the insurance policy provided by her husband's job at the Lockheed Corporation, which paid for a second round of heart surgery in 1979. But when he left the job because of a disability, she was left without insurance, and the medical debts began to pile up. "We have $1,000 on the credit card from when I had to go to the hospital for a kidney problem for eleven days, and we're paying that off by the month," Moore said. "We owe our doctor $1,600, and I still owe $400 from when I fell off a ladder in November. And then my husband owes some too. We've gotten so far behind on the doctor bills, it's going to be a while to get caught up." After calling ten insurance companies, Moore finally found a $179-a-month policy for herself, but it did not pay for any heart-related problems for the first year. So Moore had to hope with a quiet desperation that she would not need further heart surgery any time soon. She said she would not really rest easy until she reached sixty-five and the safe harbor of Medicare.

But it does not take the threat of heart surgery to worry the uninsured. Even minor illnesses or injuries can pose huge problems. In March 1991, when William Price hurt his ankle playing basketball, he and his wife, Paula, went through the informal process of family triage that is becoming all too common in their Mebane, North Carolina, household. The Prices had no health insurance for themselves and their two sons because Price was self-employed, and they decided they could not afford the available policies. So with each new medical problem, they juggled their priorities and their budget. That winter they spent thirty-five or forty dollars every two weeks for their son Ben, then seven, to see a doctor about his allergies.

More recently the Prices had to decide whether it was more pressing to take Ben to the dentist to get a cavity filled, to get Mrs. Price an ultrasound scan that might help diagnose her abdominal pains and fertility problems, or, as they decided after overnight ice packs left Mr. Price still unable to walk, to get an X ray of the hurt ankle. "My wife said I had to see a doctor, so we tried to figure out whether it would be cheaper to go to the doctor and pay fifty dollars right away, and then probably get sent to the hospital for an X ray and have to pay another bill, or just to go to the emergency room and do it all in one visit," Mr. Price said. "That's what I did, and I think it was the cheapest alternative, but the bill was one hundred forty dollars." The Prices already have more than $1,000 in medical debt to pay off, but their real worry is how they could afford treatment for an emergency. Indeed, concern about being uninsured caused a good part of Mr. Price's hesitation earlier in 1991, when he left the job he had held for five years and went out on his own selling satellite dishes.

"I really wanted insurance in case something major happened," Price said. "I looked into buying my own insurance a while ago, but it was three hundred fifty dollars a month for a family, and that's more than we can manage. I'm hoping that the place where my wife works will get a group policy, which they're trying to do. Until then, we just have to hope the family stays healthy." [TL]

HOW BUSINESS SUFFERS

THE Second World War was only a few months old. The nation was mobilizing. With millions of young men in uniform, civilian workers were in short supply, and the War Labor Board, to avoid inflation, put a ceiling on wages. So the trade unions proposed "hidden" raises. Money earmarked for raises would pay for health insurance instead. And the board gave its approval. Thus was born, accidentally, the job-linked health-insurance system that dominates medical care in the United States today, providing coverage for nearly 150 million people. Businesses soon became enthusiastic supporters, viewing company health plans as a recruiting lure and a "comfort factor" for employees. And the unions saw health care as a rich benefit to be won in collective bargaining.

For a time the system worked well for most companies and most workers, although since it was voluntary, many small companies never participated. Now, as medical costs climb, and companies and insurers seek ways to limit their obligations, the insurance system is in turmoil, and new questions are being raised about its economic and social costs. "Corporate America thought that health care was a cost they would not see, and for many years this was the case," said Eli Ginzberg, an economist at Columbia University. "As health care expanded, companies passed on the expenses in higher prices for their products. Now they can't pass them on very easily, and they are alarmed."

Arguing that health costs are putting them at a competitive disadvantage, a few big companies such as the Chrysler Corporation and Caterpillar, Inc., have even suggested that national health insurance might be a less expensive and more efficient alternative. Many economists say that if the country were starting from scratch, they would not choose to tie health insurance to employment. But the system is deeply entrenched and seems likely to survive, if only because a majority of the nation's largest companies still want it to. "Companies take a lot of pride in being able to offer health benefits; it is something they have done traditionally, and some of them have made big investments in systems that try to manage costs," said Sharon Canner, director of employee benefits for the National Association of Manufacturers. "It would be very hard to just dump out job-based health care."

Most of the proposals for change now being debated try to build on the system rather than scrap it, seeking ways to counter its adverse effects on the economy and people. Among other problems, the current system depresses take-home pay; gives large companies an advantage over small ones, which have to pay higher premiums for health insurance; provides some workers with better health care than others; and leaves tens of millions of Americans, some of them jobholders and some unemployed, with no insurance. Intensifying all of these effects, economists note, is the rapid rise in health-care costs. They contend that the job-linked insurance system, as it has been run in the past, has fueled that inflation by offering open-ended coverage. Employers, insurance companies, and government are all now experimenting with ways to slow the rising costs, in effect trying to place ceilings on what Americans spend for health care.

Among American companies, the push for change is led mostly by big, long-established manufacturing companies, including

Bethlehem Steel Corporation, Chrysler, Caterpillar, and others. They say soaring health expenses make them uncompetitive in world markets, or will once they run out of ways to offset rising bills. The outspoken companies tend to share three characteristics: their work forces are mostly people in their forties and fifties who require more health care than younger workers; their health plans cover a much larger number of retired workers than do those of newer companies such as computer or airline concerns; and they make products that must compete on world markets. "Our cars are not priced higher than others; you have to stay competitive," said Walter Maher, Chrysler's director of government relations. While Chrysler offsets most of the increases in health costs by reducing wage increases, this cannot go on indefinitely, Maher said. Moreover, he pointed out, profits are being squeezed, which might eventually dampen investment.

The biggest concern of Chrysler, Bethlehem, and companies like them is that of retirees. Chrysler has one retiree for every active worker. At Bethlehem the ratio is two retirees to each worker. Until now, companies with coverage for retirees paid the retirees' health-care bills as they were incurred and listed the outlays as a corporate expense. But under new accounting rules set by the Financial Accounting Standards Board, a private institution whose rulings are accepted by industry and government as if they were law, companies must estimate health-care costs for present and future retirees and enter these on their books. IBM entered the entire amount, $2.26 billion, in the first quarter of 1991, which cut sharply into profits. Chrysler and others were likely to spread the entry over twenty years. Whatever the method, the requirement meant damage to profits, a point that Walter F. William, Bethlehem's chairman, emphasized in a statement to Congress.

But so far it is the workers more than the corporations who are largely footing the mounting health-care bills, data show. Corporations subtract the cost increases from the money available to pay salaries. "Such cost shifting has been showing up as slower wage growth, and not as higher labor costs for employers," said Alan Krueger, a labor economist at Princeton University who has studied the phenomenon.

A consequence is that while health-insurance payments and Social Security taxes, adjusted for inflation, rose by 1.9 percent in 1990 for most of the work force, wages fell by 2 percent, the Labor Department reported. Such offsets have kept total employment costs, combining wages and benefits, from rising since 1985. But this process cannot continue, Maher said, echoing the views of many executives and their trade associations. Corporate officials expressed their alarm by noting that the health-care costs in 1989 equalled 56 percent of pretax company profits, as against 8 percent in 1965. Or they pointed out that health-care spending consumed 7 percent of total compensation for employees in 1989, as against 2 percent in 1965.

But economists charge that such comparisons are often misleading. Uwe E. Reinhardt of Princeton University says that in Germany health care is financed through a payroll tax that is 12.8 percent of a company's total employment costs. "I tell executives, 'You should be in Germany or Japan, where health-care spending is a higher percentage of total compensation.'" And Mark Pauly, a health economist at the University of Pennsylvania's Wharton School, says the real competitiveness issue is not health-care costs but productivity. If a German worker can turn out, say, one hundred calculators a day and an American only eighty, then the revenue from selling the twenty additional calculators finances more compensation for the German. "The true competitiveness issue is whether our companies are productive enough to support a high level of compensation," said Pauly. "How the compensation is split between health care and take-home pay isn't relevant."

The preference of business leaders for retaining health insurance that is tied to employment, and their recognition of the system's inadequacies, emerged in a 1991 poll of chairmen and chief executives at one thousand of the nation's largest companies. Seventy-five percent of the executives said they wanted to keep employers, not the government, as the chief brokers in funneling money into health care. But 67 percent said that while they did not want national health insurance, they did want the government to pay for the growing number of Americans who lack any coverage.

For the companies, the burden of runaway health costs is compounded by the bills for society's uninsured. When a patient cannot pay for medical care, doctors and hospitals can make up some of their loss by adding to the fees they charge patients who do have insurance. Since insured patients are mostly covered by company policies, the companies pay higher insurance premiums. Similarly, as payments from Medicaid and, to a lesser degree, Medicare have failed to cover the costs incurred by their poor and elderly clients, uncovered hospital costs have been shifted to private insurers.

The battle between corporate owners and workers over who will pay the mounting bills has made health care a major issue in collective bargaining. The AFL-CIO estimates that three-fourths of the days lost to strikes in 1989 involved disputes over health care. The American Telephone & Telegraph Company and several steel companies, for example, agreed in 1990, after strikes, to maintain health benefits. But the extra expense curtailed wage increases, which in each case were fixed to rise by less than 3 percent a year, or less than the expected inflation rate.

To help save the system and hold down their own health costs, the major employer organizations want the government to fill the gaps in the current system. Groups such as the Business Roundtable, the National Association of Manufacturers, the National Federation of Independent Business, and the United States Chamber of Commerce propose that the government provide better coverage for the elderly, the poor, and those who are now uninsured. Since many of the uninsured work for smaller businesses, there is also wide support for new regulations aimed at providing cheaper policies to small groups. "There is always the notion in the United States that government is encroaching on the private sector," Dr. Reinhardt said. "But the government is also being asked to be a shovel brigade, bailing out employers in health care."

The current system produces inequities that have increasingly given some Americans more health care than others. Generally, workers at large companies do better than employees of small ones, and unionized workers fare better than nonunion. Among small companies, there is a growing third tier. As health-insurance premiums rise, the many companies that want to pay roughly eight dollars an hour or less to cover both the pay and benefits for most employees discover that they cannot divert more money to health care without reducing wages below five or six dollars an hour, a level frequently unacceptable to workers. So such companies, including many restaurants and other service concerns, often do not provide medical insurance.

Three-fourths of the Americans without health insurance are workers or their dependents, federal data show, and the number is rising. Most of these work for small operations of fewer than twenty-five people. But some low-wage workers at fast-food chains and other big retail operations also lack health insurance. "There is just so much money to pay employees, and at some level of pay, you can't take money out of the pay package anymore to put it into health insurance," said William Dennis, research director of the National Federation of Independent Business, representing 550,000 companies, most of which employ fewer than twenty people and pay, on average, less than ten dollars an hour.

The job-based insurance system distorts the economy in additional ways. One is the uneven pattern of insurance premiums, with small companies forced to pay much more for each employee than, say, General Motors, General Electric, or International Business Machines. The national average is $2,300 a year, but a company the size of IBM, with tens of thousands of workers, can come in below average by spreading the cost more easily than a company with fewer than five hundred employees. IBM has enough healthy, young workers who do not require much medical care, that their payments subsidize the older employees, who might require more medical attention than their payments can finance. As a result, smaller companies, particularly the vast number with fewer than fifty employees, often have to pay more than $3,000 a person for an annual health-insurance policy, said Karen Davis, chair of the health policy and management department at Johns Hopkins University. That forces the companies to either charge higher prices to cover health costs or offer employees less pay, economists say. Both alternatives can make a company less competitive.

Various schemes have been proposed to reduce insurance premiums for these smaller companies, which employ more than half the nation's work force. One frequent proposal, put forth by the insurance companies themselves, would set up an insurance pool, privately operated, offering back-up coverage to insurers, who would then feel more secure about providing coverage for thousands of workers in small companies. The goal would be to simulate the sort of broadly based insurance that large companies with thousands of employees can provide, said Carl J. Schramm, former president of the Health Insurance Association of America. Ten small companies might have ten different health-insurance carriers, but each of the ten carriers would in effect sell part of the risk to a "reinsurer." The reinsurer, forming a pool that covered many employees, would spread the risk and thus lower rates.

As part of the plan, the insurance companies would not be allowed to deny insurance to a small company's employees, a restriction that is likely to prod insurance companies into trying to negotiate fee ceilings with doctors and hospitals, Schramm said. But whatever the rule changes, some inequity in premiums is likely to remain. For one thing, low-income workers, concentrated in small companies, are less healthy than higher-income workers in larger companies. For another, the costs of administering a small company's health insurance eat up 30 percent to 40 percent of the premiums, as against 10 percent or less for plans covering many more employees, Dr. Davis estimated.

The system favors big over small companies in another way. Corporations are allowed to deduct their contributions to health care from profits, a deduction that saves them billions of dollars in taxes. Small, unincorporated companies do not qualify for this tax break. "The small-company market, no matter how you cut the cards, will end up with rates that are higher than those paid by larger employers," Schramm noted.

Another drag on the economy in the current insurance system is its tendency to limit an insured worker's ability to switch jobs and still have health insurance on the new job. Economists consider such "portability" vital to the efficiency of a free-enterprise system, with workers free to seek better pay, and companies more productive workers. But switching jobs and insurance is becoming harder for workers who have chronic medical conditions or histories of ailments such as cancer. Proposed changes in insurance regulation would address the problem.

Such built-in inequities and inefficiencies have led some conservative theorists, as well as liberals who want national health insurance, to propose scrapping the current system. The conservative Heritage Foundation, for example, has urged eliminating the tax break for corporate policies, instead giving personal tax credits so that people can buy their health insurance directly.

While most companies have so far managed to remain competitive by shifting most of the rising health-care costs to employees rather than into higher prices, this approach tended until recently to make companies lazy about cost control, Dr. Reinhardt and others say. "When I talk to business, I say, 'Look, you're not using your money, you're using employees' money,'" Dr. Reinhardt said. "I've asked, 'Did you stop to think that you might be taking such and such a percentage of your employees' money and blowing it wastefully on health care?'" The money "wasted" by generous, open-ended health plans that encouraged overuse, in this argument, could be used more productively by society to support education, public works, the environment, and high-tech machinery. Or it could allow higher pay, which would eventually show up in more consumer spending.

Companies and their insurers are now trying to hold down costs with strategies such as making workers pay higher deductibles and urging more workers into health-maintenance organizations or other "managed care" plans. And while they wait for better solutions, some companies are trying to negotiate cost controls on their own. Some have tried to improve their bargaining power through service contracts with networks of doctors and hospitals. The doctors and hospitals are offered thousands of insured employees as patients if they agree to ceilings on their fees and other controls. The Hewlett-Packard Company, the computer giant that has twenty thousand workers in the San Francisco area, has such an arrangement with El Camino Hospital there. But even that big a worker pool provides El Camino with only 2 percent of its patients. "We picked that hospital because it was already a low-cost, quality provider," said Robert Hungate, director of government affairs and health care at Hewlett-Packard. "But we can't leverage the hospital much. We are not trying to force discounts."

The General Electric Company, with an aircraft-engine plant in Cincinnati and eighteen thousand workers there, teamed up with the Procter & Gamble Company, which is headquartered there, to increase their leverage with a network of doctors and hospitals that have contracted to care for thousands of employees of the two companies. But for all their size, General Electric and Procter & Gamble fail to provide most of the network's patients. "The group practice we are attempting is in an early stage, and there is still a fair amount of uncertainty about how much it will have to evolve to be effective in controlling costs," said Charles Buck, G.E.'s director of health-care management. [LU]

MEDICARE MADNESS

MEDICARE has emerged from ten years of aggressive cost-control efforts as one of the fastest-growing major programs in the federal budget. Experts see little chance of slowing its growth as the elderly become more numerous and live longer while costs, led by payments to physicians, continue to rise relentlessly. The nation's bill for Medicare, the federal health-insurance program for thirty-five million elderly and disabled people, grew 13 percent in 1992, or nearly twice as fast as Social Security, which serves a similar population.

Medicare outlays totaled $129 billion, or 9 percent of all federal spending in 1992. By comparison, military spending accounted for 22 percent of the federal budget. One of the biggest factors in Medicare's increased costs has been a dramatic rise in the volume of physicians' services used by the average Medicare beneficiary. Critics say doctors have themselves generated some of the extra business by prescribing additional and sometimes unneeded services to compensate for cutbacks in Medicare reimbursement. During the 1980s, Medicare outlays for inpatient hospital care grew an average of 9.9 percent a year, while spending for doctors' services rose 15 percent a year, quadrupling in ten years. Growth in the volume of physicians' services completely offset the effects of a federal law that froze Medicare physician fees from 1984 to 1986, the Congressional Budget Office found.

The growth of Medicare reflects several other trends as well:

• The elderly population grows slowly but steadily: 2 percent a year, or double the rate for the United States population as a whole. Moreover, the elderly population itself is aging, with a larger proportion consisting of people over seventy-five years old, who require more care than those sixty-five to seventy-five.

• Doctors' fees, hospital charges, drug prices, and other health-care costs have risen rapidly, outstripping the consumer price index for all items.

• A cutback in one type of service, such as inpatient hospital care, often produces a surge in other services; for example, outpatient care in clinics and doctors' offices.

Medicare covers 40 percent of all hospital patients and accounts for more than 25 percent of the average doctor's income from the practice of medicine. Two-thirds of hospitals report that they lose money treating Medicare patients. Doctors' incomes, which averaged $170,600 in 1991, are about five times the average for all workers in the United States, just as in the early 1970s. And while the government has moved to restrain payments to hospitals, a number of experts say the savings have been largely offset by increases in payments to doctors.

Medicare spending for doctors' services is "absolutely out of control," said Dr. Philip R. Lee, former chairman of the Physician Payment Review Commission, established by Congress in 1986 to advise lawmakers on the payment of doctors under Medicare. (President Clinton has appointed Dr. Lee to be an Assistant Secretary of Health and Human Services.) Dr. John M. Eisenberg, chairman of the department of medicine at Georgetown University, said: "I would estimate that ten percent of physician services are of no real value to the patient. A larger proportion of services, perhaps twenty to twenty-five percent, are of some small value to the patient, but it's not clear whether they are worth the cost in society's eyes."

For their part, doctors insist that Medicare payments often fail to cover their costs. To make up the difference, doctors may increase their charges to other patients and to private insurers. Doctors also complain that Medicare is crushing them with paperwork and inappropriately second-guessing their clinical judgments. "Medicare makes it difficult for me to care for my patients," said Dr. Nancy W. Dickey, a family physician in Richmond, Texas, expressing the concern of many of her colleagues across the country. "In its efforts to control utilization and cost, Medicare denigrates the doctor-patient relationship, suggesting to my patients that I am incompetent, doing unnecessary procedures, and charging too much."

The dispute underscores the broader questions being asked about Medicare among lawmakers, hospital groups, and representatives of the elderly. Has Congress failed in efforts to control Medicare costs? Has the increase in spending produced a commensurate improvement in the health of Medicare beneficiaries? In 1992 the government introduced a new method of paying doctors, with a national fee schedule meant to reduce wide disparities in the prices of specific procedures. The government has also set overall goals for the growth of Medicare spending on physician services. The system, mandated by a 1989 law, is not explicitly intended to save money at first but could easily be used for that purpose in later years. Since Medicare started paying hospitals a fixed amount for each admission in 1983, the growth of Medicare spending for hospital care has slowed considerably, and a national study concluded that the quality of care did not suffer.

Other components of the Medicare program are surging. The use of diagnostic tests and procedures has increased dramatically because of new technology and equipment. In addition, many doctors perform extra tests to protect themselves against malpractice suits. From 1986 through 1990, Medicare payments to independent laboratories doubled, to $1.4 billion. Payments for home health services have risen as Medicare prods hospitals to discharge patients sooner, sometimes even before they completely recuperate.

For the government, the administrative costs of Medicare are relatively small, amounting to less than 2.5 percent of total Medicare outlays in recent years. But doctors and hospitals say Medicare imposes a substantial administrative burden on them. After years of congressional efforts to curb its growth, Medicare is so complex that patients, doctors, and hospitals can no longer calculate how much they are entitled to receive for any service. The complexity creates countless opportunities for doctors, hospitals, laboratories, and suppliers of medical equipment to manipulate the system and maximize their reimbursement, often with the help of consultants who tell them how to do it.

Dr. Lee said that many surgeons "unbundle" services, billing the government separately for three or four procedures that should be reported and reimbursed as a single operation. A total hysterectomy, for instance, might be listed as several separate procedures, including exploration of the abdomen, removal of the ovaries and Fallopian tubes, appendectomy, and cutting away scar tissue in the pelvis.

Likewise, Dr. Lee said, doctors often bill Medicare for a more costly service than they actually perform. A doctor might charge thirty-five dollars for an extended office visit, though entitled to only twenty-seven dollars for a shorter visit. Such "upcoding" is possible because doctors have wide discretion in deciding whether to classify an office visit as brief, intermediate, or extended. In a study of Medicare records, John F. Holahan, a health economist at the Urban Institute, found that the number of claims for brief office visits was decreasing while claims for more expensive extended visits were increasing, with the result that Medicare payments were rising. In each medical specialty there has been a shift toward "the highest-paying procedures," Holahan said.

Whatever strain the federal budget experiences with the ballooning Medicare costs, the burden of medical expenses for the elderly remains. Medicare generally does not pay for outpatient prescription drugs, and it covers little of the cost of nursing-home care, which averages $25,000 a year. Households headed by an elderly person spent 12.5 percent of their after-tax income on health care in 1988, up from 7.8 percent in 1972 and 1973. As long as that trend continues, Congress will find it politically difficult to cut Medicare benefits or require any but the most affluent beneficiaries to pay more for their coverage. [RP]

INNER-CITY MELTDOWN

WHILE Americans elsewhere are living longer, healthier lives, residents of the inner cities inhabit islands of illness, epidemics, and premature death. After decades of gradual improvement, the health of the urban poor took a turn for the worse in the late 1980s and has now reached critical condition. Experts blame new depths of urban poverty and inadequate medical services for the situation. Struggling for day-to-day survival, people have little time for niceties such as doctors' visits. Poor nutrition and overcrowded housing create ideal conditions for the spread of disease. The arrival of AIDS and crack pushed chronic hardship into crisis, shattering families and monopolizing scarce health dollars.

In the past three years, cities have reported skyrocketing rates of tuberculosis, hepatitis A, syphilis, gonorrhea, measles, mumps, whooping cough, complicated ear infections, and, of course, AIDS. The number of cases is still often small, but most of these diseases were considered on the verge of eradication only five years ago after steadily declining since the beginning of the century. Many of them are virtually unknown in middle-class or wealthy neighborhoods.

Dr. David Wood, a pediatrician at Cedars-Sinai Medical Center in Los Angeles, called 1990 a "gangbuster year" for inner-city epidemics. "If you look at maps of measles outbreaks in Los

Angeles and where the poverty is, they are the same," he said. Studies also show that impoverished city dwellers with cancer, heart disease, and other serious conditions die far more quickly than their middle-class counterparts because treatment begins so late. "I never saw a woman die of cancer of the cervix until I came to the Bronx," said Dr. Carolyn Runowicz, a gynecologist at the Montefiore Medical Center. "On Park Avenue women get Pap smears, which prevent it." The death rate among the poor is also higher. In 1988 deaths from diabetes-related illnesses totaled five times higher in central Harlem than in New York City's wealthier neighborhoods.

But statistics, which at best count deaths and infectious diseases, capture only a glimpse of the big picture. They do not tally unnecessary suffering or the lifelong handicaps that result when treatable conditions such as asthma and epilepsy go unrecognized or neglected. "I've seen horrible things," Dr. Wood recalled. "Kids who have such frequent seizures that they can't go to school. Kids with asthma who don't get medications and can't play outside because they get coughing fits. It's like years ago when people with unsalvageable conditions were hidden away."

Dr. Harold P. Freeman, chief of surgery at Harlem Hospital in New York, caused a stir in 1990 when he reported in the *New England Journal of Medicine* that a black man in Harlem was less likely to reach sixty-five years of age than a man in Bangladesh. While violent crime is part of the problem, the paper said high rates of disease were the primary cause. "When sixty-seven people die in an earthquake in San Francisco, we call it a disaster and the president visits," said Dr. Freeman. "But here everyone is ignoring a chronic, consistent disaster area, with many more people dying. And there is no question that things are getting worse."

In Newark, Dr. Beatriz Arpayaglou has learned to be a pessimist. "We're seeing scenes here straight out of underdeveloped countries, diseases that haven't been seen in the United States since the turn of the century," said Dr. Arpayaglou, a pediatrician with the University Hospital in Newark's Children's Health

Project, which sends medical teams to low-income housing projects in vans fitted like medical offices. "It's really very frightening."

In the next room of the medical van at the Stella Wright Apartments, a nurse, Anne Young, was seeing Kison Chauvers, a two-year-old boy with anemia from nutritional deficiencies. The day before the team had rushed a five-year-old girl to the hospital with a life-threatening kidney infection, the symptoms of which had been neglected for several days. Her grandmother, the stoic guardian to seven children of two daughters who died of AIDS, could not get the child to a doctor sooner.

Different cities have fallen prey to different diseases. In New York City, 1,017 babies were born with congenital syphilis in 1988, up from only 16 in 1982. New York City accounts for about half the cases nationally. Newark had a 35 percent rise in the number of new tuberculosis cases from 1988 to 1989, and the pediatric clinic at Newark's University Hospital reported a fourfold increase from 1987 through 1990. In the country as a whole, tuberculosis cases have increased dramatically, largely in urban areas.

In Los Angeles in 1990 several hundred people were hospitalized for measles, and more than two dozen died. The number of measles cases nationwide rose to seventeen thousand in 1989, from a low of fifteen hundred in 1983. The city also played host to an outbreak of rubella, or German measles, which left at least nine babies with serious birth defects. Rubella is a mild illness in adults but leads to blindness in the offspring of women who catch it while pregnant. Washington, D.C., suffered a three-year mumps outbreak. After seeing fewer than half a dozen cases a year for a decade, the city had about two hundred reported cases in both 1988 and 1989. "These epidemics are sentinel events for the crumbling of our public health services," Dr. Wood said. Measles, mumps, rubella, and whooping cough are entirely preventable with vaccines, but many people do not get the shots.

Nationally, asthma rates have undergone a dramatic and somewhat baffling rise, one that doctors say is more pronounced among the urban poor. Dr. Michael Wietzman and colleagues at Boston City Hospital found that black children were twice as likely as white children to have asthma. In many studies, scientists compare black and white rather than rich and poor to eke out information about health-care differences, since it is easier to figure out race than salary from medical records, and far more blacks than whites live in the inner city. But most experts say it is primarily poverty, not race, that raises the risk. "It's mostly the social dimensions of being black," said Dr. Weitzman, now chief of pediatrics at Rochester General Hospital in Rochester, New York. "It's being poor, living in overcrowded housing, having a low birth weight, being exposed to household toxins."

Experts say the growing number of people who live in substandard housing with poor sanitation creates conditions favoring the rapid spread of infectious disease. "Diseases transmit more effectively and rapidly in crowded living conditions," said Dr. Shirley Fannin, associate deputy director of disease-control programs for Los Angeles County. "A few years ago we went out to investigate a typhoid case, and we found twenty-seven people living in one house sharing a bathroom."

As middle-class people worry about clean air and the deteriorating ozone layer, many scientists blame indoor pollution for the high rates of asthma and other diseases among the poor. In the Boston study, the factor most tightly linked to a child's risk of developing asthma was smoking by the mother, Dr. Weitzman said. Poor young women from minority groups are the country's fastest-growing group of cigarette smokers.

Living in decaying housing, 68 percent of very poor black children and 36 percent of very poor white children in central cities have blood lead levels greater than 15 micrograms per deciliter. The Centers for Disease Control now defines toxic levels at above 25, but the agency advises local health officials to take action when children have lead levels higher than 10.

Diets rich in fat and low in nutrients also take a toll. Many poor children have chronic anemia, a low red blood cell count caused by a lack of iron in their diets, leaving them perpetually tired. Once sick, poor people in the inner cities tend to suffer serious complications. Dr. Wood remembered examining a nine-year-old girl with a facial tic and discovering 20/200 vision and profound hearing loss from damage done by untreated ear infections. "She was holding her face funny partly because she couldn't see," he said. "Her parents had seen a few doctors and used up their money. No wonder she's failing in school."

For poor people in the cities, access to care is part of the problem. To be treated in a public clinic for sexually transmitted disease in Washington, D.C., a patient has to be in the clinic by nine-thirty in the morning and often must wait most of the day, said Dr. Reed Tuckson, former commissioner of health for Washington. The typical wait to schedule a pediatric appointment in inner-city clinics was several months, according to a survey done by the New York Children's Health Project, a medical outreach program affiliated with the Montefiore Medical Center in the Bronx.

But many experts say an even greater issue is the quality of care. The Community Service Society of New York polled 248 primary-care doctors in poor neighborhoods in the Bronx as to whether they offered twenty-four-hour coverage, had twenty or more regular office hours a week, accepted Medicare, and had admitting privileges at a hospital—all what the society defined as minimum components of a decent medical practice. Only six met the criteria. The society's study also found that more than 60 percent of doctors providing prenatal care could not actually deliver babies because they had no hospital affiliation; the mothers were referred to an emergency room.

"The family says, 'Yes, we're seeing a doctor,' but when you look, the care is not well organized," said Dr. Karen Burke, medical director of the New York Children's Health Project. Experts say that clinics in poor neighborhoods focus on acute illnesses and ignore routine care such as Pap smears, anemia screening, and vaccinations, which are generally less profitable.

Pediatricians are particularly worried about how early lives plagued by health problems will affect children as they age. Babies born in central Harlem are four times as likely to have very low birth weight than babies born in more prosperous New York neighborhoods. The consequences can last a lifetime, since babies under three and a half pounds are more likely to have seizures, mental retardation, heart problems, asthma, blindness, deafness, and learning disabilities. In today's inner cities, drug abuse and poor prenatal nutrition often converge to yield tiny babies.

"A kid in a middle-class suburb who has an ear infection gets antibiotics and gets better," said Dr. Irwin Redlener, director of the New York Children's Health Project. "A poor kid with an ear infection doesn't, and progresses to chronic infection, hearing loss, and language delays." In both Newark and New York, most of the preschool children seen in the mobile vans are not fully vaccinated, leaving them vulnerable to serious diseases.

Other inner-city children have been wastefully, though not harmfully, vaccinated over and over again because of a lack of medical records. At a health van in Harlem, fifteen-year-old Jewel S. had no records because his life had been a flurry of different welfare homes and schools as he and his mother fled an abusive father. The surging number of poor children and the rising costs of medicines have stymied vaccination programs, Dr. Wood said. In the early 1970s, the total cost of a child's vaccinations was under five dollars; now it is several hundred dollars.

In a study published in the *International Journal of Epidemiology* in 1990, scientists at the Washington, D.C., Commission on Public Health estimated that blacks in Washington were more than four times as likely as whites to die prematurely, before sixty-five, of heart disease, asthma, pneumonia, and some cancers. While the death rates for blacks in Washington have climbed steadily since 1982, the rates for whites have not changed. "We looked at conditions that people shouldn't be dying from in the prime of life," said Dr. Eugene Schwartz, an author of the study and the chief of the Washington Bureau of Cancer Control. "And remember, death is a very crude measure. It's the tip of an iceberg, the end of a long chain of illness and disability that we don't have a handle on."

Dr. Freeman tells of the shock of moving to Harlem Hospital from Memorial Sloan-Kettering Cancer Center, also in Manhattan, but four long miles downtown. "When I came to Harlem Hospital in the late sixties I suddenly found I was seeing extremely advanced cancer, and that hasn't changed," he said. Because they come so late to treatment, only 30 percent of women diagnosed with breast cancer at Harlem Hospital live five years, compared to 70 percent of white women and 60 percent of black women overall in the United States. Dr. Freeman has set up free cancer screenings at Harlem Hospital two mornings a week.

The fates of blacks and whites, rich and poor are diverging. The National Center for Health Statistics first started comparing black-white infant mortality in 1950, and the difference has never been greater than it is today, with black babies dying at twice the rate of white babies before their first birthday. While the life expectancy of whites rose to 75.6 years in 1987, that of blacks fell to 69.2.

Doctors involved in outreach efforts hope they will save a few lives but know these are frail, jury-rigged solutions. "We're using Band-Aids, and things are getting worse rather than better," Dr. Freeman stressed. "You have to see disease in the context in which it occurs: poor education, unemployment, homelessness, hopelessness." Dr. Tuckson added, "It's hard to tell young black men in the inner city to practice safe sex or not to smoke. They'll laugh: 'You're telling me not to smoke so I won't get cancer when I'm fifty? Hell, don't tell me about fifty, 'cause I'm not gonna make it out of my teens.' There are an extraordinarily large number of Americans who don't believe in any concept of a future and so don't believe in investing in it." [ER]

THE CRISIS OF CHRONIC CARE

CARE of the frail and chronically ill elderly, long a private burden of families, is fast becoming a public obsession and a volatile political issue as the older population increases and members of the baby-boom generation face the aging of their own parents. The nation's current system of long-term care leaves many elderly people in fear and some destitute and demoralized, in the view of many experts and families who have struggled with the problem.

A shortage of affordable community programs—a visiting aide to watch a wandering Alzheimer's patient, or a day center to provide meals and society to the frail and isolated—forces some people into nursing homes unnecessarily. It also means too little relief for the millions of relatives, usually wives or daughters, who care for the disabled at home, often at the expense of their own lives. And haunting most of the elderly is the specter of financial ruin. Accounts abound of people who watched in despair as nursing-home bills consumed the savings of a lifetime.

So far, there is no agreement on where private responsibility ends and public responsibility begins, nor on how much money government should, or could, spend to ease the burdens. In Washington and in state capitals, well-organized groups are demanding more government support. "We have insurance for retirement, and we have insurance for acute medical care," said

John Rother, the chief lobbyist for the American Association of Retired Persons, referring to the Social Security and Medicare programs. "It doesn't seem logical to leave out the thing that can wipe families out, long-term care."

Politicians are taking up the cry, but even the most sympathetic shudder at the thought of a major new government obligation, one for which the cost is certain to rise dramatically in the decades ahead. Officials are only too aware of the strains that programs such as Medicare are already placing on the federal budget. The numbers are daunting. Those eighty-five and older, who are most apt to need assistance, are increasing more than three times as fast as the population as a whole. A 1987 federal study projected that the total number of elderly Americans needing some type of help, then about 6.5 million, would climb to 19 million by 2040.

Yet the number of family members able to aid the disabled at home—still the mainstay of the nation's care system—is expected to decline, not only because of the changing demographic structure, but also because more women hold jobs and more families are smaller or scattered. Both are especially true of the baby-boom generation, whose parents are now reaching old age.

Only a minority of the elderly ever face huge bills for chronic care. People sixty-five years old have a 44 percent chance of entering a nursing home at some point in their remaining years. Only 13 percent, or about one in seven, can expect to spend a year or more in a nursing home, according to a study by LifePlans, a private consulting group on long-term care in Waltham, Massachusetts. But a prolonged stay in a nursing home or extensive paid assistance at home often means financial disaster. Nursing homes cost an average of close to $30,000 a year, and the cost is more in regions such as New York. A 1987 study by the House Select Committee on Aging found that two-thirds of single elderly people would see their incomes and assets depleted to the federal poverty level if they paid for one year in a nursing home. Half of all elderly couples would be similarly impoverished in a year.

One who knows what nursing-home bills can do is Mabel Crim, a ninety-two-year-old widow in Margate, Florida. She and her husband, Russell, a former plant manager for Standard Oil, had felt secure on their retirement in Florida, given his pension, Social Security benefits, and the $35,000 they had saved "to take care of us when we got old," as she put it. Then, at age eighty-eight Russell Crim had a heart attack and a series of strokes that left him seriously incapacitated, and he spent his last two years in a nursing home.

"The nursing home took all my savings," Mabel Crim said. "I was glad I had it and could pay it, but it left me high and dry." Once her funds were exhausted, the state's Medicaid program took over. Now, her husband gone, she maintains herself and her one-bedroom apartment with Social Security benefits and financial help from her daughters. "I get along," she said without bitterness. But one daughter, Iona Gilbert, is angry. "My mother is turning ninety-two this month, and they left her without a cent," she said. "She had daughters to help her, or she'd be out in the street. I don't know what happens to those little old ladies out there with nobody."

While Medicare and private health insurance will usually pay for medical treatment, neither covers custodial care of the type needed by those with chronic physical or mental disorders. Increasingly, private insurance is offered for long-term care, but only a small number of people have bought it so far, and policies are beyond the financial reach of most elderly people, experts say. Instead, except for the poor, chronic-care bills must be paid out of pocket. Middle-income people often pay until their assets are so depleted they can qualify for Medicaid, the federal-state welfare program for the poor. This process of "spending down" has achieved a fearful notoriety among the elderly; spouses of the disabled have sometimes even resorted to divorce so they could preserve their standard of living. For a widowed or single person, too, the quick loss of a lifetime's savings and of any chance of passing on assets to children is a wrenching blow. "Spending down is horrendous," observed Nancy Lombardo, a director of the Alzheimer's Association, who has talked with hundreds of families with a member affected by the irreversible brain disease. "It kills people."

Recent changes in the law have increased the amount that spouses, like Mabel Crim, can keep before getting Medicaid help. The rules differ by state, but federal guidelines allow spouses to keep the couple's house and, in 1990, at least $856 a month in income and at least $12,516 in assets. States may allow as much as $1,565 in income and $62,580 in assets, though most have chosen the lower limits. While advocates of the elderly cheer these changes, they say the limits still force a real decline in living standards and security on some surviving spouses. And single people are still left with virtually nothing: they can usually keep a small spending allowance and little more than $2,000 in assets. Those who are able to return home after spending time in an institution are often left with little.

The critics also argue that reliance on a welfare program, Medicaid, to meet a basic, predictable need of millions of middle-class Americans is a distortion of that program and a source of humiliation. "Here's a man who always paid his taxes, who raised four daughters, a World War I veteran, and he ends up on charity," Mrs. Gilbert said of her father. "That's the part that really hurt."

Protecting assets has become a fixation for many older people who figure that should they be incapacitated, they will need to rely on Medicaid but who want to preserve their spouse's standard of living or their children's inheritance. The improvement in the law should reduce the number of divorces, but still, more than a few widowed older people are avoiding remarriage to avoid putting their assets in jeopardy, said Fernando Torres-Gil, an associate professor of gerontology at the University of Southern California.

Although the government says it violates the spirit of the law, many people find legal ways to transfer assets to relatives or to use trusts or other devices to shelter funds. "Financially sophisticated people who are accustomed to dealing with attorneys, accountants, and financial planners can find ways to protect their assets and still qualify for Medicaid," wrote Stephen A. Moses, a former official of the U.S. Department of Health and Human Services, in the February 1990 issue of *The Gerontologist*. "Others, with less financial savvy, often lose what little they have before they learn how the system works." This means that fewer families of nursing-home patients are bankrupted than would be suggested by income data alone. But it also means that the burdens of care and the benefits of public aid are being apportioned inequitably.

At least Medicaid pays for nursing homes once people have used most of their own money or if they were poor to start. But for everyone, nursing homes are the answer of last resort. A much larger problem is the lack of home services and aid for the family and friends who care for the disabled elderly. The stereotype of callous children notwithstanding, most of the country's disabled are cared for in their own homes or those of their children.

With the aging of the population, "increasingly the caregivers are old too," noted Stephen McConnell, the director of public affairs with the Alzheimer's Association. "More and more, it's the sixty-five-year-old woman taking care of eighty-five-year-old parents." Relatives often go to extraordinary lengths before they send a loved one to an institution. Social workers say they know of too many daughters working themselves to exhaustion trying to attend to an infirm parent while raising families of their own, and too many devoted wives and husbands, frail themselves, struggling for years to provide grueling twenty-four-hour aid to a chronically ill spouse.

Uldene Ditter, seventy-two, of Ferndale, Michigan, considers herself among the more fortunate of those caring for a disabled spouse, but her daily strains and especially her financial insecurity have led her to become an outspoken advocate of change. Her husband of half a century has been in bed for the last five years with advancing Alzheimer's disease. She is determined to keep him out of a nursing home. "He doesn't have a bedsore," she said proudly. "I feel like I'm doing the right thing."

Mrs. Ditter's job is an unpaid one almost without end. She gets away for four hours on Tuesdays when a volunteer comes, and another four hours on Wednesdays when a hired woman comes, but apart from that, she said, "I'm here twenty-four hours a day." These brief hours of respite are crucial. "It just lifts me up to get out. Sometimes I get real down." She also gets help from a nurse who comes three times a week to bathe her husband. But money, and thus her own future, are constant concerns. "Just bed pads and diapers cost me $135 a month," she said. "I'm getting into my savings. You think you're doing well, then something falls apart in the house. And, of course, with him here I have to keep the furnace up a little higher."

Of fifteen billion dollars in federal Medicaid funds to be devoted to long-term care in the 1990 fiscal year, less than 3 percent went for home services. Many states and localities are now experimenting with a host of promising programs designed to help disabled people stay in the community. But overall, "there are very few services available to people caring for older relatives and friends," said Bette Mullen, the director of the women's initiative program of the American Association of Retired Persons. "And there's a lack of knowledge of the services that do exist."

Demographic and social change portend an enormous rise in the need for expensive care. The problem is not just the aging of the population, but also "the aging of the elderly population," observed Kenneth G. Manton, a demographer at Duke University. Those over eighty-five are rapidly increasing in number. At the same time, there will be relatively fewer relatives available to provide care at home. And this, Dr. Manton warned, almost inevitably means "a shift from voluntary, family sources of care to paid care" such as professional home services and nursing homes.

Now, on any given day, about 5 percent of the elderly are in a nursing home, or a total of 1.4 million in 1987, according to federal data. Three-fourths of the nursing-home residents are women, mostly widows, reflecting the tendency for women to outlive men and the related consequence that they are less likely to have a surviving spouse to care for them at home. But these numbers mask the enormous differences in the conditions of the younger and older ones among the elderly. Of those age sixty-five to seventy-four, only about 2 percent are in nursing homes and of those seventy-five to eighty-four, 6 percent. But in the eighty-five-plus age group, 23 percent, or more than one in five, are in nursing homes, according to federal surveys.

Simply because so many more of them suffer severe dementia or physical infirmities, the rapid growth of the group over eighty-five means that a rising share of the elderly will require nursing homes or other close, expensive care. It also means there will be more infirm elderly people relative to healthy elderly people who could assist them, Dr. Manton pointed out. At the same time, the tendency of more women to hold jobs and other changes in the family mean that relatively fewer children are likely to be available to help. Without a corresponding increase in professional home-care services, there could be "a deterioration in the ability of the disabled to stay in the community," Dr. Manton warned.

For a variety of economic and cultural reasons, blacks, Hispanics, and other minority groups are dramatically under-represented in nursing homes relative to the proportion of the population they make up. Many Hispanics and Asians, for example, still see nursing homes as "a strange and unnatural system," said Dr. Torres-Gil. A tradition of extended-family ties and care in the home, as well as financial concerns, has meant that the disabled from minority groups were especially likely to be kept in the community. But now the elderly from minority groups too are increasing rapidly, and traditional family ties are often breaking down. This, he asserted, only underscores the desperate need for home-care services and other alternatives tailored especially to minority communities.

One reason nursing-home costs come as such a shock to so many people is simply that they have not planned for them. Saving for retirement is part of the American way, but Americans have not traditionally thought of saving or buying insurance to cover the expenses of long-term care. Yet government policy explicitly requires people to devote nearly all available resources to such care before receiving aid. Given these clashing assumptions, it is not surprising that those who encounter the large expenses of chronic care feel bitter and betrayed.

Broader government support of long-term care costs could take the form of universal coverage without considering recipients' resources, such as Medicare, or remain linked to recipients' ability to pay. Any new program is apt to encourage wider use of private insurance by the more affluent among the elderly. Even the most sympathetic politicians warn, though, that any new federal aid is unlikely to be generous, given concerns over the budget deficit and competing social needs. More and more, experts say, planning ahead for the possible expense of chronic care will have to be a customary rite of aging. [EE]

The Insurance Nightmare

A QUESTION OF FAIRNESS

CRITICS of the health-insurance industry like to collect horror stories. There was the group of sixteen hundred real-estate agents in New Jersey who were dropped by Blue Cross. The company said their health claims were too costly. There was the executive of Aetna Insurance who left to start a small company, only to discover that he could not get insurance for himself and his employees because a woman who worked for him had heart disease. And there is the case of Kathleen Renshaw of Leucadia, California, whose family's annual health-insurance premiums soared to $16,000 after her daughter was found to have only one kidney, with about 60 percent of its normal capacity.

These critics say that such stories indicate that at least some sectors of the insurance industry have lost their sense of what insurance is supposed to do: spread the risk around. The Health Insurance Association of America counters that despite some problems, the system works well for most Americans. Spokesman Donald White said the horror stories are almost exclusively confined to small groups and individuals. Most Americans who have health insurance get it through medium to large groups, he said. "No one asks them about their health habits. Their premiums are set by the entire group's experience." White said the association is proposing legislation that would limit the ability of insurance companies to charge excessive rates to high-risk individuals in small groups or drop them altogether.

But the real question, critics say, is whether health insurance should be governed by an ethic that says, "I am my brother's keeper," or whether it should be "actuarially fair," meaning that those who are healthy should pay less than those who are sick or likely to become sick. "This is a philosophical question," said Uwe E. Reinhardt, a Princeton University economist who studies the health-insurance industry. "You have to ask yourself, what is health care? Is it to be viewed like food, where basically you say that food is every family's own problem? That is the right wing's perception of health care. It is the view of those who call patients 'consumers' and who call getting care in hospitals 'consuming health care.' " The alternative, he said, is to compare health care with elementary education, a social good whose cost should be collectively borne.

Among those favoring the idea of actuarial fairness is Dr. John Goodman, president of the National Center for Policy Analysis, a research group in Dallas that is partially financed by the insurance industry. "The absolutely fairest way, for a new buyer entering the market, is to price insurance according to expected costs," he maintained. "If you don't do that, you are forcing healthy people to subsidize the payments of sick people." He added that if some people cannot afford health insurance, the government may want to subsidize them. Picking up on Dr. Reinhardt's analogy, he compared health insurance to food. "We recognize that poor people may need help in buying food, so we give them food stamps. If we are going to try to help people out, we ought to do it in relation to financial need."

Dr. Goodman said it is unjust to spread the costs of health insurance, because then poor people and rich people are forced to pay the same higher premium to take care of sick members of the group. "If a poor person gets sick, maybe you and I would want to chip in," he said. "But if Ross Perot gets sick, that doesn't mean that you and I should give him money." Dr. Goodman said health insurance should be like life insurance. Companies would charge new applicants according to their perceived risks. But once they were insured, he said, the company should continue to cover them no matter what.

In a paper published in the *Harvard Law Review* in 1987, two lawyers, Karen Clifford of the Health Insurance Association of America and Russel P. Iuculano of the American Council on Life Insurance, made a similar argument. "An insurance company has the responsibility to treat all its policyholders fairly by establishing premiums at a level consistent with the risk represented by each individual policyholder," they wrote. For group insurance, they said, the insurer must evaluate the risk for the entire group.

Others distinguish between health risks that are no one's fault, such as diabetes, and health risks that people bring on themselves. Mark Hall, a law professor at Arizona State University who has studied the health-insurance industry, said that people who do not take care of their health should pay more for insurance. "To say a smoker should not have to pay anything more is morally indefensible." Hall added, however, that it can be difficult to decide whether, and when, to blame the victim. "Maybe we can only do this on a larger, symbolic level. We can take things such as smoking or illegal drugs—things people generally agree are bad, as opposed to something like not exercising—and impose a modest tax on them." But these arguments, said Dr. Norman Daniels, an ethicist at Tufts University, distort the very concept of insurance. "The idea of insurance is to share the risk," he said. "The social function of health insurance is to protect everyone."

Dr. Donald Light, a sociologist at the University of Medicine and Dentistry of New Jersey, said that if those few people at high risk are made to pay more, the sick will have their premiums raised astronomically in order to lower everyone else's premiums just slightly. Dr. Reinhardt favors the philosophy of the Canadian government. "The Canadians say that in a civilized society the pain of getting sick is bad enough, but the cost should be borne by society at large." He noted that he has heard many insurance executives cite an argument similar to Dr. Goodman's, saying, in essence, "I am pricing according to use. If you, society, worry about equity, let the government tax and redistribute the money." He calls that argument "von Braunian motion," after a line the songwriter Tom Lehrer wrote satirizing the rocket scientist Wernher von Braun: "Vonce ze rockets are up, who cares vere zey come down? Zat's not my department," says Wernher von Braun.

But, Dr. Reinhardt remarked, "the sad part of it is that the executives of most insurance companies vote for politicians who do not make these income redistributions." [GK]

DIVIDE AND PROFIT

PRIVATE insurers, which once spread the cost of health
insurance equally across all groups, are increasingly charging different rates for different kinds of people. The young, single, health employee and the couple who both work are
benefiting at the expense of the older worker whose spouse does
not work and who has illness in the family. All told, the difference between the highest and lowest rate paid by employees at
the same company for health insurance can now exceed two
thousand dollars a year and is expected to widen sharply in
coming years.

Some experts on health economics are troubled by such
changes, arguing that everyone should be charged the same for
health insurance. "One might call it the desocialization of American health-care financing," said Uwe E. Reinhardt, a professor
of political economy at Princeton University who specializes in
medical economics. "It used to be that this nation said we're all
in this together, and the healthy subsidize the sick, the young
subsidize the old, and so on. Now we are caving in to an ethic
that says sick people should pay higher premiums than healthy
people, and why should I be forced to subsidize someone who is
sick?"

But many insurers—the employers themselves, in the case of
larger companies—say the move away from universal rates has

been reasonable. It makes workers more aware of the cost of medical care, they say, which in theory makes them more careful consumers, just as with other purchases. And it makes the price of the insurance better reflect the employee's costs to the plan, which is fairer. "Just as workers with a spouse and three kids expect to pay more for clothing and other expenses, their higher health costs are increasingly being viewed as their responsibility as well," said Rich Ostuw, a vice president at TPF&C, a unit of the consulting firm Towers Perrin.

The change takes many forms. Workers with a spouse and children, who often paid no more for their insurance than workers with only a spouse, or even single employees, now must pay more in many plans. People who take early retirement once paid the same rate as those who continued working; now they are being charged a higher rate. Nonsmokers, who always paid the same rate as smokers, are now paying less.

Workers are also being offered a wider choice of health coverage at different prices. An employee covered by a working spouse's plan can now sometimes choose not to take insurance and instead receive a cash refund or benefits such as more life insurance or extra vacation days. Employees who want health insurance but are healthy and confident that they will not need medical care can choose the least expensive health plan. Such a plan requires only a small monthly contribution or none at all, but carries higher out-of-pocket payments when care is actually received. These plans also do not always cover as many kinds of treatments, and increasingly offer only doctors and hospitals in an insurer's network. But employees whose medical bills will be higher—or who need coverage for psychiatric care or other treatment not provided in the lowest-cost plan, or who want to use doctors not in the network—must now pay extra to belong to a "richer" plan.

Among the companies that have recently adopted such arrangements to some degree are Citicorp, American Telephone & Telegraph, Champion International, Procter & Gamble, Baker

Hughes, Chubb & Son, Southern California Edison, RJR Nabisco, Chevron, Mobil, Monsanto, and Sears, Roebuck. They are promoting the plans for the freedom of choice they offer. The changes have for the most part applied to nonunion workers; unionized workers have usually resisted.

For the last decade, employers burdened by rising medical costs have in growing numbers asked workers to pay a portion of not only their medical bills but also their insurance premiums. But only recently have a significant number begun to divide their workers into many groups, each paying a different monthly amount. "The effort to segregate the work force into more than one group is being extended to areas that traditionally have been left alone," observed Ken Sperling of Hewitt Associates, a benefits consultant.

At the same time, some insurance companies for small businesses, which once based their rates on the claims experience of a large number of people and offered everyone one price, are increasingly placing the groups they cover in different categories. Each group is charged a different rate, based on factors including occupation, location, age, and sometimes health of the members. All told, the rate for one group can be five or even fifteen times that of another group the same size. In one extreme example, a painting business in the Los Angeles area with three employees in their early sixties could pay more than five hundred dollars a person monthly, as against about fifty dollars a person for an accounting firm in Vermont with three employees in their twenties, said Richard W. Hill, a vice president at Prudential Insurance.

While a few insurers, including Blue Cross and Blue Shield plans in New York and Pennsylvania, still charge a universal rate, others say they have had to move away from it in order to retain the business of groups with lower medical costs that want lower rates. Some insurers of small businesses have also begun to exclude high-risk members of the group or waive coverage for certain medical conditions. Bob Wills, who heads an accounting and computer-services business in Enterprise, Alabama, said his insurer refused to cover an employee's two-year-old child because of a heart murmur.

To be sure, health insurance covers a lot more than it did thirty years ago. And many employers are softening the blow of higher medical costs by setting up "flexible spending accounts" that allow employees to pay their share of medical expenses with pretax earnings. Indeed, while these changes mean "it's not as good as it was, you're still getting very good protection," said Susan K. Koralik at Hewitt Associates. "You won't lose your house."

In fact, health benefits are a growing portion of an employee's compensation. That creates a problem for employers who think workers should be paid according to their productivity. "Some employers have considered plans in which the amount they contribute for medical costs is based on the employee's performance, not just on factors like family status," said Lawrence B. Leisure, a vice president at TPF&C.

The year-old insurance program at Baker Hughes, Inc., a Houston-based oil-field-services company with twelve thousand United States employees, is one of the more dramatic new plans that differentiates among employees. It includes many features adopted recently by other companies. Baker Hughes switched from two classifications—employee and employee with family— to four: employee only ($26 a month for the most popular plan), employee and spouse ($55), employee and children ($51), and employee, spouse, and children ($80). Baker Hughes offers a $20-a-month refund to employees who choose no coverage because they are covered under a spouse's plan.

The company added a $10-a-month surcharge for employees who smoke. And it awards $100 a year to employees who not only do not smoke but also pass three of four tests: on cholesterol and triglyceride levels, blood pressure, and a weight-height ratio. Baker Hughes also now offers a choice of health plans at different prices. One plan with a lower monthly rate, $7 for a single employee, has a $500 deductible before the insurance kicks in, against $250 in the plan with a higher monthly rate; and an annual maximum of $2,000 before the company starts paying 100 percent, compared with $1,300 in the more expensive plan. Baker Hughes also began to charge higher monthly rates for early retirees, who are not old enough to receive Medicare benefits. Also new: The less time an early retiree spent with the company, the higher his or her monthly payment. Whereas an active employee pays $26 a month for the most popular plan, an early retiree with twenty years of service pays $32, and one with only ten years pays $81.

All factors included, a worker covered by a spouse's insurance plan receives a refund of $240 a year, while an early retiree with ten years of service who fails the wellness checkup, has an uninsured spouse, and chooses the highest-benefit plan pays $2,292. Explaining the changes, Patsy Clemons, Baker Hughes's benefits administrator, said: "Like many companies, we had seen increases of more than twenty percent a year. We didn't want just to cut benefits. We hoped to control costs by encouraging our employees to be healthier, and we wanted to make employees' payments more in line with their costs."

Many Baker Hughes employees accept the changes. "I think it's pretty fair," said Diana Choma, a financial analyst who pays more because she covers her husband (a student) and a child under the most expensive plan. But a few Baker Hughes people, particularly retirees, have complained. "We hear from them," said Jeff Dodd, a benefits specialist. "They're worried about the cost."

Like most employers, Baker Hughes recognizes that asking many employees to pay more will not alone hold down costs sufficiently. So the company is looking into joining an insurance-company network of doctors and hospitals that offers lower rates in return for employees' business. Many other companies, on their own or through insurance companies, already offer such networks. Employees choosing a health plan featuring a network often pay a lower monthly premium and have lower payments for medical care. When such networks become better established, insurers say, the difference between the cost of using them and choosing a plan with no such arrangement will increase sharply. [GPK]

PUNISHING THE SICK

A FEDERAL appeals court has ruled that employers who serve as their own health insurers, without using a private insurance company, may change their policies and sharply reduce coverage for workers who develop costly illnesses such as AIDS. In the case before the court, an employee with AIDS saw his maximum benefits drop to five thousand dollars from one million dollars. The November 1991 decision by the United States Court of Appeals for the Fifth Circuit, in New Orleans, is legally binding in Louisiana, Texas, and Mississippi, and is sure to be cited by judges who consider the same question in other parts of the country.

In the case in New Orleans, a Houston music store with a conventional group health-insurance plan converted its coverage to "self-insurance" in August 1988 and simultaneously slashed the maximum benefit for AIDS-related claims to five thousand dollars, causing severe hardship for an employee who had already begun filing claims for treatment of AIDS. The plaintiff, John McGann, died in 1991, before the case was decided.

Before the change in coverage, the group plan provided an employee with lifetime medical benefits of up to one million dollars. When the music store limited payment for AIDS-related claims, it also made other changes to control its costs, such as eliminating coverage for alcohol and drug abuse. But the court observed that "no limitation was placed on any other catastrophic illness."

Attracted by the lack of regulation and the chance to cut expenses, American companies have increasingly dropped commercial insurance plans, assumed the financial risk of health insurance for their employees, and used their own assets to pay claims. More than half of all employees in the United States work for companies that are fully or partly self-insured, according to the Health Insurance Association of America. Under the federal law that regulates pensions and other employee benefits —the Employee Retirement Income Security Act of 1974, known as ERISA—such self-insurance plans are exempt from the normal regulation by state insurance commissioners, although they must comply with certain federal standards.

Under the federal law, the appeals court said, self-insured employers are "free to create, modify and terminate the terms and conditions of employee benefit plans without governmental interference." The appeals court concluded that a self-insured employer has "an absolute right to alter the terms of medical coverage available to plan beneficiaries." The decision was issued by a three-judge panel of the appeals court, which cited many precedents to support its interpretation of the law. The 1974 statute says: "It shall be unlawful for any person to discharge, fine, suspend, expel, discipline or discriminate against a participant or beneficiary for exercising any right to which he is entitled under the provisions of an employee benefit plan." The appeals court said this section of the law "does not prohibit welfare plan discrimination between or among categories of diseases." Nothing in the law prevents an employer from refusing to cover AIDS while it continues to cover other catastrophic illnesses, "even though the employer's decision in this respect may stem from some 'prejudice' against AIDS or its victims generally," the court said.

While the Houston case involved a company that was switching from conventional health insurance to self-insurance, the logic of the decision would allow any self-insured company to reduce or eliminate coverage for a particular illness. Under the law, the court said, discrimination by self-insured companies is "illegal only if it is motivated by a desire to retaliate against an employee or to deprive an employee of an existing right."

But in June 1993, a federal agency, the Equal Employment Opportunity Commission, declared that employers may not refuse to hire people with disabilities because of concern about their effect on health insurance costs. It also said that disabled workers must generally be given "equal access" to any health insurance provided to other employees. The new policy says that a 1990 law, the Americans with Disabilities Act, "prohibits employers from discriminating on the basis of disability in the provision of health insurance to their employees." Moreover, the policy statement suggests that an employer may not set a lower level of benefits for a specific disability like deafness, AIDS or schizophrenia or for "a discrete group of disabilities" like cancers or kidney diseases.

In the 1991 decision, the appeals court said that the store in Houston, the H&H Music Company, was trying to save money for its health-benefits plan, not to retaliate against McGann. In June 1991 McGann died, said his lawyer, Thomas B. Stoddard, who was executive director of the Lambda Legal Defense and Education Fund, a nonprofit legal organization that specializes in gay rights and AIDS. Stoddard said that the implications of the decision went beyond AIDS and could imperil access to health care for anyone who happens to develop a catastrophic illness. "This case demonstrates the need for total reform of the American health-care system," claimed Stoddard, who added at the time that his organization would appeal to the United States Supreme Court. (In November 1992, the Supreme Court declined to hear an appeal of the McGann case, so the New Orleans ruling stands. But the Equal Opportunity Commission may challenge similar actions by employers in the future.)

"Employers like H&H Music choose to escape government regulation by adopting self-insured group health plans," Stoddard said. "Such plans are not subject to state regulation, and if this decision stands, they are not subject to much federal regulation either. Under this decision, self-insured employers can be as discriminatory or mean-spirited as they want in excluding an illness from health-insurance coverage."

Mark A. Huvard of Houston, a lawyer for H&H Music, said the company cut back coverage of other services when it limited claims related to AIDS. For example, he said, the company eliminated coverage for treatment of alcohol and drug abuse. Huvard emphasized that the company, which has several hundred employees, was not retaliating against McGann and had tried to accommodate his needs while he was able to work. Employers would not offer health-insurance benefits if they were required to provide the same benefits forever, he said. "Who is going to offer health benefits if you can never change the terms?" Huvard asked. "Health benefits are not a property right. The benefits and the premiums are predicated on claims experience."

William S. Custer, research director of the Employee Benefit Research Institute, a public-policy group in Washington, said that "an increasing number of companies are moving toward self-insurance." He listed four reasons for the trend: (1) There is virtually no state regulation of self-insured health benefit plans; (2) a self-insured company keeps dividends and other returns on the investment of money that it sets aside to pay health claims for employees; (3) a self-insured company is exempt from state taxes on insurance premiums, which are levied in most states; (4) a self-insured company can be more flexible than a private insurance company in designing benefits to meet the needs of employees.

"Self-insured companies are regulated by ERISA," Custer said, "but ERISA grants employers more latitude to design the benefit package than states grant to private health insurers." Nothing in the federal law specifies the benefits that must be offered to employees by a self-insured company, he added. By contrast, there are hundreds of state laws requiring coverage of specific services in insurance offered to groups of employees by commercial insurers or by Blue Cross and Blue Shield plans.

Stoddard, noting that McGann was homosexual, said: "It comes as no surprise that this issue arose first in the context of AIDS, but the principle at stake applies equally to leukemia, cancer, multiple sclerosis, and other catastrophic illnesses. Self-insurance is the route to discrimination for employers." [RP]

THE BETRAYAL

AT LEAST twenty-three large companies have abandoned the health benefits that they were providing to thousands of retired employees. Dozens more have announced that they will not provide coverage for future retirees, and most employers who still offer the benefits are reducing their share of the costs, which have been climbing steeply. On January 1, 1993, a new accounting rule went into effect that forces employers to subtract from their profits the future costs of providing benefits to retirees.

The Primerica Corporation, a large financial-services concern that grew out of the former American Can Company, set December 23, 1992, as the deadline for sixteen hundred retirees to agree either to pay the full cost of continuing coverage or to go without it. Groups of retirees from some companies, including Primerica, McDonnell Douglas, the aerospace concern, and Unisys, the computer maker, have initiated class-action lawsuits contending that the changes violate the terms of the companies' retirement agreements. When retiree health benefits are offered, they may include a continuation of previous benefits for retirees under sixty-five and, for those sixty-five and older, policies that fill gaps in the federal Medicare program.

Some retirees were shaken by the turn of events. "They told

us, 'Either you take it by December twenty-third, or you drop out and cannot be reinstated,'" said Marie Esposito, a sixty-eight-year-old retired American Can executive secretary in Brooklyn. "Was it a scare tactic? If it is, they're doing a good job on me. I'm single. I live alone. I have no one I can turn to." Esposito, who worked at American Can for nineteen years until her department was shut down, said medicine to treat her blood pressure and stomach ulcers costs $177.67 a month, of which she was paying $17.77 at the time of Primerica's action. Continuing the same level of coverage would now cost $144 a month, swallowing most of her $240-a-month pension. "I can't swing the $144 for medical coverage, which I desperately need."

Under the new accounting rule, Financial Accounting Standard 106, employers must put a value on future retiree health costs and combine them with current medical costs as an expense. Previously, companies were required to recognize only the cost of benefits they had actually paid. Although the cash expenditure does not increase, the resulting annual expense must be subtracted from income in a company's financial reports. This expense can rise sharply under the new rule, often quadrupling the reported health-care costs for industrial companies that have many older employees or whose retirees were promised generous benefits. The new rule thus has the effect of reducing a company's annual income, a figure that is closely watched by securities analysts and investors.

The new accounting rule was intended to make a company's health-care liabilities clear to investors. It allowed companies to take a single charge against earnings before the first quarter of 1993, or to spread the charges over twenty years. As a result of the rule, the Ford Motor Company said it would take a $7.5 billion charge against its earnings in 1992. General Motors estimated that it must account for $16 billion to $24 billion of benefits.

Advocates for retirees have accused employers of using the

new rule as an excuse to shirk their obligations. "Companies have had several years' notice that they would have to comply with the accounting rule," said Cathy Ventrell-Monsees, a workers' rights manager at the American Association of Retired Persons. "To come out in the last quarter of 1992 and say, 'We are compelled to eliminate benefits because of F.A.S. 106 accounting,' is the weakest excuse for hurting people just to save money."

Rep. Ron Wyden, an Oregon Democrat who is a member of the House Select Committee on Aging, has asked the General Accounting Office to investigate the cancellation of retiree health benefits. "My sense is that we're going to see more and more scheming to use F.A.S. 106 and other accounting sleight of hand to dump seniors and get out from under paying health benefits," he said. Alain C. Enthoven, a health economist and professor of management at Stanford University, said that curtailing retiree benefits was "a very unfortunate consequence of costs being out of control." The cutbacks underline the urgency of fixing the health-care system, he said.

Unisys announced in November 1992 that it would phase out contributions to the medical plans of its retirees over the next three years, and McDonnell Douglas said in October that it would pay health benefits for salaried retirees from surplus pension funds, but only for the next four years. That will cut in half the approximately $1.2 billion accounting charge that McDonnell Douglas would have had to take. In the Primerica case, retirees were told in October 1992 that they had to decide whether to accept any of three benefits packages the company had arranged, to take advantage of a group rate. But even under the most expensive of those plans, retirees' medical coverage will be reduced. Instead of $10,000 in free life insurance, they can buy a $2,000 life-insurance policy. A Primerica spokeswoman conceded that the new policy would be "expensive."

Primerica, which is based in New York, has not said how much it would cost to continue to pay retiree benefits, but said that such benefits had not been a major expense in the past. In 1991 it spent $8.7 million for medical benefits for retirees, including the American Can group. That is less than the 1991 compensation package of Primerica's chief executive, Sanford I. Weill, which compensation expert Graef S. Crystal estimates at about $10.2 million in stock options and $2.2 million in salary and bonuses. It is also less than 2 percent of Primerica's profits in 1991 of $478 million on revenues of $6.61 billion. Large companies spent $2,345 for each retiree, on average, for health costs in 1991, said Patricia Wilson, a principal with A. Foster Higgins, a benefits consulting firm.

Like other companies, Primerica had previously tried to shift part of its medical costs to retirees. It began asking retirees to pay more for benefits shortly after Weill acquired the company in a 1988 merger with his Commercial Credit Group, Inc. The dispute involves 1,600 American Can retirees who say they had been promised certain benefits. Another 6,200 retirees of Primerica already pay their own way. Primerica raised the monthly premium paid by the American Can retirees to fifty dollars, from five dollars in January 1989. Trying to block the increase, the retirees and a group of former executives, including William F. May, American Can's chairman from 1965 to 1980, filed a class-action lawsuit in the United States District Court in Newark charging that they had been assured of receiving the five-dollar-a-month medical package until they died, when their heirs would then get ten thousand dollars in life insurance. But Primerica said the terms of the agreement allowed it to cut or end the benefits. A booklet describing the health plan said the company "expects to continue this Plan indefinitely, but necessarily reserves the right to amend, modify, or discontinue the Plan in the future in conformity with applicable legislation."

Jack McGoldrick, a retired American Can executive and a party to the lawsuit who had helped prepare the plan descriptions, said the clause meant only that changes might be made if required by new laws. The next paragraph said that "full consideration will be given to appropriate modification" if the federal government changed the Medicare program. The company argued that the wording allowed unrestricted changes. As of May 1993 the courts had not yet resolved the dispute. [MF]

INDUSTRY TURMOIL

A DINOSAUR sat on the desk of Carl J. Schramm, who was in his final days as president of the Health Insurance Association of America. The plastic toy was an apt symbol of an industry struggling to save itself from extinction as the political climate changes. Schramm, chief lobbyist and spokesman for the nation's commercial health-insurance companies, said many people tell him "this is an industry of dinosaurs."

The trade association, often perceived in Washington and elsewhere as a symbol of intransigence, is trying to deal with tumultuous economic, social, and political changes shaking the worlds of health care and insurance. But it is not easy for a risk-averse industry whose culture and mentality have been shaped by actuaries. In a break from past practice, the Health Insurance Association, representing 270 commercial insurers, has called for a new federal law that would require coverage of all Americans, define a basic set of benefits, and limit tax breaks for the purchase of its own product, health insurance.

The association, founded in 1956, often seems to be on the defensive, under siege from consumers, labor unions, state regulators, members of Congress, state legislators, and other politicians. Critics say the industry wastes billions of dollars on overhead costs. In addition, they denounce the industry for raising premiums, cutting coverage, and discriminating against people with potentially expensive medical conditions, the very people who most need insurance.

Through aggressive lobbying and advertising, the association appears, for the moment, to have bested liberal Democrats such as Rep. Marty Russo of Illinois, who wanted to establish a system of national health insurance managed and financed mainly by the government. But the insurers know that bigger battles are coming, and their new proposal signals a willingness to work with President Bill Clinton.

Schramm, a former health-policy researcher, resigned at the end of 1992, after five and a half years as president of the association, to become executive vice president of Fortis, Inc., the American arm of an international insurance and financial-services company. His successor is Bill Gradison, a former Republican member of Congress from Ohio. That is appropriate. The insurance industry and its trade association are entering one of the biggest political battles of the decade as Congress joins Clinton in trying to revamp the nation's health-care system.

The insurers' new proposal reflects a commitment to controlling health costs and providing coverage for all people, the main objectives of Clinton's health program. A requirement for universal coverage would help thirty-seven million people with no health insurance, but it would also create a big, new market for private insurers. The proposed limit on tax-free health benefits is not in the insurers' short-term interest, but they find it more palatable than efforts to control costs directly through federal regulation. (Under the association's proposal, employees would have to pay income tax on any health benefits exceeding the value of a standard health plan to be defined later.)

While the association's proposal might seem to imply unity among member companies, in fact the industry no longer speaks with a single voice. Between mid-1992 and the end of 1992, three big companies, Cigna, Aetna, and Metropolitan Life, announced that they were withdrawing from the association. The three said they believed they could be more effective in lobbying, public advocacy, and building coalitions outside the association.

There is also a widespread perception of tension between big and small companies inside the association, where each member has one vote regardless of size.

The three defectors have a strong commitment to "managed care," in which insurers coordinate networks of doctors and hospitals serving large groups of workers and their dependents. The association appreciates the importance of such networks and, in recent years, has placed more emphasis on managed care. But it apparently did not move fast enough to satisfy all the big companies. The trade group also had to consider the needs of smaller companies that still emphasize conventional forms of insurance and have difficulty making the big investments needed to organize managed-care networks.

Michael J. Morrissey, chairman of the board of the Firemark Group, an insurance research and consulting concern in Parsippany, New Jersey, suggests another reason for tension between the big insurers and some of the smaller companies. The big companies, he said, are more willing to accept laws that spread the cost of health insurance across all members of a community and prohibit insurers from charging extremely high premiums for people who are deemed to be at high risk or have chronic ailments such as diabetes.

Several states have passed laws limiting variation in health-insurance premiums, and many members of Congress favor federal legislation to require such "community rating," as it is known. "Most big companies feel that community rating is inevitable," Morrissey said. "They want to be part of shaping that process, rather than fighting it." Some of the small insurance companies have found a lucrative market by distinguishing good risks from bad ones and refusing to write coverage for the bad risks. They are reluctant to abandon this practice, known as cherry-picking. Some of these insurers could be put out of business if Congress bans the practice.

The chairman-elect of the Health Insurance Association, G. David Hurd, chief executive of the Principal Financial Group, in Des Moines, said, "Small companies always have suspicions about big companies. Big companies have suspicions about small companies." But Schramm said it was simplistic to portray the tensions within the association as a spat between big and little companies. Some small insurers have made large investments in managed care, just like the big companies, he said.

If the association has had difficulty defining itself, that may be because the definition of an insurance company is blurring. More and more insurers are in the business of providing or managing health care. Some administer health-benefit plans for companies that insure themselves. Many commercial insurers have established health-maintenance organizations, which offer a wide range of services in return for a fixed monthly fee. Thus, for example, John D. Moynahan, Jr., executive vice president of the Metropolitan Life Insurance Company, said, "Our role has changed dramatically from providing the standard type of insurance to being a manager of care. We're on an irrevocable march in that direction. We can operate more effectively as an independent company than within the structure of the industry trade association."

Soaring health costs and the shift to managed care have affected the bottom line at many insurance companies. A. Michael Frinquelli, a managing director at Salomon Brothers, Inc., who follows the insurance industry, said, "Most of the big insurance companies are making money on their health-insurance business, but the profit margins are slim, only one percent or two percent of premiums and equivalent income. The health-insurance business has strained the capital positions of these companies, partly because of the large capital investment needed to start managed-care networks." The challenge for the Health Insurance Association is like that facing the American Medical Association: how to reorient itself, adopt new positions, and create a more progressive image while still protecting the financial interests of its members. [RP]

Roots of Inflation

THE TECHNOLOGICAL
IMPERATIVE

DR. George M. Segall held up a set of multicolored images of a patient's heart. On one side the red was not as sharp, indicating that blood flow to that part of the heart was lacking. The pictures were taken with a machine, one of only fifty in the nation, that had just been installed at the Palo Alto Veterans Administration Hospital, where Dr. Segall is deputy chief of nuclear medicine.

The machine, known as a PET scanner, can peer into the workings of internal organs, providing doctors with previously unobtainable information. It can tell, for instance, whether heart tissue is alive or dead and whether it is worthwhile for a cardiologist to attempt open-heart surgery. But such information doesn't come cheap. "You're talking about a $5.5 million investment," said Dr. Segall, who is also an assistant professor at Stanford Medical School, referring to the cost of the scanner and of a cyclotron that makes the radioisotopes administered to the patient for the test. "It's by far one of the most expensive technologies available now."

Once, an advance like the PET, which stands for positron emission tomography, would have been welcomed into the nation's arsenal of medical tools. After all, Americans want, and feel entitled to, the best medical care, regardless of cost, and doctors want to provide it. And with insurance companies or government programs paying the bills, neither patient nor physician has had much reason to weigh the costs and benefits. But the future of the PET scanner in medical care is far from assured. A move is afoot, driven by strapped federal health agencies and insurance companies, to rein in what some have called a medical-technology arms race. Their hope, a revolutionary one for American medicine, is to limit the uses of costly machines and procedures to instances in which the benefits have been shown to be commensurate with the expense.

Fueling this move is a growing recognition that the uncontrolled use of high-technology medical equipment and procedures—from coronary-bypass surgery to new scanning machines to lithotripters that blast kidney stones with shock waves—helps drive the relentless increase in medical costs. PET scanning comes on the heels of other major advantages in diagnostic imaging. CAT, or CT, scanning, which stands for computerized axial tomography, appeared in the 1970s and represented a great advance over conventional X rays, but at a cost of up to $500 per scan. Magnetic resonance imaging, or MRI scans, appeared in the mid-1980s and offered advantages over CAT scans, but again at a higher cost, up to $1,000 a scan. PET scan fees are higher still, reaching $2,500.

Moreover, there is widespread agreement that many advanced, expensive medical procedures are overused. Coronary-bypass surgery, for instance, is performed three hundred thousand times a year in the United States and accounts for about one of every fifty dollars spent on health care. But a study by the Rand Corporation a few years ago found that more than 40 percent of such operations did very little, if anything, for the patients. MRI scans, doctors say, are often done to rule out a minute chance of brain injury, for example, and perhaps most of all to protect the doctor from malpractice suits.

The United States relies far more heavily on technology than other advanced nations. A 1989 study by the American Medical Association found that on a per-capita basis the United States had four times as many MRI machines as Germany and eight times as many as Canada. American doctors performed open-heart surgery 2.6 times as often as Canadian doctors and 4.4 times as often as German doctors.

Technology is only one factor in soaring health-care expenses, and diagnostic imaging is only one factor in medical technology. Still, an examination of how such imaging machines are sold, paid for, and used reveals much about the medical and business issues feeding the growth in medical technology and how difficult it would be to rein it in. "The pressure of the introduction of new technologies is inexorable," said Dr. Seymour Perry, director of a program on technology and health care at Georgetown University. "Every day there's a claim of a new breakthrough. Our society wants that. We are different from other societies in the world."

The National Institutes of Health spends billions of dollars each year on medical research. A huge medical-technology industry is also in place, spewing out streams of innovations and marketing them heavily, with profit rather than social utility often its prime motivator. Nor should society try to stifle new technology, experts agree. In addition to providing better health care, technology can lower costs. A new technique for removing gallbladders, known as laparoscopy, can be finished in a day compared with the older approach, which required up to a week in the hospital.

The case of medical imaging is an example of how technology can spread virtually unchecked by considerations of cost. One reason PET machines are undergoing scrutiny is that the last great innovation in diagnostic imaging, the magnetic resonance imager, spread rapidly after it appeared in the mid-1980s. Although offering wonderful benefits, MRI scans are often used to achieve marginal gains, experts say, and sometimes under conditions that raise at least a suspicion of conflict of interest.

There are now two thousand such MRI machines, which cost $1 million to $2 million each, in the United States. Analysts estimate that more than five million MRI scans were performed in the nation in 1990, at prices of $600 to $1,000 each. That means that magnetic resonance imaging alone is adding about $5 billion to the nation's health bill.

"People want this smart test," said John Caronna, professor of clinical neurology at New York Hospital–Cornell Medical Center in Manhattan. "There's no way to shut it off. The doctors crave it, it's reassuring, and the patients crave it." But some critics say the test is overused. "There was never any effort on the part of payers or providers or society in general to develop a rational policy on how to use them," said John L. Cova, director of medical-technology assessment for the Health Insurance Association of America, a trade group representing three hundred insurance companies. The MRI scans are "used in an inappropriate way in many instances," he charged. "It's almost a joke: 'Give him an MRI.' "

A set of forces, indicative of basic traits of the nation's health system that undermine efforts at cost control, brought about the rapid spread of MRI machines and procedures. Manufacturers constantly pushed new machines on the market. The purchase of a machine by one hospital inspired others to want to keep up. Entrepreneurs, sensing big profits, set up specialized imaging centers, often attracting doctors, who could refer patients to the centers, as co-owners.

Having bought such expensive machines, hospitals and imaging centers had an incentive to push as many patients through as possible to pay off the machines. Fear of malpractice also contributed to the machines' use. And the tests were profitable, in part because of Medicare reimbursement rates that overcompensated radiologists, in the view of many experts, and that failed to come down as the technology became more widespread.

To be sure, MRI machines can have enormous medical value. They use radio waves and powerful magnets to take pictures of the inside of the body and have been particularly useful in finding brain tumors, spinal-cord injuries, and other anomalies. Unlike the earlier CAT scan, MRI does not expose the patient to radiation. Both MRI and CAT scans have largely replaced riskier and more painful procedures, such as pneumoencephalography, in which spinal fluid is removed and air pumped into the brain.

After Medicare agreed to reimburse patients for MRI scans in 1985, sales of the machines rose to about $500 million a year in the United States. The leading manufacturer is the General Electric Company, followed by Siemens, Toshiba, Philips N.V., and Picker International. Hospitals, sometimes under pressure from their own doctors, pushed to buy machines to retain their competitive status as full-service, modern health-care centers.

Some states tried to limit the spread of machines under programs that require hospitals to obtain a certificate of need before buying new equipment. But private imaging centers, not subject to those controls, sprang up, including Medical Imaging Centers of America in San Diego and Health Images, Inc., in Atlanta. The New York State Department of Health, for instance, approved the purchase of forty-three magnetic resonance imagers in state hospitals. But there are probably an additional thirty-five private imaging centers in New York City and Long Island alone, said John Milliren, director of appropriateness review for the New York State Department of Health.

Spurring the formation of these centers was the possibility of big profits. A 1988 letter seeking investors for one such center, East Bay Medical Imaging Services in Castro Valley, California, forecast a return to investors "in excess of 25 percent per year and in many cases substantially more." Similarly, Stuart, Coleman & Company of New York solicited investors for several imaging centers with the promise of a cash distribution of 400 percent over ten years. The way to realize those profits is to run many tests. A study by the New York State Department of Health estimated that a high-volume imaging center could reduce the cost per scan below $250. Despite high volume, prices have not fallen.

To provide themselves with a steady stream of customers, imaging centers often sold part ownership to doctors, who could refer patients for tests. Critics say this practice gives doctors a financial incentive to order tests that might not otherwise be called for. "It's going to give all medicine a black eye before it's over," remarked Daniel P. Chisholm, a radiologist in Little Rock, Arkansas. "There are too many studies being performed that are not necessary." A study by Bruce J. Hillman of the University of Arizona, published in *The New England Journal of Medicine* in December 1990, found that doctors who owned X-ray or ultrasound machines did 4 to 4.5 times as many tests as doctors who referred patients to radiologists, and also charged more for each test than radiologists did—over one hundred dollars more for the ultrasound exams.

Even without the financial incentives, doctors say there are numerous incentives for ordering diagnostic tests. One is the fear of a malpractice lawsuit if a physician misses a problem. Malpractice suits are less of a threat in other countries because of different cultural traditions and legal approaches. Another factor is that there are simply no incentives not to order a scan. The patient has little incentive to refuse a test, because insurance usually covers it. And while doctors and patients might think twice if the imaging procedure were painful or risky, that is not the case with MRI, although some patients become claustrophobic inside the device during the nearly hour-long test.

"Because it's so good, it's done all the time," said Dr. Caronna. The New York neurologist added that 90 percent of the time that neurologists order MRI scans, no structural damage to the patient's nervous system is detected. Still, he said, ruling out such problems is valuable information in itself.

In addition to worrying about overuse of such tests, some say their prices are needlessly high. In part, this is because the medical system has always paid doctors more for performing sophisticated procedures than for more routine medical care. A study by Victor R. Fuchs and James S. Hahn of Stanford University found that doctors in the United States are paid 80 percent more than those in Canada for routine patient evaluation and management, but three times as much for procedures. Radiologists are the most highly paid specialists, second only to surgeons, according to the American Medical Association. The mean income after expenses for radiologists was $229,800 in 1991, as against an average for all doctors of $170,600.

One reason procedures like MRI tests start out expensive is that the technology is new. But the price did not fall even as the technology spread. Blue Shield of California, for instance, paid for 1,728 MRI brain scans in 1987 at an average payment of $647. In 1989 it paid for twice as many procedures, 3,578, at an average payment of $708. "Generally speaking, once a certain level of cost is established, it only goes in one direction from there, and that's up," said Randy Horn, a senior vice president of Mutual of Omaha, an insurance company.

Society is now trying to contain its mushrooming health-care costs. Medicare is moving toward a system of payments to doctors based on relative value of the effort involved. The system will generally reduce payments to radiologists, surgeons, and other specialists. Already payments for radiological services are being cut about 20 percent in stages, starting in 1989. In 1991 Congress voted a special 10 percent cut in the Medicare payments for MRI and CAT scans performed in imaging centers.

Medicare is also changing its rules on how it will reimburse hospitals for capital expenditures. The new rules will make hospitals "think twice" about buying expensive equipment such as scanners, said Larry Haimovitch, a medical-technology consultant in San Francisco. In what could be the biggest change, Medicare is also planning to consider cost effectiveness, not just medical effectiveness, in deciding whether to pay for procedures and technology.

But Medicare officials say they must first develop a methodology for determining cost effectiveness. Medical experts say this could involve some ethically touchy questions; for instance, how valuable is it to keep an elderly person alive for six more months? Or what is the value of a diagnostic imaging procedure that detects a disease for which there is no treatment?

Into this more hostile environment steps the PET scanner, which is even more expensive than the MRI machine and draws fees of $1,500 to $2,500. While CAT and MRI scans show the structure of internal organs, PET scans show the functioning of organs by their uptake of radioactively tagged glucose and other substances. In heart disease, a PET scan can tell whether heart tissue that appears to be dead might be salvaged. PET scans have also proven to be of great value in guiding surgery to remove part of the brain in people with epilepsy, said John C. Mazziotta, a professor of neurology and radiology at the University of California at Los Angeles. PET scans additionally show promise for being able to diagnose neurological diseases such as Alzheimer's and Huntington's, something that cannot be done with CAT or MRI scans.

But insurance companies are being cautious. So far they reimburse for PET scans only in selected cases and are carefully weighing whether to extend coverage. The Health Insurance Association of America, for instance, has organized two seminars on PET scans for insurance-company executives, the first of a series the organization plans to hold on new technologies. The Federal Office of Health Technology Assessment, which advises Medicare and other federal health-insurance programs, is also studying PET scans.

Supporters of PET scans, including manufacturers, and doctors and hospitals that have used the machines, have banded together to form the Institute for Clinical PET, to win reimbursement for the machines. The group is financing clinical trials to show how PET scans can improve the outcome for patients. It has also organized conferences and studies on cost and reimbursement issues. Health experts say the fact that such a lobbying effort has to be mounted is one of the most visible signs of the changing economics of medical technology. [AP]

TURF WARS

THE brain surgeons are jousting with the bone surgeons, the dermatologists are rubbing plastic surgeons the wrong way, and the radiologists are fighting with nearly all of their medical colleagues. Turf wars among doctors are nothing new. But now, as a growing supply of highly trained specialists confronts a stingier flow of fees, competition for the right to perform—and bill for—lucrative medical procedures is growing more intense.

The arenas of conflict are proliferating along with new technologies for inspecting or repairing the body. Underused cardiologists and cardiac surgeons fight for the right to insert pacemakers. Gastroenterologists, who refined the art of peering into the upper and lower digestive tracts with scopes, now watch in dismay as surgeons begin to do the peering themselves. These same two groups are also arguing over control of the new laparoscopic technique for removing gallbladders without open surgery.

The big money in American medicine is now in diagnostic and surgical techniques. The government and insurers are just starting to bear down on the traditionally high cost of these procedures, the way they already have on fees for office visits and hospital stays. "The proceduralists are well paid, in many instances wildly overpaid," stated Dr. Edwin Maynard, an internist at Massachusetts General Hospital in Boston and past president of the American College of Physicians.

On top of that, specialists are in oversupply in many parts of the country, in the view of many experts. Expensively trained hands and minds will not long remain idle. And who best can read a scan, insert a scope into a colon, or repair a slipped disk but a doctor from one's own specialty? "It's a matter of power, ego, and money," said Dr. John C. Hobbins, an obstetrician at Yale University.

The proliferation of new imaging techniques has left radiologists especially vulnerable to professional poaching. They long since lost their monopoly on X rays, as more doctors put machines in their offices. They have faced more recent onslaughts with the spread of magnetic resonance imaging, or MRI, ultrasound, nuclear diagnostics, and other methods. One major dispute concerns who can interpret, or "read," MRI scans, for fees that range from $150 to $250. Guerrilla warfare over this is simmering around the country—mainly between radiologists and neurologists, since MRI is often used for brain and spinal disorders—but also between radiologists and cardiologists as methods for scanning the heart are developed.

The discourse follows Rule No. 1 of the turf wars: All salvos must be fired in the name of patient welfare. "There are many neurologists reading MRI scans who shouldn't be," said Dr. James M. Moorefield, a radiologist in Sacramento and chairman of the American College of Radiology. Neurologists involved in reading scans reply that they have obtained the requisite training and that their personal interpretation of scans is vital to good care. One hospital in Atlanta negotiated a truce by granting radiologists and neurologists the right to interpret MRI scans on alternate days. The unknowing patients get their scans read by one or the other specialist simply according to when they show up. (No ill effects on one set of days or another have been reported.)

Another important area of encroachment, Dr. Moorefield said, involves use of ultrasound, especially by obstetricians with machines in their offices. Fees range from one hundred to more than three hundred dollars. "I am sure there is a lot of unqualified work going on," he said. "Not to say every one, but very many obstetricians have acquired these instruments with little or no training." The danger, he said, is that correctible conditions in the fetus or hazards for the mother will be missed. Undoubtedly there are unqualified obstetricians conducting fetal ultrasound, said Dr. Richard L. Berkowitz, chairman of obstetrics at Mt. Sinai Hospital in New York. But many more have excellent training and experience in fetal sonography. "Just because you're a radiologist doesn't mean you are well trained in this either."

"There's no reason in the world an obstetrician can't learn to read ultrasounds if he is trained," said Dr. Hobbins of Yale, who as president of a national interspecialty group on ultrasound is trying to quell the conflict, shifting the focus to qualifications rather than specialty. Some obstetricians, on the other hand, have said that a transvaginal scan, in which a probe is inserted into the vagina, is an "extension of a pelvic exam, and thus should be in the realm of obstetrics and gynecology, not radiology," he said. "That's also baloney."

And now a new player in the ultrasound game, the emergency-room physician, is stirring up both the radiologists and the obstetricians. "Everyone is somewhat concerned about the training of this whole new group of physicians," Dr. Hobbins said. "But there's no reason they can't do it too."

Plastic surgeons complain that other specialists are horning in on the performance of rhinoplasties, better known as nose jobs. The debate follows Rule No. 2 of the turf wars: Any surplus must be in someone else's specialty. "There aren't too many plastic surgeons," said Dr. John E. Christ, a plastic surgeon in Houston who advertises aggressively. "The problem is that other specialties are encroaching into the realm of plastic surgeons."

Not content to take on nose jobs and face-lifts, some ear, nose, and throat specialists are now "moving down the body," Dr. Christ said. "Some here will do fat suctioning and breast augmentation, and they are advertising heavily." Dermatologists and even general surgeons are now doing cosmetic surgery, he said, adding somewhat ominously, "All these people are wanting a slice of the pie." Dr. Christ does not believe that the poaching and the resort to advertising indicate a surplus of specialists. "We're servicing a need, and advertising helps the public find who offers these services."

To experts in medical economics, the battle for patients indicates more than a redivision of the money pot. If too many specialists have been trained, then resources have been wasted. And if they have to search for things to do, they may promote the costly overuse of procedures. "When doctors are as busy as they ought to be, they are much less inclined to do things of marginal medical value or to seek patients for elective, cosmetic services," said Dr. Arnold S. Relman, former editor of *The New England Journal of Medicine*.

But whether a procedure is marginal or a specialty is in surplus is a matter of perspective. Taking Rule No. 2 to its logical extreme, Dr. Byron C. Pevehouse, a retired neurosurgeon in San Francisco and a past president of the American Association of Neurological Surgeons, said his field suffered from scarcity: "We may have been remiss in not training enough neurosurgeons to treat all the cases. Since there are not enough neurosurgeons, the orthopedists, who produced too many, began doing neurological procedures." In many regions, he explained, there are too many orthopedists in relation to the number of broken bones that need setting or hips that need replacing, the standard work of orthopedists. And so, like Dr. Christ, he described how interlopers are creeping across the human body, invading one neurosurgical site after another.

First, orthopedists started doing peripheral nerve work on the arms and legs. "Now they think their scope of practice should include disk problems and nerve-root paralysis," Dr. Pevehouse said. "Some even want to do spinal tumors." This is bad news for patients. (Rule No. 1). "Orthopedists are not trained to the same extent to handle nervous tissue."

Orthopedists, of course, beg to differ. [EE]

A CAPTIVE MARKET

I N 1984 Atlanta had one magnetic resonance imaging machine. Now it has at least thirty. Most are owned by doctors, and not just any doctors: they are often the same ones who send their patients for imaging scans at six hundred to one thousand dollars a visit. Nobody disputes that magnetic resonance imaging, or MRI, is an invaluable diagnostic tool that allows doctors to visualize abnormalities in the brain, spine, knees, and other parts of the body. But the rapid proliferation of doctors' investments in MRI clinics and in clinical laboratories, outpatient surgery centers, and other health-care businesses has set off one of the most passionate ethical debates in medicine today. Critics, who are seeking to outlaw doctor referrals to services in which they have invested, charge that the practice is a blatant conflict of interest that encourages costly overuse of procedures. Defenders say it serves patients by speeding the availability of new technology.

Studies by the government and private groups have found that more than 10 percent of the nation's doctors have invested in businesses to which they refer patients. In Florida, where state officials worried about excess costs are urgently studying the matter, the proportion of doctors making such investments has reached one-third. The studies also find that doctors who share ownership of laboratories and other health-care businesses order more services than other physicians. Critics say many of those extra procedures are medically unnecessary. With the nation's health-care bill soaring, many experts say it is time to ban the spreading practice known in the health-care industry as "self-referral."

"You don't have to be an Einstein to see that the more patients you refer, the larger your profits will be," said Dr. Arnold S. Relman, former editor of *The New England Journal of Medicine* and a crusader against what he sees as a dangerous new business ethic in American medicine. "When you earn money by referring to a facility where you are an investor, you're just using your patient as an economic commodity."

Concerned about the spread of self-referrals, Congress in 1989 passed a law to restrict some of them. Since January 1, 1992, the government has prohibited doctors from referring Medicare or Medicaid patients to clinical laboratories in which the physicians have a financial interest. A few states, including New York and Florida, have placed restrictions on referrals to certain other doctor-owned ventures as well, including MRI scanners, and the American Medical Association has condemned most kinds of self-referral as unethical.

But defenders of the physician investments insist that they are proper and even beneficial. "It really does bring new things to the market," said Dr. Howard B. Krone, an Atlanta orthopedist who has bought shares in two magnetic resonance imaging centers, one near each of his offices. "If there's a profit involved, that's fine. It's the entrepreneurial system." Proposals to ban ownership of MRI centers or other businesses by referring physicians are "hogwash," he declared, adding, "The doctors I know in Atlanta aren't abusing this."

Physician investment in health-care businesses grew rapidly in the 1980s as the medical marketplace became more commercial and more competitive. Federal cost-control policies inadvertently encouraged such investments. Medicare's payment of flat fees for hospital stays, for example, gave hospitals an incentive to discharge patients faster, creating more demand for outpatient services. And as doctors' fees were newly limited, many physicians looked to investments to supplement their income. Such investments have proceeded fastest in the Sunbelt, where patient populations have boomed, the entrepreneurial spirit is strong, and regulation of medical investment is often not stringent. Data on the practice are most complete in Florida, where doctors now own or have invested in two-thirds of the state's outpatient surgery centers and three-fourths of its diagnostic imaging centers, according to a study by the state's Health Care Cost Containment Board.

The quick spread of imaging centers in Atlanta is typical. Magnetic resonance imaging, which did not become widely available until the late 1980s, uses magnetic and radio waves to provide sharp images of soft tissue and has become a crucial tool for diagnosing problems in the brain, spinal column, knees, and other joints. The machines cost one million to two million dollars each. About two thousand magnetic resonance scanners were operating nationwide as of 1991. Doctors hail MRI as a marvel of technology; the procedure is cheaper and safer than surgery that might otherwise be required to determine the extent of an injury. And it can save money in other ways—for example, by ruling out the need for months of worker's compensation payments to an employee feigning injury. But the procedure can easily be overused. Many experts say costly magnetic resonance scans are often used to acquire information that is marginal or can be gained more cheaply by other techniques, or to rule out slight risks as a defense against potential lawsuits.

The number of scans is climbing, creating a huge new market. In Atlanta alone, experts said MRI fees in 1991 totaled at least $60 million, up from $4 million in 1985. Physicians share ownership of more than half the area's magnetic resonance imaging machines, including many in freestanding centers and even some run by public hospitals. Dr. Maurice Jove, an orthopedic surgeon, said Atlanta doctors were imbued with the free-enterprise spirit. "The cowboys and Indians want to make a lot of money," he observed, in explaining why so many doctors had invested in the new machines. "Why should large corporations be the only ones entitled to make money in medicine?" Dr. Jove helped put together a partnership of doctors that leases an MRI machine to the DeKalb Medical Center, a 525-bed public hospital in Atlanta's eastern suburbs.

Wherever the new machines were purchased, profits depended on their heavy use, and that required a steady flow of referrals from neurologists, neurosurgeons, orthopedic surgeons, and other doctors. There could be no surer way to guarantee the supply of patients than to bring referring doctors into the business. At the same time, many doctors, whose ability to refer patients was increasingly recognized as a valuable commodity, began to ask why they should not get a piece of the new business. Direct kickbacks for the referral of Medicare or Medicaid patients are forbidden under federal law. But doctors may legally profit from part ownership of a business to which they refer patients, provided they do not receive any payment or other remuneration in return for the referrals.

"Originally I was sending my patients all the way across town to get MRI scans," said Dr. Krone, the Atlanta orthopedist. "Then I started to think, Why shouldn't there be a financial benefit if it could be done honorably?" Dr. Krone joined the partnership at DeKalb Medical Center, which opened its diagnostic imaging center in 1989. Officials of the DeKalb Medical Center say they invited local physicians to join in the new diagnostic center to avoid a situation in which two machines would exist side by side, one owned by the hospital and one owned by doctors who controlled the patient referrals. Such potentially wasteful duplication was not avoided in the south Atlanta suburb of Riverdale, where three machines are operating in an area of less than one square mile. One center, Atlanta Magnetic Imaging-South, opened in 1987 and is owned by Health Images, Inc., an Atlanta-based company that operates centers nationwide. Two more opened in 1990: one owned by a hospital, the Southern Regional Medical Center, and right next door in a small trailerlike building, Tara Magnetic Imaging, owned by a group of local doctors.

One result of the proliferation of machines is fierce competition for patients. Health Images, which runs two MRI centers in Atlanta and twenty-six others around the country, says that more and more doctors who formerly referred patients to its sites are now channeling patients to centers in which they have invested. Robert D. Carl III, founder and president of Health Images, a publicly traded company, said, "The laws of supply and demand don't operate when physicians refer patients to their own facilities. It's a captive market." These fetters on a free market may also help explain why the fees for magnetic resonance imaging have remained so high despite the growing number of machines.

Physician investments often take the form of limited partnerships. Doctors are asked to make relatively small investments with the prospect of high returns, in many cases over 50 percent a year. Critics say the high returns show that the arrangements are intended more to secure doctors (and their patients) than to raise capital.

One limited partnership, Premier Imaging Associates, opened an MRI center on the north side of Atlanta in July 1990. In a prospectus filed with the Securities and Exchange Commission as required for certain limited partnerships, Premier said, "Management hopes to develop a large base of practitioners who will be inclined to refer their patients to an MRI facility in which they have a financial interest." Premier estimated that investors would get back more than twice their original investment by December 1992. An imaging center in Texas projected even bigger profits: a return of $6,190 in the first year for each $500 of cash invested.

Dr. Robert E. Windsor, an orthopedic specialist at Sunbelt Spine and Sports Medicine, an Atlanta group practice, described his investments in four local imaging centers. The general partners in those businesses "approached us and suggested that we invest in their centers because they wanted to solidify referral patterns," he said, adding that 60 percent of his patients who need MRI scans go to the four centers in which he has invested. Dr. Windsor said that when doctors invested in a limited partnership in Atlanta, they expected to get back profits equal to their initial investment in the first two years. He recovered his $1,750 investment in Premier Imaging, which opened in the summer of 1990, within a year.

Premier was formed by Andrew M. Zeldin, a thirty-four-year-old former real-estate developer, and Dr. Jonathan S. Gallen, a thirty-five-year-old anesthesiologist. "If the doctor has an ownership interest in a facility, he has an incentive to support it," Dr. Gallen said. "He may profit from it at the end of the year." Dr. Gallen said that 75 percent to 80 percent of the patients sent to Premier Imaging came from doctors who had invested in the business. But he added that 10 percent to 15 percent of the physician-investors have never sent a patient to Premier. This, he said, showed that "patients are referred on the basis of need, not greed."

Premier, like a number of the new centers, does not take patients under Medicare or Medicaid, the federal health programs for the elderly and the poor. Such patients can be referred to other imaging centers. Premier's reason for excluding them was explained in its prospectus: This policy was adopted to insure that the firm and its owners would not violate any federal "proscriptions against self-referrals."

The investment arrangement at DeKalb Medical Center on Atlanta's east side likewise suggests that securing a steady flow of patient referrals was a prime reason for getting doctors to invest. There a partnership of fifty-nine doctors (twenty-six general partners and thirty-three limited partners) leases the imaging machine to the hospital. The 1988 partnership agreement specified that the limited partners must be doctors on the medical staff of DeKalb Medical Center—in other words, investors who could bring in patients. Since then, as concern rose about possible federal regulations on self-referral, the agreement has been amended to allow others to invest, said Dr. Russell W. Wallace, Jr., a neurologist who is a general partner.

Another provision of the agreement could also encourage a high rate of referrals. The rate of return for each scan, as well as the return to the physician-investors, rises with the total number of scans performed. Under the arrangement, if twelve hundred imaging procedures are performed in a year, the hospital pays the investors 15 percent of all revenues, in addition to a base rental fee. And if more than seventeen hundred procedures are performed, as they were in 1990, the investors receive 30 percent of the revenues from all scans. This arrangement could create a financial incentive for use of the procedure. But several partners said in interviews that they were unaware of this provision or that the additional money involved was so negligible that it would not influence their decisions.

In the mid-1980s, the heady early years of magnetic resonance imaging, the link between physician investment and the referral of patients was often explicit. Robert Carl, the president of Health Images, Inc., which opened Atlanta's first MRI center in October 1984, said, "Banks and other lenders required us to have physician-investors." Banks making loans for the new centers wanted doctors to have a stake in them in order to guarantee the flow of patients—and revenues—in what was then an untested market, said Carl and other officers of Health Images. He and his company originally took doctors as partners in several imaging centers. But they later decided to buy out the doctors after they found physicians demanding "bigger and bigger cash distributions," Carl said.

Within the medical community, radiologists were among the first to condemn the spread of investments in MRI centers by referring physicians. They have a personal stake: Many are losing business, as neurologists, orthopedists, and others invest in the imaging field and, in some cases, even take over the lucrative task of interpreting the images. Defenders of self-referral, while admitting the potential for abuse, argue that the situation is not fundamentally different from other areas of medical practice in which a doctor's integrity and judgment are the bulwark against wrongs. "To say this is a conflict of interest is like saying that every time a surgeon operates he's doing it for his own benefit," said Dr. Wallace.

Critics like Dr. Relman, while agreeing that the potential for abuse exists throughout medical practice, say there is a more clear-cut ethical problem when doctors earn money from referrals than when they are paid for personally providing care. "The whole climate in medicine is becoming more commercial and competitive," he said. "It's putting doctors in situations that force them to behave like entrepreneurs to survive." [RP & EE]

AN EPIDEMIC OF FRAUD

FRAUD and exaggerated claims are driving up the cost of workers' compensation insurance by billions of dollars a year, a variety of experts say, and have become a significant though still largely unrecognized factor in the skyrocketing cost of health care. This conclusion has been reached by regulators and law-enforcement officials in several states and by insurance officials who have begun investigations of questionable claims.

To many workers, these authorities say, lying about injuries or illness related to work has become no more sinister than crossing the street against a red light. That attitude and the resulting false claims are helping to push workers' compensation systems in some states into crisis or even to the edge of collapse. Although other factors are also contributing to the sixty billion dollars paid out by employers to public and private insurers for workers' compensation each year, officials and insurance companies in Oregon, California, New Jersey, and other states say that as much as 20 percent or more of claims may involve cheating. They say it is costing legitimately injured workers many of the benefits they deserve.

"We've found workers' compensation is riddled with fraud," said Stan Long, the president and chief executive of the State Accident Insurance Fund (SAIF), the state-owned workers' compensation insurer in Oregon, which says it has uncovered fraud in one of every four claims. "If you run a system where you give money to everybody who asks, you are going to get a lot of people asking for money."

Fraud by employers is also increasingly being recognized as a problem in workers' compensation, as is widespread abuse by doctors and lawyers. But experts say cheating by individuals illustrates a larger phenomenon in American society that government and insurance companies have often ignored: the belief that cheating on insurance is acceptable because the system always seemed to have endless amounts of money to pay for it. They say that is an attitude the nation can no longer afford.

In the last decade the costs of the insurance programs that care for workers injured on the job in the fifty states have grown more than 150 percent, or 50 percent faster than the cost of health care overall. In more than a dozen states where employers have been hit by double-digit premium increases, officials say rising workers' compensation costs have devastated small companies and sapped the competitiveness of entire industries. In states such as Maine and Rhode Island, where costs have risen more than 50 percent a year, insurance companies are abandoning programs as unprofitable.

For years experts have attributed the increasing cost of workers' compensation to growing litigation, the rising price of medical care in general, and the expanded coverage and benefits awarded by states. But until now insurers, government agencies, employers, and social scientists have rarely studied how much fraud may also be involved. Employers have often been timid in challenging workers' compensation claims they deemed dubious, many executives say, partly out of fear of being seen as attacking vulnerable workers and partly because fraud is hard to prove. In addition, they say, insurance companies often discourage investigations.

Recently, however, a small but growing number of government officials and insurance companies have begun to look into the question. They say they are finding that in some states, at least, workers' compensation has nurtured a culture of fraud in which workers regularly lie without fear or shame. In Los Angeles, pitchmen working for doctors and lawyers swarm the sidewalks outside unemployment offices, openly telling passersby they can win thousands of dollars in workers' compensation benefits simply by filing phony claims. In 1991 Pittsburgh reported a 15 percent drop in workers' compensation claims after it televised videos taken by hidden cameras of supposedly injured police officers and fire fighters working at second jobs, playing basketball, and fixing roofs.

"It is socially acceptable to exaggerate, or even lie, to insurance companies and workers' compensation agencies," said Douglas F. Stevenson, executive director of the National Council of Self-Insurers, a trade association of large corporations. "Such conduct has become so institutionalized that it no longer shocks our sense of morality." Government and private leaders in some states, however, say the type of fraud reported in California, Oregon, Colorado, New Jersey, and elsewhere is rare in their states.

Labor leaders insist that the vast majority of workers are honest. And some insurance-industry spokesmen say individuals are often not the ones to blame. "The system puts impossible pressure on people," said Eric Oxfeld, senior counsel for the American Insurance Association, an industry trade group. "An attorney says you can go back to work now and get nothing, or you can go back in a month and get thousands of dollars. I don't think it is fair to fault people when the system offers that kind of incentive."

"Say you get headaches, or backaches, or you get bad dreams," said Alexi Chau, one of more than a dozen men and women milling outside the entrances of the state unemployment office on Broadway in downtown Los Angeles. "You've got to sue your boss. You can get money." Up and down the block, recruiters plied their trade on the sunny sidewalk. Some offered business cards and glossy flyers to passersby. Others invited potential customers to sit on folding chairs and hear the rich rewards of the workers' compensation system explained.

A reporter simply asked Chau for one of his business cards. Chau responded with a two-minute discourse on how the system works: The reporter could collect $350 a week, Chau said, if he agreed to meet a doctor and a lawyer immediately. The doctor would find that he was suffering from back and neck pain caused by work. Although the reporter never mentioned anything about having health problems, Chau told him he would receive two therapy sessions a week for four months. Chau promised that after two months of treatment the doctor would help him to obtain a city pass for the disabled that would let him ride municipal buses free.

As long as the patient agrees to the diagnosis, Chau said, no one can disprove it. "Don't worry about doctor and lawyer bills," he said. "Insurance pays for it all." When later asked by the reporter if he knew he was breaking the law, Chau said that he did, but that he was planning to leave the business. He said he had been paid two hundred dollars for each successful referral.

In California, as in other states, workers' compensation is a system of insurance that reimburses employees for the economic harm from injuries and illness caused by the job. In some states the insurance is sold by private companies, in others by public agencies, and in many states by both. Workers are compensated for lost wages, medical bills, in some states job retraining, and in cases of death, benefits for their families. In most states the law requires employers to insure all workers and pay the premiums for 100 percent of their benefits.

California has seen a threefold rise in workers' compensation payments in the last decade, to more than ten billion dollars. In the highest-risk industries, employers are now required to pay premiums of more than five thousand dollars for each worker. Part of the high costs comes from real and debilitating diseases that science has linked to the workplace only in recent years, including asbestosis, hearing loss, certain types of cancer, and carpal tunnel syndrome, an affliction of people who use computers.

John F. Henning, head officer of the California Labor Federation, AFL-CIO, said that although the majority of workers file honest claims, the system does encourage abuse. "There are shyster attorneys who seduce workers to make false claims of stress," he said. In southern California, newspapers and television stations are flooded with advertisements from clinics and lawyers. One Los Angeles clinic, Boulevard Health Services, even offered to patients who attend thirty therapy sessions free trips for two to Las Vegas, Nevada, "The Fun Capital of the World."

But until recently, officials and insurance companies in California rarely spoke about workers' compensation fraud. Of the twenty-five hundred cases investigated by the State Department of Insurance's fraud unit in its twelve-year history, only forty-nine involved workers' compensation, and only five were prosecuted. Lori Kammerer, the managing director of Californians for Compensation Reform, an organization of employers, said that when businesses complained to their insurance companies about workers lying or inflating claims, they were often told it would cost more to fight such claims than to pay them.

One event that did seem to bring about a change in official attitudes was a news report broadcast on May 19, 1991, by KCBS-TV in Los Angeles. Reporter Harvey Levin posed as an unemployed data processor and was taken by a recruiter outside an unemployment office to the offices of lawyers and doctors who specialized in workers' compensation cases. Photographed by a hidden video camera, the reporter told interviewers at the law firm, the Office of Administrative Law on Wilshire Boulevard, that he was not sick. But the firm filed forms that described him as suffering from severe abdominal pain, stiff and sore neck, lower-back pain, nervousness, dizziness, blurred vision, and too much stress on the job. The law firm referred him to a medical office that charged $1,195 for initial consultations.

As a result of the broadcast and the outcry from employers, the State Department of Insurance and the Los Angeles District

Attorney have begun investigating workers' compensation fraud. The insurance department founded an investigative unit that fall solely devoted to the matter, and it now estimates that fraud accounts for more than 20 percent of the dollars paid out.

"We are just finding out that fraud is out of control in California's workers' compensation system," said Albert H. Mackensie, a deputy in the Los Angeles District Attorney's office. "Workers' comp has been a license to steal here, and there has not been a law-enforcement or police agency in place to investigate it." Several insurance companies in California have also begun aggressively investigating these cases.

The Zenith Insurance Company of Woodland Hills has asserted that one clinic certified four restaurant workers as totally unable to work and deserving of thousands of dollars in benefits because of what it described as stress and mistreatment by the restaurant's management. At the time of their medical examinations, however, the company asserted in federal court papers that the four men were fully employed at a nearby restaurant.

The clinic, American Psychometric Consultants, billed the insurance company for 18.1 hours of psychological testing for each of the four workers in one day, though the office was said to be open only nine hours a day. A lawyer representing the clinic, Richard K. Simon, disputed Zenith's charges, saying his client was a reputable organization that had violated neither the law nor professional standards. Simon said he would ask the court to dismiss the case.

Vincent Tokatlian, a Los Angeles chiropractor who worked at another clinic for six months, said he was disturbed by the fact that many patients did not even pretend to want to be treated. They asked to sign the forms and leave. "They were reluctant to spend more than three minutes," he said. "There would just be a smile or a wink but never any sign of shame."

Geoffry Burnham, a doctor's assistant who has reviewed more than twenty-five hundred workers' compensation claims for

Connecticut employers, says he is startled at how blatant cheating has become. Workers under the age of forty, Burnham said, often try to charge the system for whatever they can get, in a striking reversal of the strong work ethic of an older generation of workers. The younger workers, he said, exaggerate injuries, file for injuries that happened off the job, or for injuries that never happened at all.

In one case, Burnham said he recalled attending a karate class where he spotted an employee of General Dynamics's Electric Boat division in New London, a company where Burnham worked for several years. For three years the employee missed work three afternoons a week for medical treatments as a result of a bruise he had sustained from a fall in the snow. But as a regular karate student, Burnham said, the worker was kicked, punched, or thrown across a mat two nights a week. When confronted, the worker was neither embarrassed nor concerned that he had been caught, said Burnham.

By contrast, Burnham recalled the case of a sixty-year-old metal pattern maker who came to Electric Boat's medical office with hands that had been gnarled by years of heavy labor. He could no longer work. More typical of workers of that generation, Burnham said, the pattern maker was not interested in his workers' compensation benefits. He wanted surgery that would get him back to work as quickly as possible. "What scares me is what is happening to the American work ethic," Burnham commented.

Eugene Tish, chief operating officer at the Schuler Corporation of Salem, Oregon, said his company too had found that disability claims primarily involved younger employees, who file claims for injuries sustained on their own time. "What do you call it if you find that thirty of your claims appear in the first fifteen minutes of Monday morning?" Tish asked.

Nonetheless, officials in some states say that deceit and fraud are not a significant problem in workers' compensation claims. In New York officials say fraud does not account for more than a fraction of claims, which rose 39 percent from 1989 to 1991.

Officials in Illinois, where premiums were expected to rise 9 percent in 1992, agree. But in some other states, officials are reaching different conclusions.

Oregon officials say they did not see employee fraud as a big problem until 1989, when the state-owned workers' compensation insurer, SAIF, began an intensive and controversial crackdown. As a result of the crackdown and other changes, premiums dropped 23 percent in 1991, after years of double-digit increases. SAIF executives now say that 37 percent of claims they investigated did not deserve to be paid and that they believe 25 percent of all claims were fraudulent.

Among the more than two hundred fraud cases the company has brought to district attorneys and professional boards for action was the case of a former deputy sheriff, Jerry A. Lea, who injured his leg and finger on the job in 1982 and collected $160,000 over seven years. Lea said he was almost totally incapacitated, and appeared at hearings in a back brace, a neck brace, and with a cane. After the company's surveillance team videotaped him stacking wood and washing his car in his backyard, Lea was sentenced to ninety days in the county jail. In two other cases, workers who claimed to be fully incapacitated were taped climbing into their race cars at stock-car races.

Among the eighty-two chiropractors charged in Oregon, investigators said, several openly counseled patients on how to cheat the system. In Pittsburgh, where officials showed the videos of supposedly injured workers in seemingly fine health, the city has started a so-called safety lottery. Workers are now eligible to win $200 if they go one month without claiming an injury. "We make the lame well," joked Ben Hayllar, the director of finance of the city.

In Massachusetts, the office of Gov. William F. Weld estimates that fraud accounts for more than $400 million of the $3 billion paid out in claims. In New Jersey, the director of the insurance department's fraud division, Louis Parisi, said fraud or abuse in his state could account for some of the costs in 25 percent of workers' compensation claims. In Colorado, a study for employers found that as much as 30 percent of workers' compensation claims involved fraud or exaggeration, including outright faking and stretching recuperation periods, said Michael D. DeWitt, executive vice president of Avert, a consulting company in Fort Collins.

Authorities in Florida, Texas, and other states say that evidence is rising of employers who are defrauding the system by lying about the number of employees or by setting up deceptive leaseback agreements to "lease" their workers to other companies to reduce their premiums. In many cases, when workers are injured they find they have no coverage at all.

Fraudulent claims and abuse are by no means the only problems afflicting workers' compensation systems. The oldest social program resulting from a compact between labor and management, workers' compensation was begun in the United States at the turn of the century to blunt the often savage health dangers facing workers. By the late 1960s, however, benefits to injured workers were often regarded as so low that they failed to meet the needs of the injured and their families. In 1972 a presidential commission in the Nixon administration recommended that states sharply raise benefits. Among other recommendations adopted by most states was one to give employees unable to work a minimum of two-thirds of their gross salaries before they were injured or 80 percent of their net pay—tax free.

Since then, the total costs of workers' compensation have soared. The average premium that an employer pays for an employee has jumped to more than $500 in 1991 from the $92 it was twenty years before. The number of claims doubled in the 1980s, and the cost of claims during that time rose by 154 percent. Meanwhile, from 1975 to 1990 lost workdays attributed to on-the-job injuries doubled, from thirty million to more than sixty million; even as the economy moved from factory work to service jobs, and the increase in industrial accidents remained flat. Among the states with systems in crisis are Maine, Rhode

Island, Massachusetts, Pennsylvania, Texas, Louisiana, and Florida.

In part, the rise in costs is a result of an increase in benefits, which encourages more people to use the system. Studies show that for every 10 percent increase in the value of benefits, workers' compensation systems pay out 15 percent more money. Workers' compensation costs have also been driven up by the prices of medical care and increasing litigation. In Illinois, litigation expenses now amount to 14 percent of all the dollars paid out in claims in disputes that may not involve fraud at all, but legitimate disagreements.

One study published by the Minnesota Department of Labor and Industry in 1990 found that the same treatments for back injuries and sprains cost more than twice as much when charged to workers' compensation than to Blue Cross, and lasted longer. By comparison, the treatments for fractures, which leave less to discretion, were about the same.

Unlike people with ordinary health insurance such as Blue Cross, patients in the workers' compensation system pay no deductible and no part of the bills, giving the patients no incentive to turn down tests or treatments. In addition, few workers' compensation systems have "managed-care" and other cost-containment programs intended to prevent unneeded or overly expensive treatments. As a result, explained Orin Kramer, an economist in Princeton, New Jersey, workers who have limited health insurance or none at all, and medical professionals who have lost profits to cost-containment programs, often turn to workers' compensation. By linking treatment to a problem on the job, both can be sure employers will pay 100 percent of the bill.

A 1991 study of more than three thousand Boeing company workers by Dr. Stanley Bigos of the University of Washington found that although many workers suffer some sort of back pain, those most likely to file claims are not necessarily the most debilitated but those most dissatisfied with their jobs. While the greatest risk of back symptoms was among workers ages thirty to forty, the study found, the greatest incidence of back-injury claims was among workers ages twenty to twenty-five.

Another study, published in 1990 by the nonprofit Workers' Compensation Research Institute in Cambridge, Massachusetts, found that workers' compensation claims climb in recessions and drop as employment rises. Richard B. Victor, the institute's executive director, said people might underuse workers' compensation in good times, or use it to replace lost wages and job benefits in hard times. "A lot of the problem goes unseen because nobody is looking," said Louis Parisi of the New Jersey Insurance Department. "But we know that many people out there think workers' compensation is a bargain, and they are hitting the system for as much as they can." [PK]

AN INDUSTRY UNDER SIEGE

WHILE drug companies say they need high prices to support innovative research, health economists say that more and more of the companies' revenues are going to increasingly elaborate promotions. They include gifts for patients who take their drugs, payments to doctors as consultants, and large donations to nonprofit hospitals. And much of the research by drug companies is aimed not at innovation but at developing medicines that have the same function as similar drugs made by rivals, academics who study the drug industry have said in interviews and in testimony before Congress. Officials at the Food and Drug Administration say that of the ninety new drugs approved in 1992, only about 40 percent were a significant advance over medicines already available.

Drug costs have soared in recent years, and President Bill Clinton has lambasted the drug industry for its hefty prices and profits, contending that it spends one billion dollars more on promotion than on research and development. The drug companies say that assertion is unfounded and unfair. They argue that drug development is extraordinarily expensive and risky, and that marketing advanced drugs often requires sophisticated, one-on-one sales presentations.

But the industry has presented little hard data about its costs and pricing strategies. As a result, many health economists who admire the industry's record of innovation say they have recently grown skeptical of its claims that research would decline were it not for high prices. "The industry spends more on promotion than on research and development, so when they say they don't have enough money to develop new drugs, I don't believe them," said Dr. Barry Bleidt, a professor of pharmacy administration at Xavier University of Louisiana. "I consider myself proindustry, but I'm also proconsumer." Dr. Bleidt and others say they are concerned that drug companies are now using their promotional budgets to circumvent restrictions on marketing by federal regulators and hospitals. For example, companies are not permitted to promote a drug under development, but in some cases doctors who were paid consultants of a company have presented the merits of such drugs at medical meetings.

Although the industry willingly reveals its research and development costs—projected at $10.3 billion in the United States for 1993—drug companies often obscure what is included in the category. And like many publicly traded companies, they consider their marketing and promotional outlays to be privileged information. In documents filed with the Securities and Exchange Commission, drug companies include promotional costs in categories such as "selling, administration, general" or "cost of sales" or just "other."

"They try to keep their operating budgets as veiled as possible," said Dr. Stephen Schondelmeyer, professor of pharmaceutical economics at the University of Minnesota, "which implies that there's something they do not want to reveal. When you look at the rosy picture painted in annual reports and then hear them tell Congress they can't afford to do research, there are a lot of discrepancies." He and other health economists say that while many companies have survived on promotion, others, including Merck & Company, have an extraordinary record of innovative basic research.

The Pink Sheet, a newsletter for executives in the pharmaceutical industry, published by FDC Reports of Chevy Chase, Maryland, estimated that in 1991 drug companies spent ten billion dollars on promotion, exceeding by one billion dollars the amount spent on research. Dr. Schondelmeyer's best guess is that the gap is even greater. Based on a review of annual reports and documents filed with the SEC, he estimates that a typical drug company spends about 16 percent of its budget on research and development and as much as 20 percent on promotion. Most consumer-based industries spend about 2 percent of their budgets on marketing, although some beer and cosmetics companies spend 10 percent or more.

Dr. David A. Kessler, commissioner of the Food and Drug Administration, said he worried that much of the money spent on promotion not only was wasteful but imperiled patient care. "Our concerns about promotion go well beyond the costs it adds to drug prices," he said. "Promotion is designed to create a market for a product, and the market that's created is not necessarily the market that will benefit from the drug. So it's going to result in inappropriate prescribing, and people will be hurt."

Pharmaceutical companies say patients get value for their money. Jeff Warren, a spokesman for the Pharmaceutical Manufacturers Association, said, "We think we are unparalleled in terms of research intensity, and that bucks a trend that says that research and development are generally declining in this country." The association estimates that 16.7 percent of revenues are used for research and development. It does not keep records on marketing or promotion.

The industry defends large marketing budgets on the grounds that at least some of the promotion educates doctors and patients. Rick Honey, a spokesman for Pfizer, Inc., noted that patent protection generally lapses in ten to fifteen years, "so from a business standpoint we have to market our product aggressively. More important, this is not like marketing soda pop. Many of our employees in marketing have advanced degrees and get extensive training in how to use our products."

Drug manufacturers also stress that millions of dollars go into research on drugs that never make it to market. While pharmacologists acknowledge the enormous expense and great risk in pharmaceutical research, many say the companies owe the public a better accounting of their costs. Dr. Marcus Reidenberg, editor of *Clinical Pharmacology and Therapeutics,* said, "There's so little hard data that there's no way for an outside observer like me to be able to come to a conclusion about whether high prices are fair high prices or unconscionable high prices. I've tried to get people from drug companies to write commentaries on their costs and how they set drug prices, but haven't received any manuscripts."

The accounting standards used by pharmaceutical companies are "incredibly lax," said Dr. Peter Arno, professor of health economics at the Albert Einstein College of Medicine in the Bronx. "Their corporate reports are very vague, and they seem to fold advertising into research and development, and confuse production costs with research and development." And not all the research benefits patients. While Bristol-Myers Squibb is supporting some important basic research, it has also spent research dollars to prove that its antibiotic Duricef is effective against strep throat, a condition that is readily treated by a host of far cheaper antibiotics. Calls to Bristol-Myers Squibb for this article were not returned.

Based on a 1990 study at Tufts University, drug companies claim that it costs an average of $231 million to bring a drug to market. But only half of that is budgeted for development; the other half is what economists call "opportunity cost"—the return that could have been expected if the company had invested the money instead of tying it up in developing the drug.

In recent years the FDA and various medical societies have imposed restrictions on how drug companies may promote their products to doctors, strictly limiting the types of gifts. And an increasing number of hospitals are placing restrictions on visits by sales representatives. In response, the industry has developed more subtle promotional techniques directed at patients and hospitals. "The pharmaceutical industry is incredibly clever, and I say that from a position of both respect and disgust," said Dr.

Bleidt, the Xavier University pharmacologist. "There are fewer outright bribes to doctors these days, but they didn't decrease their promotional outlays, of course. They became smarter in how to use them."

Dr. Kessler said that many pharmaceutical companies had tried to get around the restrictions on promotion and advertising by going undercover. Instead of making the rounds to promote their products themselves, they hire prominent doctors as "consultants" who preach the virtues of the medicines at medical conventions, on hospital rounds, and in journals. New guidelines drafted by the FDA do not prohibit drug companies from paying lecturers or from sponsoring conferences but require that the ties be revealed and the terms of the contract be publicly available.

The drug companies are also increasingly sponsoring newsletters or supplements to respected journals that appear to be part of the journals. In 1991 the Food and Drug Administration took action against Bristol-Myers for printing a newsletter called *Oncology Commentary,* which was designed to look like a medical journal but discussed only the company's drugs; the name of the company was nowhere on the publication. Many companies are starting to give incentives to potential patients as well. To promote its new arthritis drug Relafen, SmithKline Beecham offered patients who visited a doctor free memberships worth about $20 in the Arthritis Foundation, a support and information group for people with the disease.

Although drug-company executives acknowledge that some abuses have occurred, they say pharmaceutical marketing often provides doctors with up-to-date information. For example, when Wyeth-Ayerst began to market the Norplant contraceptive in 1991, its marketing budget covered the cost of teaching doctors to insert the now-popular device.

Perhaps most worrisome to critics of the industry is the way drug-company money now permeates hospitals and doctors' offices, where skepticism has long been relied upon to keep overzealous sales pitches in check. Scientists and hospitals say that as research costs have risen and public funds have declined, they have come to rely more heavily on industry grants. Certain drug companies have become major charitable donors to hospitals, contributing $25,000 here and $100,000 there. Marion Merrell Dow revealed in its annual report that in the name of "strategic philanthropy," it had given an undisclosed amount of money to help establish a cardiovascular research center at the University of Cincinnati College of Medicine.

"I'm not against public philanthropy," Dr. Schondelmeyer said. "But I disagree when industry seems to raise capital far beyond what they need to produce their product. As a consumer I begin to wonder whether the hospital is acting in my best interest when they tell me I need this expensive drug."

Sam Peltzman, a business professor at the University of Chicago, said lower drug prices were not likely to lead to less promotion—or to less research either, at least in the short term. He said the drug industry acts as if high prices "are a fountain for research and development, which is just nonsense. We give companies the freedom to set price and a monopoly to sell their product for ten to fifteen years, so they are going to try to maximize their profits. That's in large part why prices have risen." He added that lowering drug prices would only threaten development of drugs that showed little promise. "Drug companies undertake these massive searches knowing there will be a big payoff if they hit a winner. We can have lower drug prices if we accept less of that searching. That's the choice we face." [ER]

THE BURSTING DAM

I N the sluggish American economy of the early 1990s, health care is one of the few industries that has rapidly grown and prospered. But not everyone in the field has shared in the bounty: As of 1991, about 1.5 million workers—mostly nursing-home aides and mostly women—were still paid close to the minimum wage of $4.25 an hour. Now industry officials say that dam is about to burst. Workers at the bottom of the health-care system should soon see big wage increases, just as governments, insurers, and health-care providers themselves are desperately seeking ways to keep costs down.

The officials say irresistible pressures are building behind the aides' wages. The population of the United States is aging, so hundreds of thousands more aides will be needed to care for the elderly in the 1990s. Unions are redoubling efforts to organize the workers. A federal law now requires formal training and certification of aides, which enhances their value. And nursing homes want to stem the rampant turnover in personnel that plagues them. "It's a real crunch issue," said Vincent Shepherd, the Texas regional human-resources director for Beverly Enter-prises of Fort Smith, Arkansas. With 860 of the nation's 19,000 nursing homes—including the College Park Care Center, a nursing home in Texas City, a town located forty miles southeast of Houston, Beverly is the biggest operator in the business.

Van Ellet, a senior analyst for the American Association of Retired Persons, said low Medicaid payments to nursing homes, more than tightfisted nursing-home operators, account for the aides' low pay. In many cases the wages are too low to lift aides above the poverty line and off welfare. "I think it's boiling over right now. You're seeing some of the pressures coming on state Medicaid budgets."

The College Park nursing home has 111 residents, up to 104 years old. Of its 95 employees, 42 are aides; the rest are registered nurses, practical nurses, kitchen and maintenance workers, and office workers. One aide, Darlene Jefferson, said she enjoyed her work, though it made most people squeamish, including many of the younger adults who have entrusted 1.5 million of their elders to nursing homes.

"I'm a bath tech," Jefferson said. "I have fifteen to bathe a day. I bring them to the shower room down the hall. They sit on a chair. I'll wash them and rinse them off and dry them. I'll wash their face, brush their teeth. It makes them feel good. It makes me feel good. I love what I do. Because of the residents themselves, the people who live here. They love you at times. Some of them are mean and hateful, but after you do things for them, they'll kiss you and hug you and love you for doing it."

Jefferson is proud of her work. She said she could manage changing adult diapers, the strains of lifting residents, and enduring the slurs of the demented. Her sole complaint is the pay. After working twenty-six of her forty-seven years in nursing homes, Jefferson earns $4.46 an hour, or $8,700 a year, from her 37½-hour work week. Separated from her husband, the mother of five with one child still at home qualifies for $66 a month in food stamps. She cannot afford the company's health-insurance plan, which would cost about $350 a year for herself and $1,300 if she included any children. So, like most Beverly nursing aides, she cannot count on receiving the kind of care that many of her patients received during their working lives— or on getting the care in her old age that she gives them in theirs.

Even at current wage levels, aides are an important factor in the cost of health care because there are so many of them. Aides are the people who work most closely with nursing-home residents in dealing with their day-to-day needs, keeping them clean and fed, and monitoring their vital signs. They make up about one-fifth of the nation's 6.8 million health-care workers, the Bureau of Labor Statistics reports. About 60 percent of them, 1 million, work in nursing homes; most of the rest work in hospitals. Some men, usually called orderlies, do the same work and are paid about 10 percent more. But 91 percent of all aides are women, and 31 percent of all aides are black.

Without Medicaid, fewer of these people would have jobs, fewer old people would have care, and fewer nursing homes would survive. More than half of nursing-home residents lack the personal resources or private insurance to pay for their beds, so Medicaid pays. But the federal government and many states set limits on Medicaid payments. These limits have been rising, but not enough to permit significant wage increases.

Medicaid in Texas pays fifty-four dollars a day for a patient at College Park, not much more than the rate for a room in nearby motels. The 10 percent of College Park's residents who are private patients pay eighty-five dollars, more than the home needs to keep them. So they, like private patients generally, help subsidize the care of the indigent.

College Park is a sprawling one-story structure in a residential neighborhood. Its patients wear white wristbands embedded with a magnetic strip that sets off a deafening beeper when they try to slip out the door. One afternoon the beeper went off every fifteen minutes. A woman in her eighties was trying to go home to Galveston and, she told aides, get married. "They've always got their minds on going home," said Glenora Keeling, eighty-four, a good-humored, brightly dressed widow in a wheelchair.

Beverly Enterprises has weathered bouts with the courts over trying to keep out labor unions and charges of mistreating patients at a few homes. But not here. "Some of the non-Beverly homes, they have no standards," said Orell Fitzsimmons, head of

Local No. 100 of the Service Employees International Union, which represents College Park workers. "Beverly has certain standards. You have to give them credit for that. This is a clean home. It is well kept up. It doesn't smell."

The staff makes it that way. Donna Hadley, thirty-one, wears a badge labeled "environmental services." She cleans twenty rooms a day along with the public restrooms and hallways. She is single and has no children. Still, she needs more money. She is thinking of looking for a second, part-time job, rather than leaving College Park for a job that pays more.

Many residents stay in their rooms because they are bedridden. Of those who can get around, the lucid among them seemed chiefly absorbed in the personal lives they have built for themselves and the activities the home organizes, such as bingo and sing-alongs. Ludmilla Thurmond, seventy-three, a widow with Parkinson's disease, seems more concerned with learning to cope for herself than with her confinement. Her knees are flat, with six-inch-long scars of deep incisions across them. "I haven't walked for eight or nine years," she said. "When I came here, I couldn't do nothing for myself. Now they still have to put on my shoes and my pants. But I take my own shower, and I put myself to bed. I push my wheelchair. When I need help, they help me."

Janet Morris, the nursing home's administrator, called the turnover among aides "horrendous." She said four of every five aides she hired were gone within a year. Paul Willging, executive vice president of the American Health Care Association, the nursing homes' lobby, said the annual turnover for the industry generally was closer to 100 percent.

The problem will become even more acute as demand for nursing-home care rises, with people living longer and with the surge of baby-boomers who will start retiring in fifteen or twenty years. At the same time, it is becoming harder to find qualified aides because federal law now requires that they have two weeks' training and be certified. Some recruits, usually unskilled women who are trained on the job to be aides, find the work demeaning and quit. Some, Morris said, take a job just to earn a little money, and then leave. Still others move from nursing home to nursing home in pursuit of tiny wage increases of five cents or ten cents an hour or bigger increases in hospitals.

High turnover can help keep a nursing home's costs down because workers who stay so briefly never move much above the minimum wage. But it also undermines one of the homes' selling points: continuous warm relations between residents and aides. Mr. Willging said turnover would probably rise because of a widening gap between nursing-home wages—an average of $5.18 an hour nationwide in 1990 and held down by Medicaid reimbursements—and hospital aides' wages of $7.20, which are less subject to Medicaid influence. To keep their employees from fleeing to hospitals, the nursing homes will need to pay more, he said.

The gap could widen even more because of new union pressure on hospital wages. In April 1991 organized labor won an important battle with the hospitals in the United States Supreme Court. Having trouble organizing hospital workers, unions argued that hospitals stacked the deck against them by permitting bargaining units of only large groups of employees who perform very different jobs and have divergent interests. Supporting a National Labor Relations Board ruling, the Court agreed that unions could split the employees into as many as eight units, each with common interests; for example, nurses, technical workers, and maintenance personnel. Unions believe the decision will make it easier to enroll workers.

A 10 percent increase in the nursing home aides' wages, now ranging from $8,500 to $12,000 a year, would add about $1.5 billion to the nation's annual nursing-home bill, or $1,000 per patient, unless the homes found ways to cut other costs or to train each aide to take care of more patients. The effect on the nation's total health-care spending, currently about $700 billion, would be small. But in health care, as in all industries, higher wages for the lowest-paid workers tend to affect the wages of workers above them. So the effect could be much greater.

The kind of worker the nursing homes covet is one like Deborah Phifer, nineteen, a single mother of two young children. She transferred from a job in the kitchen to one caring for patients. "I take their vital signs," Phifer said. "I get them up for breakfast, help them dress, feed some, make sure they're okay and dry, and looking good." She earns $4.30 an hour, or $8,385 for her 37½-hour week, which puts her $2,034 below the Census Bureau's 1990 poverty line for a family of three. Phifer could train to be a registered nurse and earn $30,000 a year. But she said she wanted a career as an aide. "I don't want to be a registered nurse," she said. "They have so much paperwork. I want to work with the people."

Along with the wages, a drawback of the aides' job for many workers is having to face the deaths of their patients. "You just do all you can when they're living," said Erma Tezeno, fifty-nine, an aide at the home for seventeen years. "All you can do is make them as comfortable as you can." [PTK]

Ethics and Economics

THE HARDEST CHOICE

T HE baby in the plastic case lies swathed in a Mickey Mouse blanket whose cartoon characters dwarf him in size. One month after birth, he has already suffered major bleeding in his head, requiring brain surgery, and still needs a respirator to breathe. Born almost four months prematurely, weighing just over a pound, the baby is sustained by a battery of tubes and machines. His skin is thin as parchment, and his eyes are sealed shut, but he is clearly a human child. A minuscule blue-and-white stocking cap prevents heat loss through his head. "Could you turn off the respirator on this baby?" asked Dr. Harry Dweck, director of neonatal intensive care at the Westchester County Medical Center in Valhalla, New York. "Could you? I couldn't. If his parents asked me to do it, I'd go to court."

Intensive care for premature infants is now keeping alive more and more infants born very early in pregnancy. But the cost is immense—more than two thousand dollars a day—and the emotional burden on parents immeasurable. Many surviving infants who weigh less than 750 grams, about 1 pound 10 ounces, at birth turn out to have physical or mental disabilities, but there is no reliable way at present to predict the outcome. For doctors and parents the treatment of these babies thus creates ever more difficult economic and ethical dilemmas.

Dr. Dweck says he has seen infants like his patient become

normal children, although he admits the chances that the survivors will be normal are less than one in four. The remainder suffer brain damage. "Some are handicapped and are a great burden to their families and to society," Dr. Dweck said, a note of sadness in his voice. It is a price he considers worth paying, and he never pulls the plug if there is a remote chance that treatment will help.

Fifty miles away, at the neonatal intensive-care unit at University Hospital of the State University of New York at Stony Brook, Dr. Leonard Kleinman adopts a more pragmatic approach. "If a baby survives a major head bleed, we'll tell the parents he is almost surely going to be damaged, and he's suffering a great deal, and we don't think we should do anything more," said Dr. Kleinman, the hospital's director of neonatal intensive care.

Although health-care economists have recently focused their attention on intensive care for the elderly, in fact most hospitals spend far more treating the very, very young. The stakes are higher too, since a premature baby who survives intact gains a lifetime, while an infant who survives with terrible damage may require decades worth of high-cost care. To complicate matters, the most premature infants, the ones who can run up bills close to half a million dollars, are also the least likely to be helped.

Doctors and parents who must weigh these vexing options have found no uniform answer. So the baby who is kept in intensive care for months at one hospital might be allowed to die at birth elsewhere. "It's a matter of style," said Dr. Alan Fleischman, director of neonatal intensive care at Montefiore Medical Center in the Bronx, noting that some doctors feel they must treat one hundred babies aggressively if there is a chance of saving one. "I don't buy that: creating one normal child by creating ninety-nine who are handicapped and disabled. We argue endlessly about which is worse: a healthy baby in heaven or a damaged baby on earth. I say neither is good, but we're going to make mistakes in both directions." Dr. Fleischman said he believed the major problem today was that babies who will not benefit from intensive care are overtreated, even when the parents do not want aggressive care.

Premature infants stay in high-tech wombs for about the same length of time that they should have remained in their mother's: four months for the most premature, who are born at twenty-four weeks gestation and weigh in the neighborhood of 500 grams, or slightly over a pound. "Above 700 grams there is clearly a great benefit to intensive care," Dr. Fleischman said. Below 700 grams, or about 1 pound 8 ounces, things get murky. Many of the very-low-birth-weight babies succumb to lung failure or severe bleeding in the brain, since these organs have not fully matured.

Dr. Michael Rie, an intensive-care specialist at the University of Kentucky in Lexington, said, "The hundred highest users of Medicaid dollars in each state are preemies who end up for months on ventilators and end up with cerebral bleeds and extremely lousy outcomes." For insurance reimbursement, the New York State Department of Health considers infants weighing below 750 grams to be the most expensive type of patient to care for, three times as costly as a person with serious burns and 20 percent more costly than even a heart-transplant patient.

Almost 50 percent of babies born weighing from 500 to 750 grams, or 1 pound 2 ounces to 1 pound 10 ounces, will survive, but the majority will have neurological damage. From 750 grams to 1,500 grams, or 3 pounds 5 ounces, about 85 percent will live, and the great majority will have no impairment. Above 1,500 grams, which has historically defined the upper boundary of very-low-birth-weight infants, babies have an excellent chance of emerging from intensive care fully intact.

In contrast, in the early 1980s it was a rare child born under 1 pound 8 ounces who even survived, and before the early 1970s, when neonatal intensive-care units began operating, few children under 2 pounds survived. But as advances allow medicine to save more and more babies, the demand for neonatal intensive care has risen, and existing units are bursting at the seams. Babies born prematurely to women who use crack or have had no prenatal care have swelled the demand. As a result, most neonatal intensive-care units have removed walls to squeeze in a few more beds, and hired nurses to work overtime. Most operate at more than 100 percent of their licensed capacity. Dr. Dweck, whose intensive-care unit serves five counties north of New York City, said he had to turn away 250 babies each year.

While pediatricians say that babies in need ultimately find a hospital that can squeeze them in, the crunch has led some to call for more public financing and others for a more "rational" use of existing beds. "Last week there was a 900-gram baby at a community hospital who we knew we could help, but we were horribly overcrowded," Dr. Kleinman said. "Meanwhile, we had a preemie with severe brain damage who hadn't moved in three weeks taking one of our beds. I'm not sure that's fair."

Some beds are occupied for months or years by the growing number of severely brain-damaged children or children on respirators who, saved from death in the intensive-care unit, are too chronically ill to go home or even move to a regular hospital bed. A 1990 New York State Health Department report on neonatal services in New York City found that in the larger units an average of two beds were occupied by such children, sometimes for years.

Situations such as these are leading people to question whether millions of dollars should be spent on intensive care for the tiniest infants, who are unlikely to live. But many are appalled by the thought. "If you were told that anyone over seventy-five years old with a stroke couldn't get care, how would that sound?" Dr. Dweck said. "That's how I feel about the 500-grammers." He said he would resuscitate fully any baby who shows signs of life at delivery regardless of gestational age or weight. In contrast, Dr. Kleinman said he did not routinely try to save babies under the 500-gram mark, but permitted the doctors who worked for him to try if they thought the baby had a chance. "We generally keep them warm and let them expire by themselves," he said. "These are not viable babies, and it's crazy to do anything more."

Others said they withdraw treatment but only once it becomes clear that their efforts would be futile. Decisions to withdraw care are usually made after consultations among doctors, nurses, and parents, but if these parties disagree, the treatment usually continues. If the parents and the doctors remain at odds about the proper course of treatment, the baby is sometimes moved to another hospital.

For doctors and parents, decisions on care of premature infants are inevitably tortured affairs, complicated by the impossibility of determining the ultimate fate of any given infant. While doctors know, for example, that about 40 percent of babies weighing 600 grams at birth, about 1 pound 5 ounces, will apparently be normal at one year, they have few clues as to which babies will fall into which group. And no one knows if babies who have normal brain examinations at one year will be developmentally normal at six or seven.

"Moms are constantly asking me, 'Is my baby going to be okay?' And I have to say, 'If you line up one hundred babies here, I can't tell you which will be doing well by kindergarten,'" Dr. Dweck said. "That's what makes it difficult for me to withdraw treatment in a willy-nilly fashion." But others say that while this may be true at birth, once premature infants experience certain complications, their odds of leading normal lives become smaller and smaller. The most serious problem is bleeding in the brain, which occurs in about 75 percent of babies under 1,000 grams—about 2 pounds 3 ounces. In many cases it will be mild and have no obvious long-term consequences, but specialists say that in about one-quarter of the cases the bleed will be severe, compressing important brain structures that in the short term leads to seizures and strokes, and in the long term to permanent damage.

"In these cases the decision is not about death," Dr. Fleischman said. "It's about severe impairment. We know the child will be severely impaired, it's only the level that's hard to predict." He said that in such cases he recommended care be withdrawn, although he said he would continue at the parents' request.

The intensive-care units for infants are technological marvels in miniature. At Westchester County Medical Center each tiny infant bed takes thirteen electrical outlets and three gas lines for oxygen and suctioning secretions from the baby's mouths and lungs. Laboratories now perform dozens of biochemical tests on a few drops of blood, tests that in the mid-1980s would have required a full vial—one-twentieth of a premature baby's blood volume—to complete.

New drugs released in 1991, called artificial surfactants, can improve the breathing capacity of the infant's normally stiff lungs. But some experts worry about overuse. Studies on infants with respiratory distress syndrome have shown that the drug can decrease the length of time on a respirator for infants over 750 grams and can improve survival in babies from 500 to 750 grams. But, encouraged by the drug's manufacturers, many doctors are using the drug in babies who are well but are felt to be at risk of developing respiratory distress. Even more worrisome to health-care economists has been the proliferation of a hugely expensive artificial lung that sits outside the body, called ECMO, whose benefits for infants remain largely unproved. Also designed to rescue infants with severe breathing problems, it pumps blood out of the infant, saturates it with oxygen, and returns it to the body.

Also driving doctors to aggressively save the tiny infants are fears. What if they withdraw treatment and the baby survives— and is left even more damaged? Dr. Dweck tells of a baby who was transferred to Westchester County Medical Center with trouble breathing and with signs of brain damage because of lack of oxygen. He had not moved for ten days. "The parents and all four grandparents wanted the ventilator discontinued," Dr. Dweck said. "If I withdraw treatment and the baby lives, how much additional damage will I have done?"

And many worry about legal obligations in the wake of the Baby Doe cases of the mid-1980s, when pediatricians were told they could be prosecuted under child abuse and neglect laws for withholding or withdrawing care from sick infants. Although pediatricians such as Dr. Fleischman insist that the law permits them to stop treating infants when treatment is clearly futile, many remain cautious. In a 1988 survey of neonatologists, half said that because of legal fears, they had performed treatments that they thought were not in a baby's best interest. Dr. Fleischman said, "I am really concerned when I see a doctor who won't stop treatment when a baby is no longer benefiting." But Dr. Rie said, "You have to go soft on pediatricians. Remember, in the mid-eighties there was an 800 number to call if you thought a pediatrician was bumping off a kid." [ER]

THE SEARCH FOR MIRACLES

NOVEMBER 1, 1991, five days after a car accident broke nearly every bone in his body, the Reverend Clair Frederick Yohe, eighty-seven years old, lay semiconscious in the surgical intensive-care unit of the Albany (New York) Medical Center. Given his advanced age, the multitude of broken bones, the collapsed lung, and the lacerated internal organs, doctors had known from the start that he had scant chance of surviving. Yet every one of his injuries could in theory be fixed, and his brain was intact. So the doctors and nurses were doing everything they could, and doing it well. Over and over they wheeled him to the operating room to sew up bleeding organs and repair shattered bones. They ran tubes into his neck, chest, and arms to feed him oxygen, nutrients, antibiotics, and sedatives, to drain fluid from his chest, and to take constant readings of his heart function and other vital signs. They put his legs in traction and wired his cracked jaw shut. Through it all Mr. Yohe lay still, the gentle seashore rhythms of his mechanical breather belying the violence of his injuries, the furiousness of his care.

As the country's health costs climb, there is serious talk about rationing high-priced care such as this, of avoiding treatment that is unlikely to succeed. And it is in the intensive-care unit, with patients like Mr. Yohe, where all the financial, technological, and ethical dilemmas converge.

On another floor of the Albany hospital, in the medical intensive-care unit, fifty-one-year-old Kathleen Cookingham also lay unconscious, her breath supplied by the mechanical ventilator that defines life in the ICU. More than a year earlier, with her body already ravaged by advancing multiple sclerosis, Mrs. Cookingham, her husband, and her doctors had all agreed that no heroic resuscitations should be attempted. Yet now she had been in intensive care for more than three months, with no end in sight. "When Kathy decided that she would not live on a machine, I had the impression it was a black-and-white issue," her husband, Earl Cookingham, later said. "It was never that. It was a very gradual type of thing. You made this decision and that decision, and all of a sudden you're where you didn't want to be."

That same November day, Sheryl Dugan, a twenty-eight-year-old mother of four, was happily tending her children at home in Morris, New York. Earlier that year she too had lain critically ill in an Albany intensive-care unit, even giving emergency birth to a daughter there. A runaway lung infection had put her so near death that her doctors gave up hope. But she recovered miraculously, becoming a vibrant example of why extraordinary measures are pursued at all.

Care of the critically ill, applying the highest technology to the sickest patients, is startlingly expensive, by some estimates consuming close to 1 percent of the gross national product. As the ability to sustain failing bodies gets ever better, the potential costs become virtually limitless. In the end, the way that society chooses to care for patients like Clair Frederick Yohe, Kathleen Cookingham, and Sheryl Dugan will set the outer limits of the country's medical spending.

It will help define society's ethical limits too. "We have to make sure we are prolonging life, not just prolonging the dying process," said Dr. I. Alan Fein, head of surgical critical care at Albany Medical Center and one of the doctors who attended Mr. Yohe. The spreading "right to die" movement, asserting the right of fatally stricken patients to forego futile care, will certainly help hold down costs and allow more peaceful deaths. On the other side, fear of legal action, or the insistence of families that cling to groundless hopes, sometimes prevents doctors from withholding care they know will be useless.

But even when the patient, the family, and the doctor are all attuned, there is often no obvious answer, as the stories of these three patients show. "Doctors can't decide these things," said Dr. Thomas C. Smith, chief of Albany's medical ICU. "Society has to tell us what to do."

Except for arthritis, Mr. Yohe (pronounced YO-hee) and his wife, Louise, eighty-one, were pictures of health. For sixty years he had served as a Methodist minister, most of them in partnership with Louise, his spouse of fifty-four years. For the last two decades the couple lived on Isle LaMotte, on Lake Champlain in Vermont, where they raised their own pesticide-free vegetables. It was an interim ministry in the late 1960s, when they helped get a small-town church on its feet, that led the Yohes to be driving one Sunday in October 1991 near Kingston, New York, some sixty miles south of Albany. A still-grateful congregation had asked Yohe back to participate in a service and share recollections. After the service, they were on their way to join a family for lunch, Mrs. Yohe driving their Geo, when another car plowed into theirs. Mrs. Yohe's right leg, pelvis, and ribs were injured. Her husband was, as she bluntly described it, "shattered."

Help came quickly, and the pair were taken to the nearby Kingston hospital. Because Mr. Yohe's injuries were so serious, doctors there sent him by ambulance to Albany, the advanced regional medical center. Traveling on a ventilator, he arrived at the Albany emergency room in deep shock, his blood pressure barely perceptible. The emergency-room doctors did what they are supposed to do when a critically ill patient arrives: They started aggressive treatment. And once treatment began, there could be no going halfway. The transfusions began immediately, and over the next forty-eight hours Mr. Yohe's entire blood volume would be replaced more than three times. He was rushed to the operating room, where his damaged spleen was removed and his stomach and kidneys were sewn up; over the next two weeks he would repeatedly be taken from the intensive-care unit to the operating room for elaborate repairs of the badly broken bones in both arms, his upper and lower legs, and his face.

The day after the accident, still in great pain herself but informed that her husband was in grave danger, Louise Yohe was wheeled to his bedside. "He was highly sedated and didn't arouse," she later recalled. But when she came back the next day, "he lifted a couple fingers, as if in a greeting," she said. "So I gather that he knew me." And later, after his jaw had been wired shut, "I was telling him a little about what had happened," she said. "I think he had a faint smile, and that gave me hope, of course. I told the doctors I wanted to know the truth about his condition. I had a little premonition that I wouldn't take him home alive. I must tell you, though, my husband was a fighter."

About two weeks after the accident, Dr. Fein would tell a caller: "He's still hanging in there, going back for his umpteenth orthopedic procedure. The odds of him actually surviving are incredibly slim. But theoretically everything is reversible. So we just trudge along and see what happens." At about that point Mr. Yohe's lungs began functioning well enough to wean him from the ventilator. No longer in need of such minute-by-minute, one-on-one scrutiny, he was transferred to a normal hospital room, freeing up the scarce intensive-care bed he had occupied for two and a half weeks.

But, as expected, he was still in perilous condition, his liver and kidneys declining under the cumulative strain, hospital-acquired infections setting in. The doctors told Mrs. Yohe how ill her husband was but said they could keep him alive on a dialysis machine. "I said no, we didn't want that," she recalled. "We had decided a long time ago that neither one of us wanted to be on life support. I had to sign a form, and that was very hard." Mrs. Yohe said she was not surprised when a doctor came to her room a few days later with the news. "They told me that he just went to sleep," she said.

If marginal care is ever to be rationed, patients in Mr. Yohe's condition might be among the first to be denied aggressive treatment. When he entered the Albany hospital, doctors believed that he had less than a 1 percent chance of surviving. Hospital bills for his final month amounted to more than $100,000, Dr. Fein said. Hospital costs are relatively low in upstate New York, and billing is limited by state regulation; in many parts of the country, or in New York City, his care might have cost several times that. In his case, auto insurance and Medicare should cover most of the fees. Had Louise Yohe insisted on continued aggressive treatment, as some relatives in similar circumstances do, her husband might have been sustained on a dialysis machine and a ventilator for another month or more, his doctors believe, at several thousand dollars a day.

Several medical teams around the country are developing "prognostic scales," scorecards for judging survival odds of the critically ill. Their goal is a tool that can help doctors avoid useless care. For patients in a lasting coma, or who are certainly about to die from, for example, widespread cancer, the futility can be obvious. In such cases, ICU directors already, without a numerical scorecard, often serve as gatekeeper, refusing entry into their crowded units those patients who can die elsewhere more comfortably, with less cost.

But refusing care is never easy, even at a hospital like Albany, where doctors are in the forefront of thinking about prudent use of medical technology; even with patients like Mr. Yohe who have declared a desire to avoid prolonged misery. "We believed he had only a one percent chance of survival, and yet we admitted him," Dr. Fein said several days after Mr. Yohe's death. "Was that the right thing to have done? Probably it was." He added, "Society still has very high expectations of what we should do for a patient like Reverend Yohe."

*   *   *

Sometimes medical care can build in a series of individually sensible steps to a senseless extreme, with no obvious cutoff point along the way. Over the last four years, Kathleen Cookingham, a mother of two daughters now nineteen and twenty-four, became what doctors sometimes call a "revolving door" patient in the ICU, in and out repeatedly with no hope of a cure and a declining quality of life. Cookingham had worked as a legal secretary until 1985, when multiple sclerosis, a progressive deterioration of the nervous system, had seriously impaired her eyes, legs, and bladder. The disease worsened in 1987, and she had to enter the hospital for intensive care. That stay lasted four agonizing months. She was unconscious at times, and the doctors said they did not believe she would survive. "She fought, and she came out of the hospital," her husband, Earl, recalled. "She was in a wheelchair, but she led a productive life." But she and her husband vowed that she would avoid a miserable life on machines.

Over the next three years, her condition deteriorating, she required several more hospital stays, some for a few days, some for weeks, usually requiring intensive care and mechanical breathing, especially as the multiple sclerosis affected nerves that controlled her diaphragm. Another crisis occurred in December 1990. By then she had also lost control of her swallowing muscles, which meant she had to be fed indefinitely through a stomach tube, just the kind of dependence she had hoped to avoid. The Cookinghams, who live on the outskirts of Albany, had developed a close relationship with hospital doctors, and the husband called Dr. Smith, a pulmonary and critical-care specialist, to discuss what to do. "The question was whether we should just leave her at home and let her die," Mr. Cookingham said.

Even then, Dr. Smith recalled, it was clear that her treatment was pushing beyond what anyone wanted. But their older daughter's wedding was just days away. As Dr. Smith remembered it, "Her husband beseeched us to keep her alive another three days, to not let her die before her daughter's wedding."

According to Earl Cookingham, Dr. Smith told him, "You can't deal with this now; bring her to the hospital." So she spent weeks in the ICU, and her chronic care escalated another unwanted step. When she went home that January a stomach tube was in place; now she needed a full-time nurse. But later, in the spring, she was able to see her second daughter graduate from high school.

A spate of seizures required several visits to the emergency room and then, in July 1991, another hospitalization. A chest infection forced her back onto a ventilator. The weeks in the ICU went by, and then still another technological step was taken. Because she never wanted to be on a breathing machine more than temporarily, Mrs. Cookingham had always refused to have a tracheostomy, in which a tube is put through the neck directly into the windpipe. Though to her it symbolized unwanted medical bondage, a tracheostomy is safer and less uncomfortable than a tube down the throat, the short-term approach. This last stay in the ICU dragged on so long, her husband said, that it seemed cruel to leave a throat tube in, so he finally consented to the tracheostomy. But soon after that she developed a blood infection, and "things really began to go sour," he said.

By early November 1991 Kathleen Cookingham's condition was worse than ever. Dr. Smith, emotionally drained himself and convinced that her care had spun out of control, decided to broach the unthinkable with her husband. "I told him we don't have to keep going," Dr. Smith recalled.

"Kathy and I had agreed that if the ventilation was only temporary, that was fine," Earl Cookingham later said. "But then it got to be two, three months." He remembered that the doctor showed him pictures of her scarred lungs and explained that her heart was now impaired. She had stopped communicating. "That's when we decided to take her off the machine," Mr. Cookingham said. "I was following her wishes."

A few days later, on November 7, a priest joined the family in the intensive-care unit and held a Catholic service at her bedside. "We all went in and held hands," Dr. Smith said. The service took about twenty minutes. Dr. Smith then gave her morphine and removed her breathing tube. Twenty minutes later she was dead.

Thinking over the last few years, Mr. Cookingham said he would not have done much differently. "She was so unpredictable," he said. "The doctors repeatedly said she wouldn't come off the machine, and then she did, and came home and had a decent life." In hindsight, he said, "maybe the last month went on longer than we intended."

Her final three-month stay in intensive care cost at least $180,000, the doctors estimated, and her care over the last several years of her life cost several hundred thousand dollars. (In some regions the costs would have surpassed $1 million.) The Cookinghams themselves did not have to pay much. The bills were mainly paid with public money—by Medicare, which covers disabled people—supplemented by their private policy. Medicaid paid for a home nurse over much of the last year.

"It was worth it," Mr. Cookingham said. "I know that's easy for me to say, because financially it didn't kill us, but I think it was worth it." The rounds of costly intensive care "gave her three years to live, three years with us, and two of the three years were very good."

Dr. Smith is still visibly seared. "The language isn't good enough to convey the emotions going on with a case like this," he said. "It's like the Eskimos having all those different words for snow. We don't yet have the right vocabulary for dying."

The ICU doctors do not give up on any patient without thinking about Sheryl Dugan, a patient who they thought would surely die, but somehow walked out of the hospital on her own feet. In May 1991 she was in her eighth month of pregnancy, when her three young children came down with chicken pox. Then she did too. Routine for children, chicken pox is potentially disastrous for pregnant women, who often suffer severe complications.

Mrs. Dugan's doctor warned her to go to the hospital at the first sign of a cough, and one night the coughing started. Doctors at the nearest hospital, in Oneonta, New York, found that the chicken-pox virus, which had already caused scratchy sores all over her body, had spread into her lungs. They sent her by ambulance on the two-hour trip to Albany. She arrived at the Albany Medical Center early on June 1, and later that day, her pneumonia worsening by the minute, was put into intensive care and on a ventilator.

The chicken-pox virus had spread not only through her lungs but also her liver, causing hepatitis. On top of that, a potentially lethal bacterium had invaded her weakened lungs, and she developed a blood infection. Her bowel shut down, and she became anemic. Most dangerous of all, she developed adult respiratory distress syndrome, an untreatable, often fatal response to infections in which fluids leak uncontrollably into the lung tissue, impeding the ability to absorb oxygen.

On her second day in the ICU she went into labor. "It was pretty hectic, with about twenty-five people in a ten-by-fifteen room," her husband recalled. Woozy from drugs and disease, Sheryl Dugan nevertheless remembers the birth quite clearly. "They didn't want me to push," she said. "They were afraid my lungs might burst. But I helped anyway." She would remember nothing more of the next four weeks. The baby girl cried when she emerged and was rushed away to prevent further exposure to the chicken pox.

Doctors fought Mrs. Dugan's infections with antibiotics, and the chicken pox with an antiviral drug, but mostly they could do little more than wait. To force more oxygen through her damaged lungs, the ventilator was turned up full throttle, risking a fatal tear of tissue from the high air pressure. She had to be paralyzed because even one cough, against that pressure, "would have shattered her lungs," Dr. Smith said. Even so, the young woman was absorbing so little oxygen that her heart began stopping intermittently, at one point failing to beat for six full seconds. Her tissues accumulated fluids, raising her weight from her normal 130 pounds to more than 200.

The baby, at the age of ten days, was in fine shape and was sent home to Mrs. Dugan's sister. "That was pretty tough, seeing her go," said her husband, who spent a month at his wife's bedside, from seven in the morning to ten at night. "I thought if Sheryl could see the baby, that might help her fight back."

One night, some weeks after the birth, Mr. Dugan recalled, "I called Sheryl's name, and she didn't respond at all. That's when I realized things were pretty serious." That day, doctors convened a conference with the family, the hospital's pastoral-care unit, social workers, and nurses. "They told me she wasn't going to make it," Mr. Dugan recalled. He went for a long walk, found a church, and sat. "We would have quit," Dr. Smith later said, "except here you had a twenty-seven-year-old with a new baby."

Then suddenly, only a couple of days after that painful family conference, and for no apparent reason, something changed. "After a while you get to know the machines," her husband said. "I saw the numbers coming round. She opened her eyes and looked around a bit, and she started to recognize my voice again." Her recovery was as swift as her decline. Doctors began weaning her from the mechanical breather on June 29. The next day is when she remembers fully waking up. "I didn't even know why I was there," she said. "The nurses talked to me like they knew me, but I didn't recognize them."

A few days later her breathing tube was removed. Three days after that she left for home, the more than fifty thousand dollars devoted to her care well spent. As she left, the doctors and nurses cried. "She got better so fast, I believe in miracles," Dr. Smith would later say. [EE]

HOPE AGAINST HOPE

IN a case that medical ethicists and legal experts say was apparently a first, a Minneapolis hospital went to court in early 1991 for permission to turn off a patient's life-support system against her family's wishes. For more than eight months, eighty-seven-year-old Helga Wanglie had lain in Hennepin County Medical Center in a world created by modern medicine: dependent a ventilator for oxygen and a feeding tube for nutrition, unaware of and unresponsive to her surroundings. Her doctors said she would never recover, and they did not want to give medical care that they termed futile.

But Mrs. Wanglie's husband and two children described her as an extremely religious woman who would have preferred even this life to death. "This is the opposite of Cruzan," said Arthur Caplan, director of the Center for Biomedical Ethics at the University of Minnesota, referring to Nancy Cruzan, the Missouri woman whose family fought for years to remove her from the feeding tube that was keeping her alive. Over the objections of the state hospital where Miss Cruzan lived in a vegetative coma, the tube was removed and she died in 1990.

"We've all worked long and hard for the patient's right to say stop," said Susan M. Wolf, an associate for law at the Hastings Center, a research center for biomedical ethics in Briarcliff, New York. "That leaves the lurking question of whether it's a symmetrical issue, and they also have the right to say 'Do everything indefinitely,' even when the doctors believe it's futile." It is a rare termination-of-care case of any kind that reaches the courtroom. Decisions to withdraw medical technology are made daily around the country. The American Hospital Association estimates that 70 percent of hospital deaths are preceded by a decision to stop some form of care. Yet Dr. Caplan said he knew of no more than forty state court opinions about ending care.

It is even rarer that a dispute finds the doctors arguing for withdrawal of life support against the wishes of the patient's family. "None of those forty address that situation," he said. "If there is such a case, it's the exception." Ms. Wolf agreed. "Maybe one other case has been reported where this kind of role reversal took place," she said, but she added that she was not familiar with one.

The reason there are few court cases of this type, experts say, is because doctors are reluctant to publicly advocate the death of a patient. Dr. Eugene Boisaubin, an emergency-room doctor who is head of the biomedical ethics consultation service at the Methodist Hospital in Houston, said circumstances similar to those of the Wanglie family arose regularly. He estimated that 95 percent of the disagreements can be resolved with talking and time. In the other 5 percent of cases, he said, "we do what the family wants, even though it goes against our medical judgment. We do know that the patient will die, but not until weeks or months later. Until this, no one had the guts to go to court." He said that he had heard of hospitals choosing to override the family and disconnect life support without a court order, but noted that his hospital had never chosen to do so.

The case that Hennepin County Medical Center took to court began on December 14, 1989, when Mrs. Wanglie tripped on a scatter rug in her hallway and fractured her right hip. She was taken to a nearby private hospital and underwent surgery. The next month she developed breathing problems and was transferred to the Hennepin County Medical Center, where she was placed on a respirator. She stayed there for five months, fully conscious and alert, writing notes to her doctors and her husband, Oliver, since the breathing tube down her throat prevented her from speaking.

In May 1990 she was weaned from her respirator and transferred to a long-term care institution across the river in St. Paul. She had been in the institution for less than a week when her heartbeat and breathing stopped suddenly. By the time she could be resuscitated she had suffered severe brain damage and was transferred back to Hennepin County Medical Center in a vegetative state. "She doesn't know anybody or anything," said Mr. Wanglie, then eighty-six. He and his children, Ruth, forty-eight, and David, forty-five, visited two or three times a week, said the retired Minneapolis lawyer. They'd stay about a half an hour and talk to the nurses about Mrs. Wanglie's condition, but they would not talk to his wife, he said, because "she wouldn't even know we were there."

Mr. Wanglie said the doctors caring for his wife first raised the question of turning off her ventilator in late May. At a meeting in a hospital conference room, he said, the family vehemently objected. He told the doctors that his wife of fifty-three years would have wanted to live. Mrs. Wanglie, a retired school teacher and the daughter of a Lutheran minister, "had strong religious convictions," her husband said in an interview. "We talked about this a year ago. If anything happened to her, she said, she wants everything done.

"She told me, 'Only He who gave life has the right to take life,'" Mr. Wanglie said of a discussion he had had with his wife before her fall. He said she had never put those thoughts into writing. "It seems to me they're trying to play God," Mr. Wanglie said. "Who are they to determine who's to die and who's to live? I take the position that as long as her heart is beating, there's life there."

Dr. Michael B. Belzer, medical director of Hennepin County Medical Center, said he sympathized with the Wanglies. But a heartbeat no longer signifies life, he said in an interview. Modern machinery can keep a patient's heart beating long after there is any hope of recovery, he said, adding, "We don't feel that physicians are obliged to provide inappropriate medical treatment that is not in the patient's medical interest.

"Since we have this explosion of medical technology, this hospital has the technology to keep fifty Helga Wanglies alive for an indefinite period of time," he said. "That would be the easy thing to do. The harder thing is to say just because we can do it, do we have to do it?"

The case of Mrs. Wanglie illustrates a broader debate over when medical care becomes futile. The broadest interpretation is that care is futile if it will not cure the underlying condition or make the patient more comfortable. Dr. Stanley J. Reiser, director of the Program on Humanities and Technology in Health Care at the University of Texas Medical School in Houston, uses the analogy of a patient who has cancer and whose family demands that he be given antibiotics or have his appendix removed.

If that would not cure him, he said, the doctors would not accede to the family's wishes. Similarly, he said, if the cancer patient was being given a certain type of drug that was not fulfilling expectations, that drug would be stopped, even if the family asked that it be continued. "Those things create no benefit in the underlying condition," Dr. Reiser said. "That is the definition of futile medical care."

Other ethicists agree with the analogy but not the broad definition of futility. Ms. Wolf and the Hastings Center have defined futile medical care as care that does not accomplish its immediate purpose. If a respirator keeps a patient breathing, she said, it cannot be defined as futile. "Once you broaden the definition and say something is futile because it's just not worth it, you're on shaky ground," she said. "A patient or a family should have the right to decide whether something is worth it, but should the doctor?"

Mrs. Wanglie's case was unusual because her family's health insurance covered her hospitalization almost entirely. "This is a pure ethics case," Dr. Caplan said. "It's not about money, but futility, and what we mean by futility. We've talked around that concept in recent years, using the smoke screen of 'Can we afford to do this?' There's been a harder question buried under that layer of blather about money; namely, 'What's the point of medical care?'"

In January 1991 Dr. Belzer said his hospital hoped to raise that question publicly by asking the county district court to allow the removal of Mrs. Wanglie's life-support system. He said it was a step hospital officials decided to take after other options failed. He said the hospital staff had met with the Wanglie family members and asked them to have Mrs. Wanglie transferred to another hospital or to file for an injunction forcing Hennepin County Medical Center to continue care. That would have brought a legal ruling without having the hospital appear to aggressively advocate a patient's death.

Mr. Wanglie and his children refused to do either. "I want her to stay where she is," Mr. Wanglie said. "And I don't think I need a court order to ask a hospital to provide medical care." Hennepin County Medical Center is a public hospital, its governing body the elected County Board of Commissioners. Before the hospital could petition the court to appoint Mrs. Wanglie a conservator or a guardian, who in fact would seek to have her life-support system removed, it needed the board's permission.

The board members approved the hospital's action, 4 to 3, with the tie-breaking vote being cast by a commissioner who has known the Wanglie family for thirty years. He announced his decision in January 1991 after more than a month of deliberation. That commissioner, Randy Johnson, said in an interview that he decided to allow the hospital to bring its request to court because "I don't think this is a decision to be made by a board of elected commissioners who happen to be trustees of the hospital. These are issues that we're going to be confronted with more and more often as medical machinery becomes more and more able to keep people alive," he said. On July 1, 1991, the Hennepin County Court ruled against the county hospital, affirming the right of Helga Wanglie's husband to make medical decisions on her behalf. A few days later Helga Wanglie died from multiple organ failure caused by infection, the hospital reported. [LB]

DOCTORS SAY YES,
INSURERS SAY NO

DR. Steven Nissen, a cardiologist at the Cleveland Clinic Foundation, was called in to consult in the puzzling case of a forty-four-year-old woman. Her chest felt tight at times, but she did not have the pain that signals the clogged arteries of heart disease. Hospitalized several times for the discomfort, she was discharged each time when tests showed nothing wrong.

Then Dr. Nissen had an idea: a new, little-used test called intravascular ultrasound, which would let him see inside the woman's arteries. Like something out of the film *Fantastic Voyage*, the test involves threading through the blood vessels a catheter with the equivalent of a tiny movie camera at the tip. "We put the probe in there," Dr. Nissen said, "and sure enough, there was soft cholesterol-laden plaque all up and down the artery," indicating serious clogging.

The other doctors in the room, who were about to send the woman home with no treatment, were shocked. They prescribed two powerful cholesterol-lowering drugs and a strict low-fat diet to try to induce the plaque to regress. The hope is to prevent a disabling or fatal heart attack, keep the woman at work, and eliminate enormous hospital bills.

Intravascular ultrasound "could be the most important change in the way we evaluate patients with coronary disease in the last thirty years," said Dr. Jeffrey Isner, chief of cardiovascular research at St. Elizabeth's Hospital in Boston. Other cardiologists agree. They say it shows the inside of a patient's blood vessels with detail so fine and images so pure, the only thing comparable is to split open the blood vessels at autopsy and look at them. But development and use of the new device has languished, doctors and manufacturers say, falling victim to the nation's struggle to control medical costs.

The bill for each intravascular ultrasound is expected to be several thousand dollars. Insurance companies are beginning to refuse to pay for such expensive tests and treatments unless it can be clinically proved that they are more effective for a particular class of patient than are the existing methods. And their costs must be justified, by improvement in the patient and also sometimes by elimination of the need for other costly treatments. The catch, cardiologists and manufacturers say, is that the only way to prove intravascular ultrasound is clinically and cost-effective is to use it a lot. And the only way that will happen is if insurers pay for it.

Health-care experts say that the story of intravascular ultrasound illustrates a growing obstacle to the development of medical technology. For years the country has relied on health insurance to pay for the diffusion of new technologies that saved or improved lives and—oh, by the way—turned a pretty profit for doctors, hospitals, and medical-equipment manufacturers and the investors who financed them. When that source is cut off, there seems nowhere else to turn.

The problem, many experts say, is that in the name of cost containment Americans may be slowing progress toward medical advances—even ones that might ultimately save on health costs by detecting disease at an early stage, curing it at a lower cost, or preventing it. "What you see here in this case, what's being complained about, is the beginnings of mechanisms of controlling a process that never was controlled," said Dr. Norman Daniels, a health-care researcher at Tufts University. "In the past you could always just go ahead and run with this ball as far as you could and see if it was worth carrying. And if it wasn't, so what? You could always get reimbursement."

Insurers say they are in a bind. Expensive technologies account for 40 percent of annual increases in health-insurance premiums, said Dr. John Cova, director of medical technology assessment for the Health Insurance Association of America, which represents many insurance companies. "We have fewer and fewer health-care dollars to spend each year and more and more to spend them on," he said. "We can no longer afford to support the diffusion of new technology through health-care coverage."

Intravascular ultrasound is far from the only treatment running into resistance from insurers. Dr. Michael Strauss, the president of Health Technology Associates, a consulting firm in Washington, said the new insurance climate has a chilling effect on investors who finance small companies. "If it takes five, six, or seven years to get payment, most companies can't hold out that long," he said. "We have retainer agreements with lots of venture capitalists, and about once a week we get a call asking what is the likelihood of payment" on a new method or device.

A 1991 survey of executives at medical product and service companies found that 45 percent of those at companies with sales exceeding $51 million thought that the new resistance by insurers, which also includes bargaining down the price they pay for various treatments, was hurting their stock price and financing prospects. The figure rose to 81 percent at the smallest companies (sales under $5 million). One-third of the company presidents in the survey, by the consulting firm Biomedical Business International of Santa Ana, California, said cuts in insurance coverage would reduce revenues by as much as 5 percent; almost half said the drop would be 6 percent to 25 percent.

Not too long ago, insurers routinely paid for devices and medical procedures that had Food and Drug Administration approval. And devices such as that used for intravascular ultrasound are usually approved quite quickly by the FDA. Unlike drugs, for which manufacturers have to prove safety and efficacy, devices need only be substantially equivalent to other devices on the market.

But FDA approval is "not enough anymore," Dr. Strauss said. The Health Insurance Association of America helps its members decide whether to pay for new technologies by convening panels of experts to discuss them. Dr. Cova said he brings together four or five advocates of a technology and four or five who challenge it. An expert deemed neutral leads the panel, and transcripts are sent to the three hundred commercial insurers in the group. The medical director at each insurer then decides whether to recommend reimbursement. Dr. Cova said the insurance association also passes its findings on to the government for its own health programs, including Medicare and Medicaid. The government assesses technology through the tiny Office of Health Technology Assessment. And like the private insurers, the government has increasingly balked at paying for certain things.

The field of cardiology, in which the intravascular ultrasound is a potential player, illustrates the way medical technology, with all its benefits and costs, has proliferated. Thirty years ago a patient with chest discomfort who went to the doctor would typically come away with nitroglycerin pills that temporarily relieve chest pain. The cost was usually minimal. Then again, a lot of patients later died of heart attacks.

In the 1960s came the wide use of angiography, in which a dye is injected into the arteries and an X ray is taken, showing constrictions. The test, improved since then, costs insurers about $1,500, says the Blue Cross and Blue Shield Association. By the 1970s surgeons were practicing coronary-bypass surgery, in which blood is shunted around a blocked artery. Such surgery typically costs $40,000 today. Now diagnostic tests also include an echocardiogram, measuring heart movement, at about $450, and a scintillation test, measuring blood flow to the heart, at $400.

An intravascular ultrasound would cost insurers about $3,000 to $4,000, said Melissa Sabino, vice president of the Wilkerson Group, a New York health-care consulting company. This includes about $2,000 to $3,000 for the hospital and about $1,000 for the cardiologist administering the ten-minute test. And that charge might come on top of the cost of the angiogram tried beforehand. Such procedures have proved lucrative for the specialists who perform them; these doctors "have increased their income quite a bit recently," Ms. Sabino said, by doing more procedures and charging more.

In an intravascular ultrasound, doctors thread a thin catheter into the blood vessels. At the tip of the catheter is a minuscule device that bounces sound waves off the artery walls. A special ultrasound machine picks up the signals and produces detailed pictures. The technique helps cardiologists determine whether the artery-clogging plaque is hard or soft. This allows doctors to more rationally consider a variety of options, including whether to do a bypass, to try to squash the plaque against the vessel wall by inflating a tiny balloon within the artery, or to try to vaporize the plaque with a laser.

In addition, cardiologists say, intravascular ultrasound allows them to learn, for the first time, whether a person has a uniform, and dangerous, buildup of plaque, as Dr. Nissen's patient did, or merely narrow blood vessels. Tests like angiography sometimes miss the plaque because they look for areas of artery constriction. The plaque buildup in Dr. Nissen's patient was so uniform, narrowing the artery so smoothly, that it appeared the artery was simply of slightly small bore. Some patients who have undergone intravascular ultrasound in the few hospitals that offer it were spared bypass surgery, saving tens of thousands of dollars, when doctors learned that they were fine. Others, like the woman Dr. Nissen saw, had huge pileups of plaque, although some patients, including the woman, could not benefit from surgery because there was no specific constriction.

If intravascular ultrasound had come on the scene just a few years earlier, cardiologists say, it would have spread quickly. Now, with no insurance payments, just a few medical centers offer it. Only large medical centers, such as the Cleveland Clinic and Duke University Medical School, are willing to absorb its costs, taking a loss or paying for it through research grants. The new resistance from insurers has left medical-equipment manufacturers dangling, said Steven Speil, director of payment and health-care delivery at the Health Industry Manufacturers Association. "Payers say, 'Give us more information on what it can do.' But you can't generate more data absent reimbursement," he said. Mr. Speil said a growing number of companies are giving up on new technologies.

The medical-equipment industry offers great potential for profitability once a device gains wide use. Ms. Sabino said gross profit would typically be around 60 percent for machines such as ultrasound devices and about 80 percent for catheters. The ultrasound machines that make intravascular images sell for $75,000 to $100,000. The catheters, which cannot be reused, sell for $400 to $800. The ultrasound machines and catheters are being made mostly by small companies, among them Intertherapy in Irvine, California, Endosonics in Pleasanton, California, and Cardiovascular Imaging Systems in Sunnyvale, California. But in 1992 Hewlett-Packard announced that it would start making the machines as well, teaming up with Boston Scientific, a Watertown, Massachusetts, manufacturer of catheters.

Doctors say they are especially saddened by the slow development of intravascular ultrasound when they compare it with other technologies that gained a foothold because insurers paid for them. For example, balloon angioplasty, introduced in the early 1980s to clear arteries by inflating a tiny balloon, spread rapidly and is now more widely used than bypass surgery. Yet only now are clinical trials under way to see which provides better long-term results.

An expensive diagnostic method, magnetic resonance imaging, also slipped in under the old rules. Dr. Cova said that if manufacturers are so set on intravascular ultrasound, they should "take some of the millions of dollars that they are spending on marketing and advertising and fund a neutral party that would assess that technology." But Dr. Daniels of Tufts said that would not be so easy. It is hard enough, he said, to do a good cost assessment of an established technology, but nearly impossible to do one for an embryonic technology.

Another possibility is for doctors and manufacturers to jointly perform clinical trials that could show the intravascular ultrasound saves money by improving diagnoses. But the studies would take years, and the handful of companies that make the special catheters and ultrasound machines are mostly small start-up companies, with limited cash to pay for clinical trials. In the past, trials were not done at all, or they were done by the government.

Dr. Isner of St. Elizabeth's said he and others like the intravascular ultrasound so much that they considered doing the studies themselves. But "it's not that easy," he said. "Maybe the fact that no one has gone to the trouble reflects our past experience that it is not necessary to go to that trouble. Maybe now we are living in an era where if we feel strongly enough about something like this, we have to do it." [GK]

A DISPUTED FRONTIER

TWO months after the birth of her second child, Marie McCook of Philadelphia discovered she had breast cancer that had spread into her neck. Her prognosis was poor, but her doctors told her she was a suitable candidate for a dangerous, unproved, and costly therapy under study: a bone-marrow transplant, which would allow them to bombard her body with huge, otherwise-lethal doses of anticancer drugs.

She grasped the slender reed. "I feel it has given me an opportunity at a possible cure," Mrs. McCook, thirty-five years old, said of the $100,000 procedure. It was performed in the spring of 1991 at the University of Pennsylvania Cancer Center, and while her cancer has melted away, she will not know if she is cured for years. The bills were paid by her health-insurance company, which is supporting the study.

Evelyn Harper, forty-seven, with two children, learned in the fall of 1990 that her breast cancer had invaded her eyes and liver. A resident of the Virgin Islands, she sought treatment in Los Angeles, where doctors said she too should consider a marrow transplant. But her insurer, like many around the country, said it would not cover an experimental therapy. The following February she appealed, sending reams of data provided by her doctors arguing that the procedure might give her a 20 percent chance of surviving cancer-free for years. At the end of May

1991 the appeal was denied. By then the cancer had spread too widely to consider a transplant.

"That might not have sounded like a big chance of success, but it's a lot better than nothing," said her husband, Dennis Harper. "It seems like the insurance company holds you off as long as possible, waiting until it's too late for a transplant. That's not right."

Whether insurers should pay for marrow transplants has already become tinder for bitter lawsuits, poignant talk shows, and an emerging political movement of breast-cancer patients. The debate exemplifies the wrenching issues that may increasingly bedevil American medicine in an era of fast-changing, enormously expensive treatments and rising concern about costs. Health experts and government leaders, as well as insurers, hope to tame runaway medical expenses through more stringent assessment of new treatments and by weighing their benefits and costs.

The concepts sound sensible and uncontroversial—until they are applied to real people with life-threatening diseases, and to promising treatments being urgently refined. Marrow transplants, grueling ordeals that put patients through at least three harrowing weeks of hospitalization, have already proved useful against certain cancers of the blood, and insurers generally pay in those cases. Doctors are now trying the therapy in patients with several other kinds of cancer, including ovarian, testicular, and especially breast cancer.

Some patients have shown encouraging responses, but many have not. The mortality rate from the procedure itself, while improving, is still 5 percent or more. All the researchers agree on the need for more research, but they put different shades on the same skimpy facts. "For the right patient, I think it should be considered a therapeutic option," said Dr. William P. Peters, director of the Duke University Medical Center's marrow-transplant program, a leader in research on transplants for breast cancer and a critic of insurance companies that refuse to pay when the procedures are performed at experienced centers.

Other experts are skeptical. "We have raised the public's expectations far beyond what is supported by the published data," Dr. I. Craig Henderson, director of the breast-evaluation center of the Dana Farber Cancer Institute in Boston, wrote in *The Journal of the National Cancer Institute*. "We have no evidence as of yet that any patient will be cured by this therapy who would not have been cured by more conventional treatment."

Hundreds of women with breast cancer each year are now enduring the transplants and accompanying blasts of drugs. Researchers believe at least ten thousand women a year of the more than forty thousand who die from breast cancer annually may be good candidates if the procedure is shown to help more than it hurts. Most women whose cancer is caught in early stages are cured with conventional treatments, including removal of the cancerous lump or the entire breast, along with drug therapy and radiation. For them there is no reason to take on the risk and travails of a marrow transplant. Many more women are ruled out as transplant candidates by age and condition. Because it is so demanding on the body, the procedure is seldom tried on women older than about fifty-five, or on those with other medical problems. Firm answers about effectiveness are several years away: Controlled clinical trials, comparing patients receiving transplants with similar women receiving conventional chemotherapy, have just begun.

The procedure is becoming safer and less expensive, but even at best, research suggests, it will never offer a miraculous cure for patients with advanced breast cancer; it will, however, raise their odds of survival. For advanced breast cancer, it appears that transplants will, at best, keep 10 percent to 20 percent of the women cancer-free, said Dr. Edward A. Stadtmauer of the University of Pennsylvania Cancer Center, who is treating Mrs. McCook in a study comparing transplants with traditional drug therapy. And that success rate may fall, he said, as more patients are followed for more years. "That still would be wonderful," he said. "But we also have to look at quality of life, toxicity, and costs. I have to say I still don't know which group in the study is going to do better."

With known therapies offering little, some patients see the unknown in a different light. "There's a whole list of things that could go wrong, and yes, it scared me," Mrs. McCook said. "But I also have two small children, and the chance of not being here in ten years also scares me."

Insurance companies have long said they do not cover unproved therapies, but they have often paid for innovative, unapproved uses of cancer drugs. In decades past too, they started paying with little question for costly new procedures, such as coronary-bypass operations, which were widely adopted with little evaluation. But today, expensive new procedures receive much closer scrutiny.

The official position of the insurance industry on transplants is clear enough. "We are not saying this is too expensive and it shouldn't be covered," said Naomi Aronson, director of technology assessment with the Blue Cross and Blue Shield Association in Chicago. "We are saying that procedures need to be evaluated so that precious health-care resources can be used for things that are effective." If studies prove that transplants improve survival, Dr. Aronson said, the companies will pay.

To speed the search for answers and perhaps fend off lawsuits, many Blue Cross affiliates and, in the Philadelphia area, U.S. Healthcare, a large health-maintenance organization, have agreed to contribute to the costs of patients receiving transplants in certain clinical trials. In practice, after hearing pleas or threats from doctors or lawyers, many insurers are paying transplant bills for some breast-cancer patients, but many, too, are denying coverage. Recently, some insurers have begun writing policies that specifically exclude coverage of marrow transplants for breast cancer.

Cancer researchers, as well as desperate patients, are angry. "It's unfortunate, because basically they are holding transplants for breast cancer up to a different standard than other costly procedures," said Dr. Karen H. Antman, director of the transplant program at the Dana Farber Cancer Institute. Insurance officials deny they have a double standard. "It will be impossible to do studies unless patients have coverage," Dr. Antman added. Ellen Hobbs, a thirty-six-year-old breast-cancer patient in Sacramento, California, said, "What's the difference between experimental and state of the art? The doctors told me that traditional chemotherapy would be ineffective.

"This country spends a lot of money fixing up people with no hope," continued Mrs. Hobbs, who had a transplant in June 1991 and became politically active after fighting for months, with the help of a lawyer, before persuading her insurer to pay. She received radiation therapy in follow-up treatment and was doing well, but, like Mrs. McCook, could not know her long-term prospects, since cancer cells can lurk in the body for years before resurging.

For such a trying ordeal, the transplants involve a series of undramatic steps. Doctors have long suspected that in some patients they could kill cancer in the body by dousing it with enough toxic drugs. The problem was that this would kill the patient too, by destroying the marrow cells that generate vital red and white cells and platelets in the blood. In "autologous" marrow transplants, some of the patient's own marrow cells are extracted from bone or blood and frozen; outside donors are not needed. The patient is then subjected to several days of intensive chemotherapy—ten times the normal dose. Her marrow cells are reinjected, and the real drama begins.

For weeks, until the reinjected marrow begins producing new blood cells, assuming it does, the patient lives without much of an immune system, susceptible to vicious fungal, bacterial, and viral infections. "It is horrible," Mrs. McCook said. "Everything just hits rock bottom. I had temperatures of 105, vomiting, bowel problems, and I needed morphine. You lose your hair and your appetite, you lose your taste buds. You get depressed."

Until recently all patients spent more than a month in the

hospital, and transplant-related mortality at some leading centers was over 20 percent, most often from infections. But the recent availability of growth factors—manufactured versions of natural body chemicals that stimulate the marrow cells—has shortened the period of critical vulnerability, reduced hospital stays to as little as three weeks, and pulled down death rates to 5 percent to 15 percent at various centers. The growth factors have also pulled down the cost, which is attributable more than anything else to the length of the hospital stay. Dr. Antman said the cost for some patients at some centers was down to $70,000 or less. Dr. Peters believes that over the next several years the price could fall to $25,000 or less.

Right now, transplants are considered worth risking for the several thousand women each year whose cancer has spread to ten or more lymph nodes, meaning that they have a high chance of relapse after normal therapy. It is also considered worth the risk for the smaller number of women with large tumors that cannot be surgically removed or with inflammatory tumors, and for the tens of thousands of women whose cancer has already spread to other parts of the body and is rarely cured. Among those groups, only some can even potentially benefit. Before a transplant is considered, a woman is given a course of conventional chemotherapy. Only those whose tumors shrink in response to lower doses, studies have found, may potentially be helped with the all-out attack of high doses and a marrow transplant.

In a positive sign, studies indicate that women receiving transplants are far more likely than others to show a good short-term response: the disappearance of detectable cancer. The open question is whether these remissions will last. Dr. Peters and other researchers point to encouraging recent results from studies involving limited numbers of patients. In one study at Duke, among fifty-nine women whose cancer had spread to ten or more lymph nodes but not more widely, three-fourths were cancer-free after four years, he said. With conventional therapy, he would only expect about one-fifth of such patients to be cancer-free.

Among a group of forty-five transplant patients whose cancer had already spread to distant sites beyond the lymph nodes, he said, 20 percent were cancer-free after an average of four years. With conventional therapy, almost none with such advanced disease would have been cancer-free at that point, he said. Of another group of twenty-two women with advanced cancer who were early pioneers with the therapy, three remained cancer-free after five to eight years.

But others say figures like these, while intriguing, may easily mislead. "The question is, what would have happened to those same patients if they had gotten conventional chemotherapy?" said Dr. David M. Eddy, a health economist at Duke University and a consultant to insurance companies. "I can show you individual patients who received conventional therapy who also survived five or ten years."

Among other problems with existing comparisons, the patient groups may have differed in important ways. "The transplant patients are very healthy, good candidates for treatment," noted Dr. Bruce D. Cheson of the National Cancer Institute. Dr. John H. Glick, director of the University of Pennsylvania Cancer Center, says four or five years is not long enough to say a patient is cured of breast cancer. "Some of the advocates are speaking too soon," he said.

By the mid-1990s the clinical trials should yield convincing evidence about the comparative effectiveness of transplants, although it will take longer to know whether cures are achieved. If a statistically significant survival benefit is shown, even for a few years, then the insurance dispute may fade away. But, depending on how dramatic the trial results are, divisive questions of cost versus benefit may persist. "If there is a big difference in survival, then it will be persuasive," said Dr. Cheson. "But if there is only a small advantage for transplants, it's still going to be an individual decision the physician will have to make with the patient."

Even the insurance industry has shied away from the more explosive but ultimately unavoidable issue for American medicine: How good does a treatment have to be to make it worth the price? In the case of marrow transplants, insurance companies have said that if studies yield proof of benefit, they will cover the procedure, whatever it costs. But some experts wonder whether this approach will remain feasible, or even wise. "I think they should take the cost into account and weigh it against the benefits," said Dr. Eddy, the health economist. "I think in five years they will do that, but they don't now.

"Somewhere, sometime, someone will have to judge what additional benefit is worth what additional cost," Dr. Eddy continued. He acknowledged that this would be treacherous new terrain for government, insurers, doctors, and patients who, like Mrs. McCook, put a value on hope itself. "Society has had very little experience doing this," Dr. Eddy said. [EE]

"DR. DEAL"

THE Tokos Medical Corporation, which sells a service that detects early labor in pregnant women, recently started a program to reward obstetricians who ordered it for their patients. In its files the company called the program "Dr. Deal." The deal: earn up to $20,000 annually on an investment of $1,000.

The program, in which three hundred to four hundred obstetricians nationwide are participating, works like this: The doctors put up $1,000 each to become shareholders in a company set up by Tokos that typically exists only on paper. In return, the doctors pocket 15 percent of the payment for any Tokos services prescribed by members of the physician-owned company. Tokos says participating physicians currently average about $5,000 a year from the arrangement; literature from one Tokos subsidiary boasted that annual earnings could reach $22,500.

When doctors do prescribe it, Tokos's home-monitoring service is not cheap. It costs $100 to $300 a day, or $5,000 or more a pregnancy. That's a hard sell among cost-conscious insurers, so Tokos has twenty employees who make the company's case—and they have had increasing success in persuading insurers to pay. But a debate is growing about the effectiveness of the home uterine monitor that is the keystone of Tokos's service. The Food and Drug Administration is also investigating Tokos's marketing claims. Separately, there is a scientific controversy about the safety of the drugs Tokos sells to prolong pregnancy.

Some doctors are concerned about not only Tokos's marketing practices but also the willingness of some physicians to take part in its investment plans. "It is a sad day for medicine," said Dr. Benjamin Sachs, chief of obstetrics and gynecology at Beth Israel Hospital in Boston. A look at Tokos's marketing efforts highlights one of the most troubling issues in health care: Medical companies often go to great lengths to encourage doctors to use their products, and to persuade insurers to pay for them. And they can succeed even when significant questions exist about a product's efficacy and safety.

Health-care experts say that nothing will change—and medical costs will never be satisfactorily controlled—without a systematic effort, whether by the government or the private sector, to study medical technologies and identify who will most benefit from them. "This is an extraordinarily pervasive problem," said Dr. Robert H. Brook, director of the health-sciences program at the Rand Corporation in Santa Monica, California. "The government has to step in to help resolve the risks and benefits of these practices and then decide what is going to be used in basic medical care."

Some experts think the problem is so great that the Clinton administration's effort to reform the health-care system by managing competition among insurers will fail unless it identifies which competing treatments and technologies are most effective. "Managed competition does not have the ability to deal with this problem," said Dr. Mark Chassin, commissioner of the New York State Department of Health.

Pressure is also growing to crack down on financial-incentive programs that may affect the way physicians treat patients. Tokos's chairman and chief executive, Robert F. Byrnes, said in a 1993 interview that his company's investment plan for physicians was both legal and ethical because it compensated doctors for paperwork and other chores for which insurers do not pay. He added that Tokos was helping to reduce the medical catastrophes associated with premature birth, and in the process holding down medical costs by keeping women out of the hospital. "We have raised everyone's consciousness about the problem of prematurity," he said. "And we are very proud of our system, because it works."

But Kirk Johnson, an attorney for the American Medical Association, said his group was investigating possible conflicts of interest posed by physician investment plans like those offered by Tokos. And in 1993, a federal task force recommended an end to plans under which physicians refer patients to businesses that they own but in which they don't participate directly. "This is a very murky area that we are very concerned about," Mr. Johnson said.

Founded in 1983, Tokos is the leading company in a burgeoning industry that has sprung up to prevent premature births, a leading cause of birth defects and infant mortality. It is by no means alone in its aggressive efforts to gain acceptance of its product among physicians and insurers. Its two largest competitors, Healthdyne, Inc., and Caremark International, Inc., also provide financial incentives to physicians to use similar services. And there are many other technologies, new and old, the efficacy of which remains unproven. Two examples: positron emission tomography (PET scan) for cardiac imaging, and the use of antigens for detection of ovarian cancer.

The need to prevent premature births is a compelling one. Each year 6 percent to 8 percent of infants are born prematurely (defined as before the thirty-seventh week of gestation), some so early that they die or suffer crippling defects. A troubled pregnancy can be devastating. And associated medical costs can reach one million dollars.

Doctors cannot predict early delivery, though women carrying more than one fetus or having a history of early labor are considered to be at greatest risk. And though women can be trained to recognize some signs of early labor, home monitoring detects contractions a woman may not feel. Also, a physician who might have hospitalized a woman for early labor, at five hundred dollars a day, now may have a cheaper choice. It is a choice most patients prefer. "If the patient knows about monitoring, God forbid if you don't provide it," said Dr. J. Joshua Kopelman, an obstetrician in Aurora, Colorado. The use of home monitoring of pregnancies is growing sharply. In 1992 Tokos, which controls about 65 percent of the market, treated approximately twenty-five thousand patients, a 25 percent increase from 1991. Through the first nine months of 1992, the company had revenues of $124 million.

To use the Tokos monitor, a woman straps around her abdomen a belt containing a sensor that detects uterine contractions. The hour-long reading is made one or more times a day and is transmitted by telephone lines to one of sixty Tokos offices staffed by nurses who analyze the data. Should the data suggest that the woman is experiencing early labor, a Tokos nurse calls her physician, who may prescribe terbutaline or ritodrine, medications dispensed by Tokos in a home-infusion kit, to relax the uterus.

A single monitor reading is $100 a day; additional readings and drugs raise that to $300. Visits by a Tokos nurse, required in the most serious cases, cost extra. As for the company's profitability, Mr. Byrnes, interviewed at Tokos's Santa Ana, California, headquarters, said it had a profit margin of 15 percent to 17 percent of revenues.

While the company's service is expensive, many people think it worth the price. Deborah Jones of Wayne, New Jersey, lost a child after going into labor early. In her most recent pregnancy, her physician prescribed Tokos monitoring, and she had a healthy girl. "I found great relief and security in the monitor," she said. Even many of the company's critics agree that intensive contact between a nurse and an expectant mother, part of Tokos's regimen, may help prolong a pregnancy.

But does the Tokos technology itself—the devices that transmit data on uterine activity to the nurses—have any benefit beyond a psychological one in producing healthier babies? That is the nub of the dispute. Some scientists argue that educating the patient to recognize symptoms or simply putting her in daily contact with a nurse would be just as helpful, and less expensive. Some insurers say they could provide nursing more cheaply than Tokos.

In the mid-1980s, studies by researchers including Dr. Michael Katz, chief of perinatology at the California Pacific Medical Center in San Francisco, and Dr. John C. Morrison of the University of Mississippi appeared to support the value of the monitoring. But in 1988 Dr. Jay Iams of Ohio State University published a study that set the battle lines. Dr. Iams said he initially assumed that his study would prove monitoring's benefits by showing that it extended more pregnancies than did simple daily telephone contact between a patient and a nurse. Instead, he found no difference. "I think everyone was shocked," Dr. Iams said.

But in recent years, much of the research both pro and con has come under attack as scientifically flawed. And, lacking a definitive study, the scientists involved in the debate have only dug in their heels. Those opposing the growing use of the Tokos service, including Dr. Sachs of Beth Israel in Boston, see it as consuming money that might be better used for patient education. But advocates such as Dr. Morrison, who is now a paid Tokos consultant, say it helps a nurse do her job better. "I think the literature is clear that you need the whole system," he said.

In 1992 the American College of Obstetricians and Gynecologists, a professional group, declined for the second time to recommend the routine use of home pregnancy monitoring for high-risk patients. The group cited, among other things, a lack of clear research showing benefits. Also, a study by a Canadian team published in 1992 in *The New England Journal of Medicine* suggested that ritodrine is not effective and in fact can cause health problems such as maternal heart arrythmia, and, in rare instances, death. The other drug used by Tokos, terbutaline, is chemically similar to ritodrine.

It is a dispute that has left insurers frustrated over what to do. While a majority of the nation's seventy-three Blue Cross and Blue Shield programs do pay for Tokos claims, about twenty plans do not. State Medicaid plans are also divided. But efforts by Tokos's team of twenty who visit insurers appear to be paying off. The company is getting about 80 percent of its orders approved by insurers, up from about 65 percent in 1990, Mr. Byrnes said.

The company's weapons have been studies such as a 1990 report by Dr. Thomas S. Kosasa of the John A. Burns School of Medicine in Hawaii that found home monitoring of seventy-nine patients reduced insurance costs by $11,500 a patient. Some insurers agreed that monitoring might avert catastrophic health problems associated with premature infants. "It is less costly to have ten patients monitored, even if only one may need it, than to have one patient with a perinatal disaster and have that baby in the hospital with brain damage for months or for the rest of its life," said Dr. Marvin Blitz, the vice president for medical policy and research at Empire Blue Cross and Blue Shield in New York. Other insurance executives, including Dr. Wade Aubry, medical director of Blue Shield of California, have looked at the data and reached a different conclusion: that there is no evidence that the monitoring—as opposed to educating the patient or offering counseling—makes a difference.

No matter who's right, Tokos's investment plans and others like it are coming under increased scrutiny. In 1992 alone Tokos established about forty physician-owned companies nationwide. Some of the groups were set up by a company known as Women's Homecare, a joint venture between Tokos and T² Medical, Inc., a concern in Alpharetta, Georgia, that pioneered doctor-owned companies in the home-care field.

The plans appear to be part of a high-stakes battle for physicians' loyalty. Dr. Victor J. Weinstein, an obstetrician in Charleston, South Carolina, who is a member of the Tokos plan, recalled his initial encounter with company officials. "We said to them, 'Why are you doing this?' They said they were afraid of losing market share to competitors. They said, 'We want to make you a part of us.'"

The major concern with such plans is that physicians will prescribe unnecessary services so they can make more money. Another problem: Doctors may form loyalties to companies like Tokos and so overlook more innovative or cost-effective treatments. Federal law bars physicians from referring Medicare and Medicaid patients to companies in which they have a financial interest. But it does not cover private patients. The Tokos plan involves only private patients.

Doctors who use Tokos's services are of two minds on the compensation. Dr. Weinstein, the Charleston obstetrician, said the investment plan was a way of compensating him for added time spent on home-care patients. But Dr. Kopelman, the Colorado obstetrician, said he and his partner decided in 1992 to turn down Tokos's offer of fees to "supervise" cases. "We did not feel it represented any additional time, so we did not feel that we needed any additional compensation," he said.

For his part, Mr. Byrnes said he was comfortable with the plans and was checking to make sure doctors were not overprescribing just to make more money. "We invite anyone to come in and look at our books," he said. He may soon find a taker. "The kind of returns these plans are offering physicians seem way out of line with the investment at stake," said Mr. Johnson of the AMA. He said that he had been unaware of the details of the Tokos plan and that the company had not sought an ethics ruling from the AMA on the plan.

Ironically, Tokos may have pushed its monitor so aggressively because of insurers' reimbursement policies. Typically, insurers will pay only for drugs and devices, not nursing services alone, Mr. Byrnes said. And insurers like Dr. Blitz said that if the Tokos monitor proved ineffective, they would use their own nurses, not Tokos's, to talk with patients. The company's claims in support of its own service have concerned some insurers. "The device was approved in a very narrow way, but that is not the way it is necessarily marketed," said Dr. Gerald Silverstein, vice president of the Celtic Life Insurance Company in Chicago, which does pay for some Tokos claims.

Indeed, the company may have overreached in some of its claims. It promotes its service—the monitor, nursing, and drugs—as effective in reducing premature births. But the Food and Drug Administration has approved only the use of the monitor, not the service as a whole, and only then to detect early labor in the small group of women who have a history of early delivery. Also, the government has never approved terbutaline as a birth-delaying drug, or Tokos's claim that its system can reduce early births.

While it is legal and common for physicians to prescribe drugs and devices for unapproved uses, a company may not market its products for such uses or make unapproved claims for those products. An FDA spokeswoman declined to comment on her agency's inquiry into Tokos's claims. But Tokos officials said they have recently moved to separate their claims about the monitor and the service. Mr. Byrnes said the debate surrounding his company had been caused by a small group of scientists opposed to monitoring and by speculators.

For all the debate, the question of whether Tokos's monitor is worth the price may never be adequately answered. What is needed, many people say, is studies that separate the benefits provided by the monitor from those offered by talking with a nurse. In recent months, the National Institute of Child Health and Human Development, a federal agency, has tried to raise six million dollars to finance such a study. But both Tokos and Healthdyne officials turned down a request to help underwrite the research, said Dr. Donald McNellis, the institute's special assistant for obstetrics. (Caremark, the smallest of the three home-care providers, has expressed interest.)

Mr. Byrnes said it was time to move beyond the monitoring debate and finance studies to better identify women at risk of premature delivery. Dr. Iams said he could understand why there was so little interest among the home-monitoring companies. "They are out marketing their services and making money," he said. "The only thing that this study can do is hurt them." [BM]

How Others Do It

CANADA: CARE AND COMPROMISE

SINCE a heart attack in 1989, Len Quesnelle has had a dozen tests to study the blocked arteries of his heart, spent weeks in intensive care because of chest pain, and finally, in March 1991, had a triple bypass. He has seen his share of doctors and hospitals, but he has never received a bill, paid a health-insurance premium, or filled out a health-insurance form. Although the price for his surgery, calculated in American dollars, was fourteen thousand dollars, he paid less than two hundred dollars, for telephone calls and renting a television.

As a citizen of Canada, Mr. Quesnelle is a beneficiary of one of the world's most comprehensive health-insurance programs, the Canadian national health plan, which uses tax money to provide medical care to everyone at no charge. But during his eighteen-month ordeal, Mr. Quesnelle often had to wait weeks for tests and treatment, and he almost had a second heart attack in the three-month wait before his surgery. Such delays, typical in Canada for certain costly procedures, would be considered imprudent, if not malpractice, in the United States.

At a time when some thirty-seven million Americans lack insurance, the Canadian health-care system serves as a taunting reminder that with a few compromises it is possible to provide quality care for everyone, and for less money. In Canada there are few machines to blast apart kidney stones, but no women go without prenatal care. There is no Mayo Clinic, but there are also no emergency rooms teeming with people who cannot afford a family doctor. "Canada is an embarrassment to the United States," said Vickery Stoughton, an American who is the president of Toronto Hospital.

But a majority of Americans, accustomed to receiving the most advanced medical care in an instant, without regard to price, may not be embarrassed enough to accept Canadian-style compromises. About the time Mr. Quesnelle had his surgery in Toronto, William Beagle had elective bypass surgery at Buffalo General Hospital, across Lake Ontario from Toronto. For a nine-day stay he received more than fifty bills totalling more than fifty thousand dollars, each of which he submitted with a claim form to Metropolitan Life, which paid all but eighteen dollars. Since his case was complicated and would tie up his surgeon for an entire day, Mr. Beagle waited a long time for his operation by American standards: ten days.

Toronto Hospital looks the same as any prestigious urban American center: computers in every room, transplant patients in intensive-care units, even the same antiseptic smell hanging in the halls. But the health-care structure behind the facade could hardly be more different. Every Canadian, rich or poor, is promised equal access to doctors and hospitals through provincial insurance plans that cover nearly all medical expenses. With the flash of a red-and-white card, patients can obtain everything from nutritional counseling to lung transplants. Patients select their family doctors, and doctors for the most part order whatever tests they like, without the paperwork required by insurers that eats up a growing share of American medical costs.

Despite the governmental largess, Canada spends an average of 30 percent less per person on health care than the United States, for a total of close to 10 percent of the gross domestic product in 1991. The American level surpassed 13 percent of gross domestic product in 1991 and continues a relentless climb. To make sure the country lives within its allotted means, the Canadian federal and provincial governments control hospital operating budgets with an iron fist and doctors' fees through bargaining with provincial medical associations. To rein in costs, the government limits the number of specialists who are trained, limits purchases of expensive equipment, and restricts costly procedures such as open-heart surgery to a few university hospitals.

To get the most for its money, the system is slow to offer expensive new machines and procedures, waiting until their medical value is solidly proved—and, critics say, proved again. And so the price of universal access is a degree of inconvenience and delay and, in fast-changing fields, sometimes settling for last year's treatment. Typical is the case of Albert Palmer, a seventy-two-year-old farmer from Scarborough, Ontario. He waited three months for an operation to improve the blood supply to his feet, which had become agonizingly painful whenever he walked. Though there was no great danger, he had to endure the pain and supervise planting of his pea fields from a chair.

While the quality of care remains generally high, Canada's health system is showing signs of distress. Doctors predict that a barrage of expensive new technologies and an aging, sicker population will strain finances in the coming decade, leaving patients with longer waits, outdated technology, and even overt rationing. "The only way you can afford universal health care is to run everything like a VW, which in the end gets you from place to place," said Dr. Alan Hudson, chief executive at Toronto Hospital. "The problem is we try to run everything as almost a Cadillac. As medical costs rise, we can't afford it."

If patient satisfaction is the measure of good medicine, then the Canadian system is a resounding success. Ask a Canadian whether he uses the national system, and you get a perplexed pause. Of course he does; medical care outside the system is virtually outlawed. But more than that, Canadians are convinced the system is without rival. "You don't want to wait when you're in pain, but there's no other choice," Mr. Palmer, the farmer, said. Far from threatening a malpractice suit, he added what is almost a Canadian refrain: "But I waited because this is the best medicine in the world."

Asked if he had ever considered going to the United States for treatment, Joseph Breglia, a fifty-three-year-old Toronto lawyer who had been battling leukemia for five years, replied simply, "Not even a thought." Even wealthy Canadians who could afford to cross the border for treatment rarely do it.

Doctors who have worked in both countries say Canadians generally shrug off the system's inconveniences in a way that Americans would not. "Canadians are used to peace, order, and good governance. We probably seem like a dull lot," said Dr. Donald Wigle, a Toronto cardiologist. "Americans go for life, liberty, and the pursuit of happiness. I don't think they would put up with the waits." Administrators at American hospitals agree. "If we can't provide bypass surgery in a timely fashion, our patients will say good-bye and fly to Pittsburgh or Cleveland," said John Friedlander, president of Buffalo General.

Like their patients, Canada's doctors are generally satisfied with the system, though there have been bruising battles with the government over fees. Doctors' charges for services are a good deal lower than what is charged in the United States, particularly in the surgical specialties, but because administrative costs and malpractice premiums are also much lower, most doctors earn salaries comparable to those of their American counterparts. "I never have a problem recruiting internists," said Dr. Arnold Aberman, the chief doctor at Toronto Hospital. "That might not be true if I was recruiting cardiac surgeons, since no one in Canada earns three million dollars a year. Once you accept the limitations of the system, it's a pleasant place to be." Doctors send the government a list of patient visits each month and a few weeks later receive payment. Lawsuits are very rare, in part because Canadian lawyers must work for a fee rather than a share of malpractice settlements, and patients cannot sue for punitive damages.

Statistics also speak well for Canadian medicine. On average,

Canadians live longer than Americans, and Canada has a lower infant-mortality rate. While Canada has little of the extreme poverty seen in American inner cities, its health statistics also reflect the good basic care enjoyed by everyone, including cholesterol checks, prenatal testing, and other services that are frequently not covered by insurance in the United States and that the poor often cannot afford. "The overwhelming good thing about this system is never having your hand tied by the patient's financial status," said Dr. Lorne Becker, a family doctor who recently returned to practice in his native Toronto after ten years of working in the United States. "It's a relief not having to fight with patients to get mammograms because they cost too much."

To promote access the government maintains a ratio of general doctors to specialists of about one to one, as opposed to one to two in the United States. But while basic care is good, it is rarely elaborate, and the Canadians are generally less aggressive about monitoring and treating chronic conditions. For example, American doctors advise cholesterol testing for everyone over the age of twenty and treat patients with levels above 200. Canadian doctors test only those with other risks for heart disease and do not pursue further testing or treatment unless the level is over 265. Canadian doctors say that medical studies support their low-key approach, but in their world of strictly budgeted resources, cost is always in the background.

If Canada is generous with the basics, it is stingy with high technology. Delays, travel, and waits for cutting-edge treatments are intentionally built into the system, like speed bumps in a road, to make sure people proceed in health care deliberately and to prevent runaway use. Except in cases of dire emergency, Canadians wait for weeks to months for a wide variety of expensive procedures, including advanced radiology scans, heart-bypass and brain-tumor operations, and the destruction of painful kidney stones with a sound-wave machine called a lithotripter. The supply of specialists and equipment for such procedures perpetually lags just behind demand.

"Everything is accessible to everyone, but not always accessible enough," said Dr. Irving H. Lipton, a cardiac surgeon in Toronto, a pile of X rays on his desk from patients awaiting surgery. He now has fifty-four patients in line for a cardiac bypass, fourteen of whom he considers urgent. Such patients are frequently having chest pains at rest and often must wait in the hospital until surgery. Ideally, he says, he would like to accommodate the urgent patients in one to two days, but realistically the wait will be one or two weeks. Patients for whom the surgery is elective wait three or four months.

Canadian surgeons also lament the scarcity of advanced diagnostic equipment, particularly magnetic resonance imaging devices, the two-million-dollar MRI scanners that have transformed the treatment of brain, spine, and joint disorders in the United States. In 1991 there were fifteen MRI scanners in all of Canada, and two thousand in the United States. The United States had more than ten times more per person.

Dr. Walter Kucharczyk, a radiologist who runs the MRI scanner at Toronto Hospital, fields telephone calls every day pleading the cases of patients and loved ones, a task that he says "stinks." A person with a quickly progressive paralysis qualifies as an emergency and promptly obtains a spinal scan to determine the source of the problem. But patients awaiting operations for brain tumors or confined to bed by ruptured disks are considered to be merely urgent and wait one to six weeks.

"These people are watched very carefully, but imagine being thirty years old and sitting around with a brain tumor growing, even slowly, in your head," said Dr. Ben Freedman, an ethicist at the Jewish General Hospital in Montreal. Dr. Kucharczyk rarely finds room for elective cases, such as patients with severe headaches or knee injuries, who would be scanned for good measure in the United States. "They wait a year, and at that point either the patient's better, had surgery, or dead," he said.

Since high technology and specialty care are concentrated at a few centers scattered around the country, sick Canadians must be ready to wait and then travel, or travel and then wait. Kiki Margaritas, a fifty-three-year-old patient from North Bay, Ontario, who has breast cancer, spent a month at the Princess Margaret Hospital in Toronto, two hundred miles from home, so she could receive radiation treatments. The government paid her bus fare and the cost of a room at a residence for patients next to the hospital, but her family could not afford to visit.

Not surprisingly, the long lines sometimes lead to charges of favoritism. Dr. Wigle said those with "influence and affluence" frequently jump to the top of waiting lists. "There's a black market for medicine," Dr. Kucharczyk said. "People who have influence in the ministry or friends at the hospital get different treatment."

In the vast majority of cases, the delays and inconveniences probably do no long-term harm, Canadian doctors agree. Mrs. Margaritas waited two months between her mastectomy and the start of chemotherapy. Such a gap would be unheard of across the border, though, and could theoretically make the difference between a relapse and a cure, said Dr. Kyu Shin, a cancer specialist at Roswell Park Cancer Institute in Buffalo.

In theory, people who run into trouble go to the front of the line, but "absolutely, people die on the waiting lists," said Dr. Lipton, the Toronto heart surgeon. Dr. Wigle, the cardiologist, has a patient who had a major heart attack while waiting for bypass surgery. Although he survived, his heart muscle was so damaged that he had to go on another waiting list, this one for a heart transplant.

Driven by the need to make money, American hospitals survive by doing more operations and ever more tests; driven by the need to conserve their fixed finances, Canadian hospitals stay afloat by doing fewer. As one of the few cardiac surgeons serving the extended Toronto region, with a population of six million, Dr. Lipton would like to perform more operations at the end of the day to erase the backlog, but cannot because the hospital cannot pay overtime to the operating-room staff except in emergencies.

If Dr. Lipton needs to perform emergency surgery, he frequently has to take a less sick patient off the day's operating list. Contrast that with the United States: "Nights, weekends, we can always twist someone's arm and do another case," said Dr. Thomas Lajos, a surgeon at Buffalo General. Flexing his technological muscle, at 5 P.M. one Friday he called to request an MRI scan. It was done that night.

To many doctors, even more worrisome than the inconveniences is the fact that newer technologies and equipment are sometimes simply unavailable. Dr. Hans Messner, a cancer specialist and chief of the bone-marrow transplant program at Princess Margaret Hospital in Toronto, says he would like to be able to use growth factors in his leukemia patients undergoing marrow transplants. These genetically engineered compounds have been shown to reduce the length of hospital stays and improve survival for the risky procedure. In the United States they have crossed the boundary from experimental and have become state of the art. "The government is reviewing the data, but there is significant inertia, since these things are very costly," he said.

In the operating room, surgeons say that they are frequently using older equipment than their American colleagues, and, in intensive care, new gadgets come once a decade rather than every other year. Although Toronto Hospital has the biggest lung-transplant program in the world, it has not yet been able to buy a fiber-optic bronchoscope, a device inserted through the mouth to transmit perfect pictures of the lungs. Even many community hospitals in the United States have one.

Canadian doctors have learned to consider cost in their medical decisions, something that many experts say will have to happen in the United States. Dr. Messner, the cancer specialist, knows his budget allows him to do only about fifty-five bone-marrow transplants per year. At $100,000 each, he says he will devote this resource to the patients most likely to survive. "You learn to be frugal," he said. "If I filled my beds with patients who had only a ten percent chance of survival, at the end of the year I'd have only five left. So instead I fill them with patients who have a sixty percent chance and end up with thirty-five."

When waits become too long, doctors and patients often decide to make do with more primitive and accessible technologies. For back surgery, when an MRI scan is unavailable, this means an X ray called a myelogram, which involves injecting dye into the spine. It is uncomfortable, complicated by allergic reactions, and requires a hospital stay.

And when desperate, Canadians have a final option: to go to the United States, whose hospitals have served as a convenient pressure valve. The Canadian system generally pays American hospitals for care it cannot reasonably provide, although patients must get prior approval. In a typical case, when James McGillis of Burlington, Ontario, developed excruciating pain from a kidney stone blocking his bladder, he was sent to a private center in Buffalo to have the stones pulverized, because the single lithotripter in Ontario was solidly booked. When the delays become unacceptably long even by Canadian standards, Ontario has paid for coronary-bypass operations in Detroit and MRI scans in Buffalo to give the health ministry time to juggle its resources.

Although Canadian doctors often wish for a new high-speed bone drill or a second scanner, some experts say that technical plenty in the United States does not always lead to better care, just to more care, while basic needs go wanting. "It's nice to have a lithotripter in Outer Snowshoe, but that money comes from somewhere else," said Dr. Adam Linton, a kidney specialist in London, Ontario. The travel required by centralization of certain procedures makes treatment inconvenient, but also more assured in quality, he added.

And treatments are unavailable to many citizens of the United States for other reasons. Studies have repeatedly shown that black Americans benefit from high technology far less often than whites, for example. Uninsured patients, or those on Medicaid, often can wait months for an elective MRI scan or even a general checkup.

Despite the government's efforts to control costs, in Canada as in the United States the press of soaring medical prices and ever-better, more costly technology threatens to tear the system apart. Although Canadians demand the best in health care, they are reluctant to pay more taxes for it. Already the Peace Bridge from Ontario to Buffalo is crowded with shoppers driving to avoid sales taxes totaling 15 percent, which have been driven up in part by health expenses. Hospitals striving to offer advanced treatments on limited budgets have been increasingly forced to make unhappy compromises. "When a hospital is given a budget and starts to run out of money, it has no choice but to cut services," Dr. Linton said.

For many hospitals, the simplest solution is to close down beds, a drastic measure in a system already running at capacity. Other hospitals have limited the number of joints an orthopedist may replace or the number of patients who may be on dialysis. So far that has resulted mostly in delays being a little longer or travel distance greater. "We have not yet had to kill anyone by not providing dialysis or a transplant, but the issue is at a flash point," Dr. Linton said. "We are running out of maneuvering room financially."

Indeed, as costly new machines and drugs are proved to treat a wide range of maladies, doctors wonder how the system will afford them. Some provinces are introducing user fees for patients, and other provinces are experimenting with health-maintenance organizations like those being promoted in the United States. "People look at Canada and think we have a panacea," Dr. Wigle said. "We do not. We both have to learn from each other." [ER]

JAPAN: CRADLE TO GRAVE,
NO FRILLS

S EVENTY-YEAR-OLD Genji Ito had to travel twenty minutes by bicycle on a drizzly morning to get to the Toho
University Hospital in Tokyo by seven-thirty, an hour before it
officially opened. But it was still a good day, he noted happily,
for his early start had landed him No. 69 in the hospital's dank
waiting room, which meant that it would take only until noon to
see the doctor about his heart condition and get his medication.

"This system is my savior," said Mr. Ito, sitting with about one
hundred others who filled the rows of vinyl-covered benches,
since Japanese physicians generally do not make appointments.
Despite the long wait and the briefness of the visits, no matter
how many times Mr. Ito goes, he pays just 900 yen a month for
his treatment—the equivalent of $7.25—which is typical for a
senior citizen. Japanese like Mr. Ito put up with waiting at
crowded clinics and seemingly impersonal treatment from physicians, but in return they enjoy what some describe as the most
efficient, comprehensive health-insurance system in the world.

The system has produced one of the healthiest societies on
earth while keeping the financial burden on corporations re-
markably light. Japanese companies pay about one-fifth of what
American concerns do for employee health insurance. But the
three-decade-old system is facing a challenge of demography
that threatens this success: the rapid growth in the numbers of

retirees healthy enough to pedal a bicycle to the hospital but old enough to need large doses of expensive medical care. The portion of the population sixty-five or older is expected to double, to 25 percent from 12 percent as of 1992, within thirty years. As a result, the portion of total medical costs that go for the aged is projected to rise from 17.8 percent in 1980 to 37 percent in the year 2000 and 41 percent in 2010.

In the past, the system has been so lucrative that government-controlled health insurers once used their surpluses to build resorts in Australia and Hawaii. Today these insurers, reflecting the kind of cost pressures seen in other countries, are preparing to slash $320 million from the budgets of 247 government-owned hospitals and clinics through 1997, close 74 other medical facilities, and merge 7. Doctors are bracing for tighter controls on their fees and the possible loss of a major source of profit: selling the medication they prescribe.

But perhaps the most important lesson for American policymakers struggling to repair the medical safety net is in the Japanese approach to solving the cost problem. In all the study councils and debates taking place there, the one bedrock assumption not being questioned is that the burden of supporting these soaring medical costs should not fall on corporations. Nearly everyone is calling for the government, and hence the taxpayer, to foot the bill. "The increase in costs is unavoidable, and we know that," said Tetsuo Yagi, a former deputy minister of Health and Welfare and now vice president of the National Federation of Health Insurance Societies, a trade group. "The issue is how to balance the burden. We know that if we go beyond a certain point we would lower the vitality of the Japanese economy. That is what we agree we have to avoid. The government has to bear this burden, and I think it will."

This kind of choice reflects a side of Japan's economic strength that is often overlooked. Americans focus on the technological prowess of Japanese automakers, computer-chip producers, and consumer-electronics giants. But one of the secrets of Japan's industrial might is that the social-welfare system delivers an impressive level of services to all while costing taxpayers and corporations relatively little. Daniel I. Okimoto, a professor at the Asia-Pacific Research Center at Stanford University, who is coordinating a major study of Japanese health care, said, "The Japanese system has lots of trade-offs, but on balance, if your objective is to control costs, it works. That is a competitive strength." Many Americans would reject some of these trade-offs as cumbersome, impersonal, or too restrictive. The complaints among Japanese range from crowded, factorylike facilities to doctors' heavy overprescription of drugs as a way of increasing restricted incomes.

Also making the Japanese health-care system work more efficiently are: the absence of a large, impoverished underclass; diets heavy in rice, fish, and vegetables that are generally healthier than those of Westerners; and an almost total absence of medical-malpractice suits. Overall, Japanese spent an estimated 21.68 trillion yen on health care in 1992, or $175 billion. That is 6.8 percent of the gross national product; total medical costs in the United States were 14 percent of the GNP. More than eighty million Americans are either uninsured or inadequately insured. Everyone in Japan is covered by the government-controlled system. While Japanese corporations pay a little more than $700 per employee on annual premiums, American companies pay $3,452, according to Hewitt Associates, a benefits consultant.

By some measures, none of these trade-offs has compromised the ultimate strength of the Japanese system. The life expectancy for men is 75.9 years and for women 81.8, the highest in the world. The infant-mortality rate is 0.46 percent of live births, said Dr. Naoki Ikegami, a health administrator at Keio University School of Medicine. "You get your money's worth in the United States, but if you don't have the money, you don't get the worth," remarked Dr. Ikegami, who has been a visiting professor at the University of Pennsylvania. "In Japan there is real equality. That is our strength."

*　　*　　*

But a visit to any clinic or hospital demonstrates just what the Japanese give up. To be a patient is to be told surprisingly little about diagnoses, the kinds of treatment being used, or the drugs administered. Doctors are not accustomed to hearing questions and give almost no information. In this regard, some Japanese doctors say their system stands roughly where the American system did twenty-five years ago.

For instance, in a landmark case several years ago, Japan's Supreme Court ruled that doctors are not required to tell patients if they are suffering from cancer. The patient, a nurse, had rejected surgery because her doctor said she had gallstones, rather than cancer. Her family sued, saying that if she had been correctly informed, she would have made a different decision, and her life could have been saved. The court rejected that argument on the ground that a doctor need not share the full details of a diagnosis. In one case it was disclosed that more than eighty elderly people died in a suburban Tokyo hospital after being infected by a kind of antibiotic-resistant bacteria common in hospitals. Relatives say they were told neither the cause of the illnesses nor that the patients were being given large doses of a new type of antibiotic that was reportedly ineffective against the infection.

"The majority of patients in Japan know nothing about the drugs they are taking," said Dr. Masanori Fukushima, a cancer specialist. "There are still plenty of doctors who clip off the name of the drug from the package given to patients. The attitudes are premodern."

No matter what the disorder, patients receive extraordinary numbers of injections and pills, making the Japanese the largest consumers of drugs, per person, in the world. This has for years included a variety of drugs for the treatment of cancer, blood disorders, and senility that some doctors say are of dubious effectiveness. Patients taking experimental drugs are not told in some cases that they are participating in trials.

Hospital stays are measured in weeks rather than days. Dr. Teruo Hirose, a heart surgeon who has practiced both in Japan and the United States and wrote a book comparing the two systems, said the average hospital stay in Japan is 39 days, compared with 5.8 in the United States. Doctors tend to encourage long hospital stays to increase fees through greater volume of business. But the cost per day is relatively modest, keeping the overall cost of the system low. For example, many patients find themselves having to ask their families to provide meals and other services while they are in the hospital.

The centerpiece of the Japanese health-insurance system is a thick green-and-white paperback book issued by the Health and Welfare Ministry, which sits on the desk of just about every health professional. The book lists exactly what doctors can charge for every approved treatment. There is almost no flexibility. An experienced specialist in a demanding area of medicine would be paid the same for an exam as a newly minted general practitioner. Besides providing no differentiation for levels of skill or expertise, there is nothing in it to allow for regional differences in costs. An appendectomy, for instance, costs $388 whether it is performed in downtown Tokyo or in rural areas of the northern island of Hokkaido.

A number of experts, both critics and supporters of the system, agree that this rigid fee schedule restrains costs, but they say it also distorts the services doctors deliver. The lack of recognition of differences in quality puts emphasis on quantity. According to a 1991 article in the *Stanford Law & Policy Review* by Aki Yoshikawa, Norihiko Shirouzu, and Matthew Holt, doctors in private clinics see sixty-four patients a day on the average, for about five minutes each.

While American doctors are generally prohibited from both prescribing and selling drugs to patients, in Japan this is a principal source of income. Japanese take at least 50 percent more drugs than Americans do, says Dr. Fukushima, who has written extensively on this matter. He also says that the system for testing drugs is not rigorous enough and thus results in the heavy use of medication of questionable effectiveness.

Dr. Fukushima said this realization took hold when he worked temporarily in Houston in 1979, and saw the high level of research being done, the quality of the services provided, and the close relationships that developed between doctors and patients —something that rarely exists in Japan. He also became aware, he said, of the concept of informed consent.

Though the green-and-white fee schedule does not recognize differences in quality, patients do. Special gratuities are often paid to gain access to the best specialists, such as surgeons. Dr. Hirose said that the top surgeons are simply offered large under-the-table payments to take on wealthier patients quickly. "It's a bribe," he said. "It's a part of things."

Every Japanese citizen is covered by one of several health plans overseen and in many instances run by the government. Slightly more than 55 percent of the nation's 125 million people are covered by corporate plans, which are run like co-operatives. There are separate plans for public employees, seamen, teachers, retirees, farmers, and the self-employed. In one of the biggest differences with the United States, the aged are covered under a separate system. Unlike their American competitors, Japanese corporations are not responsible for the health care of their retired employees. In most cases premiums are automatically deducted from paychecks. According to Dr. Ikegami, the medical-school health administrator, the Japanese pay on average 2.7 percent of their total incomes for health-insurance premiums. This is matched by employers.

The incomes of doctors, hospitals, and clinics depend on a grand-scale negotiation every two years between the medical association and the Health and Welfare Ministry. Line by line, they hammer out how much each entry in the fee book will be increased. In practice, decisions rest with the Finance Ministry, which lays down in advance the overall increase in costs that will be permitted. "The big problem is that this does not correctly account for all the costs that doctors and hospitals face," said Dr. Kiyohiko Yoshida, an executive member of the board of trustees of the Japan Medical Association. "Neither side is completely satisfied with the results, but we have to find compromises." Insurance coverage leaves some of the costs to patients, who pay 10 percent to 30 percent of their medical bills, depending on the kind of plan under which they are covered. But there are monthly caps to costs, and low-income people are heavily subsidized.

Those who know both the United States and Japan will say that the diversity, urban poverty, and the strong medical lobby in America would make it impossible to apply Japan's system. "Delivering medical services in Japan is something like dealing only with the middle class and up in California," Dr. Fukushima said. "Our system is very backward in many ways, but it does show how effective a strong consensus can be." [JS]

GERMANY: CURBING COSTS
WITH PRESSURE

I F THE most critical problem in providing national health care is getting control over rapidly rising costs, as President Bill Clinton has often said, he may find some intriguing ideas in the German health-care system, which offers coverage to all at a much lower price than Americans pay. Germany's much-admired system of health care, provided through nonprofit but private "sickness funds" that are legally mandatory for nearly 90 percent of the population, leaves patients with freedom to choose their own doctors and their own hospitals, and freedom from almost all medical bills.

Germans spend only a little more than half as much per person on health care as Americans do, $1,659 in 1991, compared with $2,867 for the United States. As a share of gross national product, health spending in Germany in that year was 8.5 percent, while in the United States it was 13.4 percent. American health experts and politicians have flocked to Germany in recent years to try to learn how they could apply at home what they see there. But they have found little that could simply be copied from a country with different cultural traditions.

Visiting a German hospital or doctor's office is much like visiting a good one in the United States. Many German hospitals are regarded as among the best in the world, and few have the crowded emergency rooms and waiting areas that are common in urban American hospitals because people have no other source of medical care. Neither do they have to increase bills for insured patients to cover those who cannot pay, because in Germany insurance covers virtually everybody, including foreign workers and asylum-seekers.

For years the German government has tried to keep medical expenditures from growing faster than the economy as a whole, not so much by limiting benefits as by pressing drug makers, doctors, and hospitals to contain fees—an approach that has worked fairly well. The biggest savings have come from government-mandated programs that brought down the prices of German pharmaceutical products, once the highest in Europe, by ordering insurance funds to pay only what generic drugs cost. Doctors administer their own payments from the health-insurance system, and since 1985 they have agreed to annual caps on total payments, which they share depending on the number of treatments performed.

In another effort to curb costs and to counter what is generally seen as a surplus of physicians, doctors were told that from now on they would have to retire, as far as the sickness funds were concerned, at age sixty-eight. New practices can be set up only in localities where the government agrees there is a need for them. The restrictions have stirred some unhappiness among doctors. German general practitioners earn an average of $95,565 before taxes, which puts them among the country's highest earners, but their incomes have not risen as fast as average wages over the last two decades. "Many people go into the medical profession with expectations that are too high," said Dr. Karsten Vilmar, head of the national physicians' association in Cologne. "But these kinds of limitations seem to us to violate the constitutional guarantees on professional freedom."

Another factor in keeping down costs is that malpractice suits are less common in Germany than in the United States. So are extraordinary life-prolonging measures for patients judged to be terminally ill. "If an elderly patient is clearly dying of natural causes, I treat her at home," said Dr. Ursula Friedrichs, who like most of her colleagues still makes house calls. "I know a hospital stay wouldn't do any good." According to a recent study by John K. Iglehart in *The New England Journal of Medicine*, "On the average, German hospitals have fewer pieces of high-technology equipment than most big urban hospitals in the United States." But Germany concentrates its most expensive medical technology in teaching hospitals such as the University Hospital in Bonn, where the basic daily room rate can be as high as four hundred dollars, but remains far below American rates.

Still, with a mounting demand for medical services, costs have been soaring, putting the insurance funds billions of dollars in the red in 1992. To try to bring costs under control, the government, with a determination worthy of Otto von Bismarck (the chancellor who expanded the sickness-fund system in Prussia in 1883 to keep the socialists at bay), has recently run roughshod over the lobbies of doctors, dentists, hospital administrators, and drug manufacturers, all of which are seemingly far less powerful in Germany than they are in Washington. A law that went into effect January 1, 1993, imposed more across-the-board reductions in the price of most medicines, tightened the caps on doctors' fees, and changed the way hospitals are paid in ways devised to encourage efficiency and lower costs.

Germany's system bears little resemblance to Britain's state-run system of cradle-to-grave national health care, adopted after World War II. It is also very different from the American health-insurance system, which leaves some thirty-seven million people uncovered. The main difference between the German system and the American one is that most Germans have no choice about whether to join a health-insurance plan and no problem finding coverage, either. Unless they are either very poor or pretty well off, the law requires them to become members of one of 1,147 "sickness funds" in the country. Some of the funds are connected to private employers, while others are quasi-public institutions.

The funds are supposed to break even, and each one sets a monthly premium rate as a percentage of a wage earner's monthly salary. The rates among the funds now vary between 8 percent and 16.8 percent of salary, and have reached a historically high national average of 13.1 percent. The premiums are shared equally by employer and employee, and are paid by payroll deduction. The rate is the same for single and married wage earners, with or without dependents, in any given sickness fund.

"Everybody knows exactly how much health insurance costs, and when the figure climbed above thirteen percent, everybody in the system knew they had to get costs under control, or the public would be after them," said Uwe E. Reinhardt of Princeton University, an economist who is an expert on the German system. Nearly all employers are required to participate, including small businesses and low-wage industries, which in the United States often say they cannot afford to offer health benefits. The funds cover not only workers and employees but retirees and people on welfare. Government agencies pay the premiums for the elderly and the indigent, as well as for the three million Germans out of work as of 1993. Changing jobs, or losing them, does not mean losing insurance coverage, even for a minute.

Germans who have the basic, mandatory insurance never see doctor or hospital bills. Starting in 1993, most of them had to pay more for medicine, but only up to a maximum of seven marks—less than $4.50—every time a prescription was filled. Hospital patients must pay only $6.80 a day in western Germany, and $6.25 in the formerly Communist eastern part, and only for the first fourteen days. After that, even this charge is dropped.

"All I had to do was fill out a health-care coupon from my sickness fund and present it to the doctor," said Marianne Wettlauffer, sixty-eight, who had a slight heart attack several years ago and also spent six weeks in a rehabilitation cure in the Black Forest. All but a nominal amount was paid for by her sickness fund. Her husband, Hellmut, sixty-eight, also had a heart attack ten years ago while he was a government employee. His current care too costs him nothing out of pocket, though he supplements his government pension plan with an inexpensive private policy that provides additional benefits such as private hospital rooms.

Their physician, Dr. Friedrichs, has a small second-floor practice in a modern building in Bad Godesberg. From the small waiting room to the two consulting rooms, every room is white and antiseptically modern. Dr. Friedrichs takes privately insured patients as well as those in the sickness funds. The private patients bring in bigger fees, but the funds provide the bread and butter, with a minimum of administrative headache, she said. "I get the payment automatically when I turn in the coupon, with the services performed marked on it," she said.

In 1993 Germans who earned more than $40,000 a year ($29,450 in the formerly Communist eastern part of Germany, where wages and salaries are still lower) were not required to buy health insurance, but almost all of them—about 6.3 million people—purchase it anyway. Because 88 percent of the population is covered by the sickness funds, risk is more evenly distributed among them than in the United States, and private insurance is also relatively cheap by American standards.

How to reduce waste and inefficiency has been a preoccupation of German governments since the mid-1970s. In 1990 changes were effected that were supposed to put the health system on a secure financial basis for the next century. Sickness funds were ordered to pay for generic drugs wherever possible, dental benefits were curtailed, and hospitals were directed to increase efficiency. But costs kept rising anyway, much faster than the rate of inflation or the funds' income from premiums. Either the rates had to be raised or costs had to be cut. And for German politicians, raising health premiums was about as desirable as raising taxes.

Since the system is set up to be self-financing, the German government did not bail out the funds with taxpayers' money. Instead it enacted a draconian new law that went into effect on

January 1, 1993, with the backing of all the major political parties. Among other new controls on the pharmaceutical industry, the law mandated a one-year across-the-board reduction of 5 percent in the price of most nongeneric medicines sold in the western part of the country, and a price freeze through 1994. In the poorer east the law required all medicine to be sold at a 20 percent discount.

The law also reduced orthodontists' fees by 10 percent, mandated that hospital fees rise during the next two years no faster than incomes, and barred clinics or private practices from buying expensive new "major equipment" without government approval. The law eliminated the traditional practice of reimbursing hospitals' costs and letting them bill the funds at a daily rate. Many doctors concede that this practice often led to admissions on Fridays, so hospitals could collect fees over the weekends even though no treatment was given, and discharge ten days later on Mondays for operations that need only have taken a few days.

By 1996 German hospitals and physicians are to work out new fees based on the procedure, not the length of stay. To hold down doctors' fees, the new law provides that reimbursements from the sickness funds rise only as fast as income from premiums. The funds pay doctors by the number of services they perform at a rate negotiated with the sickness funds, so by limiting the total "pot," the payments can be limited too.

In all, the government says that the new law will save $6.5 billion in 1993 and that premiums will not have to rise faster than inflation. Government and health officials all insist that they do not want to be forced to delay care, the way the British National Health Service does for "elective" operations such as hip replacements and heart transplants, with waiting lists that can delay them for years. Nor can they understand why Americans accept a system with what they see as Darwinian traits.

"We are not entitled, particularly with our German past, to decide who is entitled to survival and who is not," said Dr. Vilmar, who heads the national physicians' association. "All we have to ask ourselves is whether we really need a system that provides one-hundred-percent coverage to everybody. There should be a system of perceptible cost sharing." He is among the critics of the new law who question if providers of medical care will ever have a strong reason to keep costs under control as long as most consumers never have to even think about how much their care costs.

Regardless of the new law, serious challenges will remain. As in the United States, for example, there is debate about how to cover the costs of long-term care, such as nursing homes, for the growing population of disabled elderly. Nursing care for the elderly at home is partly covered under the German system, but only up to four weeks and only if it is connected with an illness or accident. Nursing homes cost about as much in Germany as they do in the United States, and those who cannot pay usually have to sign over their assets or rely on help from welfare. Children with incomes can also be required to pay for nursing-home care for their invalid parents.

Labor Minister Norbert Blum has proposed a new state-run old-age insurance plan to cover nursing-home care, to be paid for by payroll deductions and by eliminating one national paid holiday. But opposition from churches as well as labor unions makes it doubtful whether the plan will become law by 1996, as Mr. Blum wanted. Only one thing seems sure: With a rapidly aging population (the proportion of those over sixty will grow by 19 percent by the end of the century, while the segment between twenty and forty is shrinking by more than 12 percent), the pressure from medical costs will continue to mount. [CRW]

States and Cities
Experiment

HAWAII: IT CAN BE DONE

RESIDENTS of the Hawaiian islands, more than twenty-four hundred miles from the American mainland, have long complained that they are left out of major debates that ripple across the nation. But on at least one big issue—how to provide adequate medical care to all citizens—health-policy analysts say Hawaiians are well ahead of the rest of the country, and their state is being studied in Congress and by other state governments as a potential national model.

The fiftieth state is the only one that can boast of near-universal health care. Under a program that requires employers to pick up the cost of insurance premiums for any person working more than twenty hours a week, most of Hawaii's 1.1 million people have some kind of medical insurance. The unemployed, seasonal workers, and those whose jobs do not include insurance are taken care of by state medical subsidies. In all, 98 percent of Hawaiians have some kind of medical insurance. By contrast, in the country as a whole, 14 percent of the population, or thirty-seven million people, lack medical insurance and get no government subsidy. Most are wage earners who work for small or low-paying businesses.

Perhaps most surprising to many experts, Hawaii's near-universal access to health care has not led to soaring costs. While Hawaii ranks near the top of the states in cost of living, its average health-insurance premium is near the bottom. For example, a typical family in Hawaii pays a premium of $263 a month, about half that of other states.

To be sure, Hawaii differs from the other forty-nine states in many important ways. The population is small, the climate is healthful, and the state has a long tradition of providing generous benefits to workers, most of whom belong to unions. Even during the early-1990s recession in tourism, Hawaii had the lowest unemployment rate of any state, 2.8 percent; its insurance companies have to pay little compared to other states for hospital care for the unemployed. Its insurance industry is dominated by a few big companies, which can exercise strong bargaining power to keep doctors' and hospitals' fees down. It is in the middle of an ocean, so businesses that might object to paying health care costs—up to $1,000 a year per employee—cannot simply move across a state line.

But while these oddities help explain Hawaii's success in keeping rates low while providing care to nearly everyone, advocates there and experts on the mainland say the state has much to contribute to the current national debate. "One criticism I hear is that we are different, as if we're all sipping mai tais on the beach and dancing in coconut-shell bras," said Dr. John Lewin, Hawaii's director of health. "We have a lot of poor people in Hawaii. We have all the health problems of the rest of the states. But what makes us different is that we decided to do something about it."

Dr. Lewin, energetic and outspoken, has become a sort of evangelist for universal health care, which he calls a basic human right. He has spoken to numerous congressional officials and to leaders in states such as California and Washington, where similar plans are under discussion. The thrust of his argument is that the states can provide health insurance for all citizens and keep down costs if preventive care is emphasized, and if there is competition among the major insurance companies to go after the uninsured.

Dr. Karen Davis, a professor of health policy at Johns Hopkins

University, agrees. "What Hawaii has demonstrated, to a lot of people's astonishment," she said, "is that they have covered all their people while minimizing economic disruption." By contrast, Massachusetts's plan for universal health insurance, also considered a pioneer of sorts, stalled amid concern over the state's soured economy and the opposition of small-business owners, who would be required to offer employees insurance or pay the state to do it.

The Hawaii plan took effect in 1974, when much of the country was in a severe recession. The world of health care was much different then. For one thing, mandatory insurance coverage by employers was not considered particularly radical; one of its leading advocates was the Nixon administration. For another, no one had heard of AIDS, crack addiction, or many of the high-technology advances that have driven up the cost of medicine. Before Hawaii's plan went into effect, 17 percent of its residents were without medical insurance—a greater percentage than that represented by the thirty-seven million Americans who lack coverage today.

In the Hawaii plan, the employee pays a portion of the insurance: no more than 1.5 percent of a person's gross wages, or half the premium, whichever is less. For someone making two thousand dollars a month, the fee can work out to around thirty dollars a month. The requirement applies even to people who hire domestic workers for twenty hours a week or more, and any business that does not comply can be fined or shut down. State officials say they have had few problems with compliance.

Some business groups still complain about the cost. "For the smaller businesses, it's somewhat of a problem," said Mary Jane Van Buren, a spokeswoman for the Hawaii Chamber of Commerce. "It can make a difference, for some people, between going under and staying profitable." But she added, "People accept it, like everything else, as the cost of doing business here."

As the President and Congress debate whether to require all

employers to provide health coverage, the main argument against such a measure is that it puts too much of the burden on small businesses. It could lead to higher inflation, the critics say, and create still more bureaucracy to bedevil small businesses that are already snagged in government-generated red tape. But Hawaii's example, experts there say, has belied the argument.

The state's economy is run by small businesses; more than 90 percent of Hawaii's 27,271 individual enterprises employ fifty people or fewer, according to the state labor department. Jean Pinc, who runs the B&L Bike and Sport Shop in Kailua, on the big island of Hawaii, said the additional cost of paying health insurance for three full-time employees has not been a drag on the business. "We want to keep our good people, and one way to keep somebody loyal is to give them good benefits," she said. "Everybody who runs a small business is pretty much in the same situation."

Not everyone is covered by the Hawaii requirements. In the most important exception, employers do not have to pay for care of dependents. But business people there say the competition for workers is so strong that most dependents are covered. There are ways to get around paying insurance premiums. Some businesses hire only part-time workers, avoiding the twenty-hour threshold. "We could do that if we wanted to, and I know some people do," Ms. Pinc said. "But again, it comes down to trying to run a business with people who will stay loyal and do a good job for you."

The fact that Hawaii has virtually full employment means that companies have to compete, with various benefit packages, to keep good workers. As it is, "some employers are desperate for workers," said Rich Budnick, a spokesman for the labor department in Honolulu. In 1990 a second part of the Hawaiian health plan, intended to cover the 5 percent of the population that falls between the cracks, went into effect. People who otherwise have no insurance pay a small fee for each doctor visit and a portion of the insurance premium. The rest is picked up by the state. The poor are covered by Medicaid, the state-federal program, as in other states. As of 1991 the State Health Insurance Program was running below its projected budget cost, insuring slightly more than ten thousand people at an annual cost of under one thousand dollars per person. But it provides only basic benefits, covering no more than five days in a hospital per year and limiting care in other ways.

The question most frequently asked about Hawaii's system is how the state has managed to control costs. With Hawaii's isolation and expensive real estate, the cost of living is about 30 percent above the national average. But in 1991 its health-insurance premiums for a single person per month averaged about $94 a month—well below the $154 average cost for a similar policy in New York, California's $141 premium, and the $282 average for Kansas. The infant-mortality rate, down 50 percent from its high of sixteen per thousand in 1974, was among the nation's lowest. Life expectancy, at seventy-eight years, was near the top.

"The secret of our success, the secret that many in the American medical establishment do not want to hear, is prevention," Dr. Lewin said. "We have twice as many outpatient visits—that is, people see their doctors several times a year—and half as many hospital stays as the national average." People are encouraged to go to the doctor early and often, he said, thus minimizing the chance of costly operations for maladies that could have been prevented. "The emergency room is not the place to get prenatal care," Dr. Lewin said.

Another cost-saving aspect is that the pool of workers covered by a given insurance plan is not drawn from a single workplace but from the entire population. If the premiums were based on the health of ten people at one office, and two of those people had life-threatening diseases, the costs for everyone else at that office would skyrocket. But because the risk pool comprises all state residents, the costs are much lower. "This has reduced the administrative expenses for insurers and, together with the spreading of risk, made insurance premiums affordable for all but a handful of small employers," wrote Molly Joel Coye, the head of California's department of health services, in the summer 1991 edition of *Issues in Science and Technology*.

But just as Hawaii was being studied by people outside the state, Dr. Lewin feared that an onerous new federal system might be imposed on Hawaii. The federal government should establish a minimum set of benefits, Dr. Lewin said, then step aside and let the states craft their own programs. [TE]

OREGON: SOCIAL TRIAGE

I N MARCH 1993 the Clinton administration approved Oregon's novel proposal to guarantee health services for all poor people while eliminating coverage of low-priority treatments, a form of rationing that has sparked wide controversy. But the federal government said the state must revise its ranking of medical services to eliminate the possibility of bias against disabled people as it sets priorities and determines what will be covered and what will not. The administration also imposed stringent conditions on Oregon to try to limit federal costs and, at the same time, to prevent sharp reductions in services for poor and disabled people.

Under the plan, all poor people in Oregon will be eligible for Medicaid, the federal-state program that now serves 240,000 Oregonians, including only about two-thirds of the poor. Oregon officials rejoiced at the federal action, which clears the way for a five-year state experiment that will be closely watched by federal officials and health policy experts. "We will be an absolute beacon for the nation," Sen. Bob Packwood of Oregon said in an interview. "What we want to try is what the nation will come to. We cannot pay for every conceivable procedure that every conceivable person could conceivably want."

The next hurdles for the state are fiscal and political. The restrictions on what Medicaid will cover are not intended to produce large savings, and the state must come up with at least $100 million to extend Medicaid to 120,000 newly eligible people. Oregon is already facing a deficit in its state budget and is considering new taxes on doctors, hospitals, and other providers of health care.

While approving Oregon's plan, Donna E. Shalala, the Secretary of Health and Human Services, imposed twenty-nine conditions and restrictions, including several to prevent discrimination against disabled people. The Bush administration rejected a similar proposal from Oregon in 1992, saying it appeared to violate a 1990 law, the Americans With Disabilities Act. Some spokesmen for the disabled maintained that the disabled might be denied medically necessary services under the plan. Oregon revised its proposal to take into account the federal objections. In ranking medical services for coverage under Medicaid, the original proposal weighed the contribution of the services, if any, to a patient's quality of life. State officials say they eliminated the use of that measurement because federal officials objected to it.

In preparing its latest proposal, Oregon, drawing on years of public hearings and research, ranked 688 medical procedures according to their costs and benefits. The state said its Medicaid program would pay for services ranked 1 through 568. But it would not pay for procedures lower on the list, supposedly the least beneficial and least effective. These include treatments for conditions that are self-limiting; cosmetic procedures; and treatments whose effectiveness is unproved. Services falling below the new cutoff include liver transplants for people with liver cancer, nutritional counseling for obese people, and fertility services, as well as medical treatments for the common cold, chronic back pain, infectious mononucleosis, phlebitis, and acute viral hepatitis. Some critics of the Oregon approach say that any such formal ranking of medical treatments cannot take full account of individual circumstances. As a result, they say, some people who could benefit may be denied useful care while others who are unlikely to benefit from a particular treatment may receive it.

Oregon officials defend rationing, or "setting of priorities" as they prefer to call it, as a corollary to their efforts to guarantee access to health care for all poor people in the state. Under the plan, Medicaid would be available to Oregon residents with incomes less than the federal poverty level ($11,187 for a family of three in 1992). The Medicaid director in Oregon, Jean I. Thorne, said three groups of poor people currently ineligible for Medicaid—single men, women without children, and childless couples—would be covered under the state plan.

Oregon has often been a pioneer in social policy, from its efforts early in this century to regulate workers' hours to its recent attempts to protect the environment and guarantee access to health care for its residents. Apart from the explicit rationing, the Oregon health plan resembles in many ways proposals being considered by the Clinton administration for the nation as a whole. It encourages Medicaid recipients to use health-maintenance organizations and other forms of "managed care." It will require employers to buy or provide health insurance for their employees. It defines basic health benefits to which state residents will be entitled. And it will probably reduce access to services beyond the standard package. The state law requiring employers to arrange health insurance coverage for employees is scheduled to take effect in July 1995. Oregon officials say 280,000 of the state's three million residents will gain coverage as a result of this requirement.

In a letter to the White House, seventy national advocacy groups had urged President Clinton to reject the Oregon proposal. They said it would set dangerous precedents and would violate the Americans With Disabilities Act of 1990, which generally prohibits discrimination against disabled people. Among those listed as endorsing the statement were the United Cerebral Palsy Associations, the Spina Bifida Association of America, the American Association on Mental Retardation, the AIDS Action Council, and the American Civil Liberties Union.

After the federal government approved the Oregon proposal, Robert Griss, senior health policy researcher for the United Cerebral Palsy Associations, said, "We are not thinking of initiating a lawsuit at this point because we believe there has been technical compliance, on paper," with the 1990 law. But he added: "Disabled people may not get the services they need when a real individual walks into a real doctor's office."

Under the original proposal, Oregon could have shortened the list of covered services if it ran short of money. But the governor of Oregon, Barbara Roberts, assured Clinton administration officials that the state would not make such cutbacks for two years and would seek federal permission before reducing benefits for three years after that. Representative Henry A. Waxman of California, a formidable critic of the Oregon plan, said that he would not fight it in view of Governor Roberts's commitments. Waxman is chairman of a House subcommittee responsible for Medicaid.

Representative Ron Wyden of Oregon, a liberal Democrat who supports the state plan, said: "Critics persist in saying that Oregon is rationing health care or limiting health-care benefits. But you cannot ration health care to people who get none." [RP]

NEW YORK: MANAGED CARE
AND THE POOR

O N AN icy winter morning at the Livingston Income Support Center in Brooklyn, a handful of men and women sat in a back corner of the office listening quietly as city workers explained a new requirement for those seeking public assistance. "Do you have a satisfactory ongoing relationship with a doctor?" one worker asked Hyacinth Maryshaw, thirty-six. "No," Ms. Maryshaw answered. "Do you have any experience with managed care?" the worker continued. "No." Half an hour later, Ms. Maryshaw left the center enrolled in the Health Insurance Plan of Greater New York (HIP), a large private health-maintenance organization. Though she had gone to reapply for welfare, Ms. Maryshaw became the latest participant in New York City's first foray into mandatory "managed care," the initial phase of one of the most ambitious entries in a growing national movement that seeks to provide better health care for the poor and, ultimately, contain costs.

Traditionally, Medicaid, the federal-state health program for the poor, lets patients be treated wherever their membership cards are accepted. Because of Medicaid's low reimbursements, that often translates into shabby clinics and crowded emergency rooms. Managed care, by contrast, aims to provide better, more complete care by requiring patients to choose from preselected lists of doctors and hospitals. Begun in October 1992 as an experiment in southwest Brooklyn, but scheduled to be extended to the entire city within five years, the New York program is too new to be fully assessed. Still, several days of interviews in welfare centers, doctors' offices, and hospitals offered a broadly drawn picture of public response and of how the switch from traditional Medicaid to managed care may force the poor to change their actions and expectations about health care.

City welfare officials say that some people have resisted signing up, saying they do not want to lose the independence Medicaid gives them or that they already have doctors they like. But most of the Medicaid users, who tend to end up in emergency rooms instead of doctors' offices, have joined enthusiastically, saying they are tired of sporadic care, faceless doctors, and long emergency-room waits. They also say they are happy to have a doctor who knows their name, a central office that keeps up with their medical records, and access to a variety of services not offered by Medicaid.

Greta Johnsen, thirty-seven, of Bay Ridge offered a toothy smile as an example. Not long ago her mouth was filled with chipped, decaying teeth, and she was unable to find a dentist who accepted Medicaid. Now enrolled in Health Care Plus, which has its own dentists, Ms. Johnsen has had four teeth capped and a root canal performed. Now getting regular dental and physical checkups, she said, "I'm getting a lot of my health back to where it should be."

Managed care plans, which include health-maintenance and "preferred provider" groups, are now used by thirty-six states for more than 3.6 million Medicaid recipients, or 12 percent of the nation's Medicaid population. The Brooklyn experiment, which covers 25,000 welfare recipients—all poor families with children from Sunset Park, Bay Ridge, Bensonhurst, Borough Park, Coney Island, and Gravesend—is a response to a state law passed in 1991 amid mounting Medicaid costs and reports of dismal care for the poor. It requires that half the state's 2.6 million Medicaid recipients be moved into managed care within five years. While the measure is meant to contain costs, its biggest goal is better care for the money.

"The law should help the state achieve long-term savings," said Paul Tenan, director of community health insurance and finance systems for the state health department. "But its main purpose is to expand Medicaid recipients' access to the kind of health services that private insurance provides to most people."

Within five years, officials in New York City hope to be providing managed care to half the 1.5 million residents on welfare, with numerous insurance groups participating. Ultimately the officials expect some small savings: perhaps $50 million a year from the $2.75 billion currently spent on medical services for the poor. For most plans the city will pay monthly per-capita fees to managed-care providers that equal about 95 percent of what patients' care now costs. The 5 percent difference is the savings.

While other states have tried versions of the managed-care plan, New York City has one of the most ambitious plans because of its sheer number of Medicaid recipients. Florence H. Frucher, director of the Mayor's Office of Medicaid Managed-Care, said, "The magnitude and the pace of this is what makes this so interesting." In the mandatory program's first four months, more than five thousand people enrolled, including many who arrived with reservations about what the change might mean.

At the Livingston Center, Sherry Dowling, a twenty-eight-year-old single mother, had said she "wasn't interested," but changed her mind because "there is coverage I didn't know I was eligible for." She said in recent months she had stopped treatment of a kidney infection because she couldn't pay the doctor's $1,300 bill. That treatment would be covered under the new system, a city worker explained to her. "Maybe this will be better," she said.

But such a wholesale shift in the pattern of care does not come easily for everyone. For many it requires a shift in attitudes. Except in true emergencies, for example, patients must consult their selected primary-care physician before seeing specialists or entering the hospital; the plans will not pay for unneeded visits.

As a result, an undetermined number of users are seeking exemptions from doctors and hospitals.

Exemptions are given to anyone who can verify a relationship with a primary-care doctor who meets the same requirements as doctors in the managed-care programs, or who can prove special circumstances. Those who don't enroll are automatically assigned to a plan. Medicaid users elsewhere in the city can also enroll in the plans if they are available, but their enrollment is not required. "I don't want to join a plan, because my son's doctor is my neighbor, and she is a good pediatrician," said Yimel Hennis, nineteen, as she struggled to hold her squirming fourteen-month-old son, Luis, at the Livingston Income Support Center, where she asked for an exemption form.

In the waiting rooms and doctors' offices of Sunset Park, the early verdict from patients and doctors was similarly mixed. At the Sunset Park Family Health Center, a clinic attached to the Lutheran Medical Center, patients filled the tiny waiting rooms marked by signs such as Pediatrics, and Women's Health. As she stood in line outside a window to exchange vouchers for $2.50 in bus fare, a provision of Health Care Plus, Alemania Hidalgo, thirty-seven, praised the Brooklyn experiment as an improvement over Medicaid. "I didn't like having so many doctors before," said Ms. Hidalgo, who had arrived at the center to have a tooth filled. "Now I have just one, and my children have one too. This is better."

Rosa Villanueva, thirty-three, had the opposite response. "I don't like this mandatory plan," she said as she sat in the waiting room at the Lutheran Medical Center clinic. "With Medicaid I could go to different hospitals. Now I can't. And I like faster service." She glanced around the crowded room. "Here I have to wait, sometimes for two to four hours." Ms. Villanueva also said that she had been going to Spanish-speaking doctors whom she had liked and who accepted Medicaid. Her new doctor, she said, does not speak Spanish, and "the chemistry was not right." A health-care worker, who was standing by, explained that she could change doctors. Ms. Villanueva had not known that.

For doctors taking part in the Brooklyn project, many with cramped but popular offices on Fifth Avenue in Sunset Park, mandatory managed care has brought its share of blessings and headaches as well. The plans offer a steady client base and a more organized way of keeping up with payments and complete medical histories. But they also give the doctors less autonomy, smaller fees in some cases, and reams of new lists and requirements. Some doctors say they feel constrained by the need to check many of their treatment decisions with the company.

"With our plan fully developed, we make it easier for primary-care providers to take care of people," said Dr. Merle C. Cunningham, medical director for the Sunset Park Family Health Center. "But every plan has its own rules. And it has gotten to be an onerous hassle to keep up with which benefits go for which patients in which plans."

Dr. Rabindar Sinha, a Sunset Park pediatrician who is taking part in two of the six plans now offered in Brooklyn, says the change to managed care has had a noticeable impact on his practice. Ninety percent of the nearly two hundred patients he sees each week in Brooklyn are on Medicaid, he says, and an increasing number are enrolled in the managed care plans. One part-time secretary had to be hired full-time to handle the paperwork. And he says that reimbursements from the managed-care plans don't always cover his basic office expenses. "To keep our client base, we have to join," he said, noting that several of his long-time patients had been assigned to other doctors in other plans. "What will happen in the future, we don't know." [MBWT]

ROCHESTER: AN AMERICAN
SUCCESS STORY

I N THE search for ways to slow the surge in national medical
spending, policymakers and economists are paying growing
attention to Rochester, a prosperous industrial city of 232,000 in
upstate New York. Health-care experts say Rochester is one of
the few American cities with systems that work. Although medical costs have also been rising rapidly in Rochester in recent
years, they are still at least 25 percent lower per capita than
national levels. And in Rochester, only 6 percent of the population does not have insurance, according to a survey by Louis
Harris & Associates—far below the 14 percent national rate.

By cooperating closely, instead of scrambling for advantage as
they do in most cities, the doctors, the hospitals, and the local
businesses have kept the quality of care high, with a relatively
low level of waste and unnecessary care. The General Accounting Office is preparing for Congress a report on the Rochester
system. "Rochester is a jewel in a sea of health-care despair," said
Stephen Skorcz, a Toronto hospital executive who was president
for four years of the Rochester Area Hospitals Corporation, a
nonprofit planning and research group that the hospitals established.

The Rochester program has served the interests of the city's
largest employers, including Eastman Kodak and Xerox, by
holding down the growth in costly health-care benefits. But the

chief beneficiaries have been the families and small businesses that typically would not have access to affordable care because they were not part of a larger group. Under the Rochester plan they pay the same monthly premiums for each person as Kodak and Xerox, for equal benefits. And unlike most health-care plans for small groups, no one pays more or is refused coverage because of age, sex, or a previous medical condition.

Doctors and business and hospital executives around the country say one reason the Rochester system works is that local industry, vigorously led by Kodak, which has thirty-nine thousand employees in the Rochester area, cooperates closely. All but a few employers buy their insurance from Rochester Area Blue Cross and an independent health-maintenance organization, instead of following the national pattern of insuring themselves in separate arrangements. This self-insuring can reduce a large company's costs, at least for a time, but it often increases the burden for small companies, which have few employees over which to spread the risks.

David E. Edwards, Kodak's benefits director, compared the company's community-first philosophy to the maxim "the family that prays together stays together." Kodak's 1991 health costs averaged $2,100 an employee in Rochester, which was 25 percent lower than at the company's operations in other cities. Kodak's total cost last year for all employees, retirees, and dependents was $240 million.

Rochester Area Blue Cross and Blue Shield said the cost of health-care coverage per employee in company plans was $2,378 in 1991, about one-third less than the $3,573 reported in a national survey of employers by the A. Foster Higgins benefits consulting firm. Those numbers include both employer and employee contributions. In addition, Blue Cross administrative costs were 7 percent of revenues, much lower than national estimates of 14 percent to 24 percent for most insurers. Rochester Area Blue Cross officials said the reasons for their lower costs included the efficiency of their electronic claims processing, the high productivity of their employees, and the relatively low spending on advertising.

More than half the region's one million people are in health-maintenance organizations, which are prepaid health plans that offer comprehensive coverage, including regular checkups, and try to help their members avert expensive hospital stays. Even the handful of self-insured employers, including Bausch & Lomb and General Motors's Delco Chassis and AC Rochester units, say most of their Rochester people are in one of the two local HMOs, one of which is offered by Blue Cross. Blue Cross HMO premiums in 1991 were as much as 25 percent lower than those for comparable traditional coverage.

Another area of industry cooperation has included close oversight of the area's seven hospitals, which represent a large portion of the costs of health care. Backed by state health-planning laws that require approval for big projects or purchases, the Rochester business executives who sit on the hospital boards have kept a tight lid on new buildings and technology. "No one proposes a Taj Mahal," said Albert D. Sharbonneau, executive vice president of the Genesee Hospital in Rochester, which has 424 beds. "It's not worth your time." No additional hospital beds have been authorized since the 1960s, so more than 90 percent of the beds are always occupied. With all the patients they can handle, "the hospitals haven't had to get into helicopter wars," said Arthur Liebert, president of the 526-bed Rochester General Hospital, referring to the helicopters some hospitals deploy in emergencies.

Avoiding expensive duplication, the hospitals have agreed over the years on which institutions should perform certain specialized services—among them, organ transplants, open-heart surgery, pediatrics, psychiatry—usually with related teaching programs at the University of Rochester medical school. Under industry pressure, the hospitals agreed to let the Hospital Corporation set communitywide budget ceilings for a time in the early 1980s. This forced them to squeeze down spending. Then, because costs were lower than the going rates paid by Medicare,

Rochester voluntarily gave back to surprised federal officials a total of $4.8 million in 1984 and 1989 to prove the effectiveness of its approach. "When we took the check down to Washington, they didn't know what to do with it," said Dr. James A. Block, who headed the Hospital Corporation at the time and is now president of Johns Hopkins Hospital in Baltimore. "Nobody had ever returned Medicare money before."

But when the hospitals began to experience operating losses in the late 1980s, they rebelled against the budget ceilings. Other developments, including expensive new diagnostic equipment and surgical procedures, soon were pushing up medical costs in Rochester as rapidly as in other cities, albeit from a much lower base. "Costs have been creeping up in the past few years," said Patricia M. Nazemetz, Xerox's benefits director. But she said that local business executives were trying to get planning back on the table, with all the interested parties taking part in the discussion.

To keep the hospitals cooperating, Donald D. Zrebiec, a retired Xerox executive, is helping to direct a program in which management experts from Kodak, Xerox, General Motors, and IBM are advising eight Rochester-area hospitals on how to improve the quality of their service. With hospitals closely controlled in New York State, more health-care spending has moved to physicians' offices and clinics, which often buy their own computerized scanners and magnetic-imaging machines. The Rochester Area Blue Cross and Blue Shield is considering an innovative plan that would put pressure on these buyers to get approval as the hospitals do.

Another cornerstone of the Rochester plan is the single-price approach, known as community rating. Under community rating, everybody—young and old, healthy and infirm—is grouped together so the risks and costs are spread evenly across large numbers of people. By contrast, when they become sick or grow old, most individuals and members of small groups have to pay higher premiums or drop their coverage, joining the uninsured.

Al Ross, a fifty-nine-year-old home-maintenance contractor,

kept his Blue Cross coverage in Rochester after he moved with his wife and two children to Hilton Head Island, South Carolina. "Here they charge according to your age," he said of South Carolina, "and there is an additional charge for each child. I'd feel crushed if I had to pay that."

Only a few other places, notably Hawaii, had kept community rating, which was common before insurers began to compete for the business of small groups with varying rates. This and other kinds of competition in health care came into vogue in the 1980s in hopes that the pressures of the marketplace would slow rising medical costs, but the practice has tended to favor groups of healthier people and exclude people who are at risk of incurring higher medical bills.

Recently, modified versions of the single-price approach have been adopted by some states, including Maine, Vermont, Oregon, New Jersey, and New York. Community rating is also under study in several other state legislatures and in Congress. Commercial insurers who oppose community rating say the system would force them to raise premiums beyond the reach of many young and healthy policyholders. That has not happened, however, in Rochester. But Chris Petersen, a senior counsel with the Health Insurance Association of America, a commercial insurers' group, contends that the Rochester system can function only because Blue Cross plans in New York are exempt from state taxes and get discounts on hospital charges.

Policymakers in Washington and across the country express interest in adopting at least parts of the Rochester system. But experts disagree over how many of the Rochester advantages could be replicated elsewhere. People in Rochester "have been out in front in showing how they can behave as a community," said Dr. Merlin DuVal, a former assistant secretary of health, education, and welfare who is dean emeritus of the University of Arizona College of Medicine. Dr. Block of Johns Hopkins said the Rochester approach could be transferred to any city if local business leaders would join in supporting a unified regional insurance program. Kodak executives said they were discussing similar approaches in several cities where the company has large plants.

But Humphrey Taylor, chief executive of Louis Harris & Associates, was doubtful. "They have a sense of community in Rochester, which just doesn't exist in most places," he said. Even if the Rochester program cannot be translated exactly, it may well offer some useful lessons to communities elsewhere. "The government can learn from Rochester's example," said Howard Berman, president of Rochester Area Blue Cross and Blue Shield. "We have an American success story." [MF]

Coping With Change

STRUGGLING WITH LIMITS

J ANUARY 1993 made it just over a year since the employees at Randall Decorators, a small Staten Island business, became part of a momentous transformation in health insurance in the United States by switching to a plan that lowers monthly costs but limits their choice of doctors. They expected to save money and they did, cutting their monthly premiums by 23 percent, a total savings of four hundred dollars a month among the seven employees who joined the plan. What they did not expect was the difficulty some have had in adjusting to the new health plan. They have had to come to terms with the fact that the intimate relationship between patient and doctor has expanded to include a third party: an insurance company.

There was, for instance, the rage of one decorator who was certain she was suffering from Lyme disease, but who had to plead with a series of doctors until one reluctantly authorized diagnostic tests, which came back positive. There was also the frustration of the office manager, who was planning to start a family, when she realized she would have to leave her trusted obstetrician and choose a stranger from her new insurer's list.

There was envious tension when several employees rejected the new health-maintenance organization entirely, relying instead on their spouses' less restrictive insurance. But there was relief for some, particularly one upholsterer who has difficulty reading and who had used the local emergency room as his doctor because he felt overwhelmed by the paperwork of his previous insurance. Now he, his wife, and two children have a doctor all their own, and there are no forms to fill out at any visit—just a payment of two dollars, regardless of what is wrong.

The experience of the employees at Randall Decorators with their new "managed care" plan is typical of that faced by tens of millions of Americans, as employers, insurers, and government struggle to slow the rise in health-care costs. Even as Washington debated proposals for restructuring health care, a major transition in the insurance system was already well under way, with effects on medical costs and quality of care that are still largely unknown.

In the long-standing pattern, patients were free to choose their doctors, often developing a close relationship with their personal physicians, though in cases of serious disease they were often referred to specialists they did not know. The doctors could provide treatment without being questioned, and insurers simply paid whatever bills they were sent. In the new era of managed care, more patients are restricted in their choice of doctors and hospitals, and insurers increasingly tell doctors what procedures are worth doing and limit the fees doctors can charge.

Already nearly half of insured employees around the country are enrolled in some form of managed care, ranging from health-maintenance organizations in which doctors provide all care for a set fee from the insurer, or in some cases work on salary, to insurer-organized networks of doctors and hospitals that have agreed to accept discounted fees as services are used. Increasingly the nation's companies, which pay for most health insurance, are nudging or pushing their employees into managed care, and government health programs are adopting it. The approach also figures prominently in most proposals for national restructuring of health care now under debate in Washington.

In interviews at the huge storefront showroom of Randall

Decorators, in Staten Island's New Dorp section, nearly all the employees said they would stick with their plan from U.S. Healthcare, the second-largest managed-care provider in the New York area. The company has 1.5 million patients in eight Northeast states, including New York, New Jersey, and Connecticut.

But they say they have learned to be more involved in their own health—partly out of fear that the added bureaucracy of managed care means they may not get individual attention and partly because they are less trusting of doctors they choose from a list rather than through the advice of a friend. They call the doctor for test results, for instance, rather than assuming that all is well, and have begun researching their ailments so they can better evaluate their care. "You have to take responsibility for yourself," said Laurie Daghestani, the company's office manager, who still has not decided whether to use her own obstetrician if she becomes pregnant, which would require her to lay out extra money.

In the U.S. Healthcare plan, a patient chooses a primary doctor from a list provided by the insurer. That doctor authorizes all the patient's medical care, including referral to specialists. The doctors, in turn, must clear most major treatment decisions with the insurer. In case of an emergency, when the primary doctor cannot be reached, U.S. Healthcare will pay for care from an unaffiliated doctor or hospital.

Primary doctors receive a set annual fee from U.S. Healthcare for each patient, regardless of the number of visits. Patients pay two dollars to visit their primary physician and nothing for visits to participating specialists or for lab tests, and they do not have to fill out any claim forms. If they choose to see an outside doctor, they must pay a deductible, plus 25 percent of the bill beyond that.

Randall Decorators began looking for a new insurance plan in mid-1992, when company officials decided they could no longer afford their health insurance. The company was founded in 1949, and the employees have always been treated like family, said Mrs. Daghestani, whose grandfather founded the business and whose father now owns it. The entire staff helped research companies whose ads they had heard or seen.

While examining the list of doctors participating with U.S. Healthcare, company manager Anthony Petro, who has worked for Randall for thirty years, recognized one name. He knew the doctor socially. Mr. Petro breeds Dalmatians, the doctor breeds miniature pinschers, and the two men often met at dog shows.

A sales representative of U.S. Healthcare was invited to make a presentation, and she arrived with a basket of apples to stress her company's commitment to preventive care. With much hesitation, the Randall employees voted to enroll in the plan. They were particularly concerned that the number of participating doctors in Staten Island was somewhat limited and that unless they used those doctors they would be required to pay for a large portion of their own care.

On the other hand, they were attracted by U.S. Healthcare's policy that patients could change doctors as frequently as they wished among those in the plan until they found one they liked. They were impressed that doctors' compensation was based, in part, on the result of patient surveys, and they were comforted that one doctor was familiar to Mr. Petro.

Most of all they liked the cost. By joining U.S. Healthcare, the group is saving $400 a month. The bill from U.S. Healthcare is $138.50 per month for each single employee and $337.60 per month for each family policy. Employees pay about $25 a month while the company pays the rest, a long-standing tradition at Randall Decorators. As a small group, the seven employees seeking coverage faced a total premium from Blue Cross/Blue Shield of $1,710 a month—a figure that would have increased sharply had they remained with that insurer, which on January 1, 1993, was granted a 26 percent rate increase by New York state.

Several employees opted not to use the managed-care plan at all. Betty Masini, a decorator, is covered under her husband's traditional plan. Anthony Petro, Jr., Mr. Petro's son, dropped his U.S. Healthcare coverage as soon as he was eligible under his new wife's traditional policy. Those who did switch to U.S. Healthcare had problems. At first everyone used the doctor Mr. Petro knew, but they found him short on time and courtesy. (The man has since closed his practice, and the employees of Randall refused to name him for publication.)

Mrs. Daghestani's husband had symptoms of what he feared was internal bleeding. When he called the office he was told the doctor could not see him for two weeks. Mr. Petro, Jr., caught the chicken pox and said the doctor told him, "You can't come in here, you're sick." Employees blame the problems mostly on the personality of that doctor, and they have all since found doctors they like. But they also believe that because doctors receive a monthly payment for each enrolled patient whether or not that patient is treated, there is no incentive for doctors to go out of their way for patients.

A more serious frustration surfaced when Patricia Petro, Mr. Petro's wife, who had been with the business for more than ten years, became seriously and mysteriously ill. She developed incapacitating joint pain that she believed was Lyme disease, an ailment familiar to dog breeders who spend time in open fields. But she could not persuade a series of doctors to test her for the disease, which is extremely difficult to diagnose conclusively even with a test. Unless a plan doctor authorizes a test, U.S. Healthcare will not pay for it. Nor will it pay for the treatment of a condition that a plan doctor does not diagnose or confirm. And the cost of treating an advanced case of Lyme disease can start at fifteen thousand dollars, Mr. Petro learned.

After several changes of doctors, the Petros found one willing to authorize the tests, which were positive. Feeling vindicated, the family then found themselves arguing with U.S. Healthcare about how she should be treated. The intravenous antibiotics that she needed could be given three ways: in the hospital, at home under the supervision of a trained health aide, or at home with no supervision.

Mrs. Petro was petrified at the thought of administering an intravenous drug to herself, but that is what the insurance company authorized, so she learned how. There were no complications, and today Mrs. Petro is feeling better physically, but both she and her husband have lost their enthusiasm for managed care. "I felt like her health was in the hands of the accountants," Mr. Petro said.

Peter Zambelli, a spokesman for U.S. Healthcare, said the company did not discourage testing for financial reasons. To the contrary, he said, "the bias under managed care is to do more tests to make sure there is no condition that can be caught early, when treatment is more successful and less expensive."

In addition to the trade-offs, however, are the benefits. Harry Himelfarb, for example, Mrs. Daghestani's father and the founder of the business, is extremely pleased with the thorough checkups he has received under his new policy. Many managed-care plans stress preventive care in the belief that keeping people healthy will lower costs later on, and checkups, vaccinations, and other maintenance seldom paid for by traditional insurance is often covered. [LB]

INSURERS VERSUS THERAPISTS

THE twenty-six-year-old woman's moods swung violently. She went from joy to anger to sadness to despair and was treated four times at a hospital emergency room after slitting her wrists. She was finally admitted to Sheppard Pratt, a psychiatric hospital in Baltimore. But after two weeks her insurance company questioned her need for hospitalization. Panicked, she threw herself down a flight of stairs.

The insurance reviewer, upon hearing this, remarked, "Clearly the treatment isn't working," according to Dr. Steven S. Sharfstein, the hospital director. Against her doctor's wishes, the reviewer ruled that the hospital would have to discharge the woman immediately, Dr. Sharfstein said. The case illustrates what psychotherapists say is one of the most profound changes in one hundred years of mental-health treatment and care. A system has been put in place that has in effect interposed a third party into the previously sacrosanct, confidential relationship between doctor or therapist and mental-health patient.

The insurance companies and American employers insist that the new system is essential to control costs. American expenditures on health care in general and psychiatric care in particular are skyrocketing, and mental-health care represents the sharpest rise in such costs for insurers. As a result, insurers have in recent years increasingly turned to "managed care," often hiring specialized companies to monitor treatments. Managed care is now expanding rapidly into psychotherapy and, where it deems appropriate, is blocking, altering, shortening, or effectively ending treatments.

Therapists are up in arms over what they regard as serious and often dangerous interference that puts severe limits on their ability to conduct their practices. It is not unfair to say that therapists and insurers are engaged in all but open warfare. Not that these two opposing forces always end up in disagreement. In the case of the twenty-six-year-old woman, her hospital fought the insurance company, which eventually agreed to reverse its decision. "We sent angry letters, and the family got a lawyer," Dr. Sharfstein said. In the end the woman was hospitalized for five months, was stabilized emotionally, and released.

Managed care in one form or another is being applied to almost all hospitals and clinics that provide psychiatric care, whether they are public or private, for-profit or nonprofit. But much of the impetus for managed care began with the rapid growth in the 1980s of for-profit private psychiatric hospitals, along with growing charges of overuse of hospitalization and misdiagnoses. Psychotherapists say the pendulum has now swung much too far, that more people who really need psychiatric care are being told they will not be reimbursed for their doctors' bills.

These insurers have "become more aggressive and restrictive about paying for psychotherapy than ever," said John Docherty, a psychiatrist at Brookside Hospital in Nashua, New Hampshire. "It's escalated enormously." Doctors also contend that managed care, with its new employees and extensive bureaucracy, has itself added substantially to health-care costs. The managed-care companies say that to the contrary, they have helped control costs, though health economists say no good overall studies have been done.

The American Psychiatric Association has installed a hot line for its members, an 800 number on which it is receiving 150 to 200 calls a month. Most are from therapists complaining that patients who genuinely need hospitalization for serious illnesses are being denied it. They complain too about what they say is the lack of sufficient knowledge or experience among some managed-care monitors. "There's a great deal of anger and frustration among psychiatrists," said Sajini Thomas, a health economist whose office runs the hot line.

The managed-care companies contend that professionals in the psychiatric-care community are the least flexible in seeking new ways to reduce costs of all members of the health-care community. These companies say they are not trying to usurp doctors' roles but are simply trying to prevent abuses or unneeded expense. Nancy Cannon, an official of Private Healthcare Systems of Lexington, Massachusetts, a managed-care company for seventeen insurance companies, called the nation's psychotherapists the "most recalcitrant professional group, the most reluctant to participate in change-making."

In general medicine, when alternatives to surgery are proposed, physicians begin to explore or make changes. But mental-health-care doctors "tend to mystify the treatment experience when it is not always so mysterious," she said. Medication with outpatient care alone is sometimes cheaper and more effective than hospitalization.

The aim of the managed-care companies, about four hundred of which have been created in the last five years, is to conduct a case-by-case consideration to try to match a patient's medical needs to the most effective but least expensive treatment. Even opponents of managed care say that when it is done well, it can serve patients better than the old system, through improved and informed review of the options. But, they add, the focus is too often placed simply on saving money, accomplished too often through capricious and arbitrary denial of benefits.

Dr. Paul Fink, former president of the American Psychiatric Association, said there was no question abuses had occurred in the mental-health field that have driven up costs and in some cases been harmful to patients. "Trying to get control over the ethical behavior of hospitals and doctors in hospitals is a tough task," he said. "The people who suffer are the patients. And the people who have caused the suffering had better clean up their acts." He said managed care, however, has done both "some good and some bad, depriving people who need care of care where extended stays would be helpful; adhering to rules instead of paying attention to legitimate needs of patients."

Whatever its strengths or drawbacks, the economics alone suggest that the new system is here to stay. The amount of money spent per person on health care in the United States is the highest in the world. From 1987 to 1988 employers' overall health costs rose 18.6 percent, while those for mental health rose 27 percent, according to the Employee Benefit Research Institute.

The fact that some form of cost containment and careful management of psychiatric care is needed is also underscored by economic pressures applied by a reduction in mental-health benefit plans themselves. As fee payments have risen, employers have been steadily cutting back their benefit packages. In 1982, 43 percent of employers' health plans had more restrictive coverage for mental-health problems than other ailments; by 1988 the figure was 71 percent, a U.S. Department of Labor study shows. The plans typically limited the duration of psychiatric hospital stays to 20 or 60 days, versus a minimum of 120—and often no limit at all—for other illnesses.

Office visits to a therapist have been restricted even more drastically, the report found. In 1982 therapy visits were already subject to limits in 84 percent of plans. By 1988 that was true of 95 percent. Because the sharpest rise in costs has been so high, "employers are asking for their mental-health benefits to be managed, where they do not ask the same for other medical problems," said Tom Joyce, a spokesman for the Prudential Insurance Company of America.

In some cases the companies are insisting that their representatives interview patients directly about their psychiatric care. "They'll make a direct suggestion to a patient," said Dr. Ruth

Yoshpe of the American Psychiatric Association. "Your doctor's not good enough. You should see one on our approved list, or we'll cut off your payments." Dr. Yoshpe contended that "sometimes the companies have people reviewing cases who are not physicians, telling psychiatrists, 'Why don't you just give some medication, without psychotherapy?' or, 'Our guidelines say four therapy sessions are enough,' when the doctor thinks the patient needs twenty." In general, the managed-care companies deny that their reviewers are not adequately trained, though they acknowledge that they often are not medically trained.

At any rate, the tighter fiscal policies have threatened the very existence of some forms of therapy. The most endangered species is the long-term, open-ended core of psychoanalysis that was the norm for decades after Sigmund Freud developed the field. There are some still willing and able to scrape together fees for four-times-a-week sessions that can continue for four or five years and cost $100,000 or more. But most cannot, and there are virtually no health plans that will help with the cost.

There are physicians in mental health who think this is as it should be. "Psychoanalysis is great, but your employer shouldn't have to pay for it," said Dr. Bernard Rappaport, medical director of American Biodyne, a managed-care company in San Francisco. "The old model was that you went into long-term therapy and more or less got fixed once and for all," Dr. Rappaport said. "The new one is that you get a brief therapy that helps you get over what you're struggling with at the moment. And when down the road something else is troubling you, you come back for another short treatment."

Even critics say that when managed care is done well, both patients and those who pay their bills can emerge winners. Dr. Sharfstein of Sheppard Pratt in Baltimore tells of a man who, at thirty-eight, had medical insurance but had been hospitalized or homeless because of schizophrenia. "He'd been tried on every medication," the doctor said, "but none worked until we included him in the clinical trial of a new drug, clozapine. His symptoms cleared for the first time." The man's problems were not over, but they were much improved.

"What he needed was a sheltered living situation," the doctor said, adding that his hospital had such a patient residence that cost $115 a day. The man's insurance covered hospitalization at $400 a day—but not the sheltered residency at $115. Dr. Sharfstein talked to the managed-care monitor, and the company allowed an exception to its rules and provided six months in the residence. "For the first time, he's not in the hospital and not homeless on the streets," the doctor said. "It makes me hopeful that managed care can work." [DG]

SECOND-GUESSING THE
DOCTORS

DR. Robert Sawyer, a Denver surgeon, has a full-time office
manager to get approval from insurers to perform operations. He also speaks to the companies every couple of days himself to report on patients' progress, spending about an hour each
day on the phone justifying his patients' care. In the case of a
patient whose extensive intestinal bleeding prompted a two-
month hospital stay, he fielded daily calls from her insurance
company requesting minute details: the volume of urine she had
produced and the drip rate of her intravenous lines. The purpose of such calls is to reduce costs by weeding out care that is
wasteful or inappropriate. But Dr. Sawyer said that in his case
the strategy had been ineffective: "With all the overhead, I'm
sure they're not saving money on me. We've spent hours on the
phone going back and forth, but in the end I've never been
turned down."

Second-guessing doctors' decisions, formally known as utilization review, has become ubiquitous in American medicine. It is
at the heart of "managed-care" plans in which close oversight is
a given, but it is also common now even with traditional, unrestricted health plans. Insurance companies say such scrutiny
saves them as much as ten dollars for every dollar they spend to
hire reviewers or to buy computer programs that help them

evaluate care. But whether such reviews are saving society any money—or costing it dearly—is a subject of wide debate.

It is clearly not saving money for the Mayo Clinic, which now has seventy full-time employees talking to twenty-four hundred different insurers. It is not saving money for Dr. Sawyer and other surgeons who have had to hire a business staff and pass the costs on to patients. It is not saving money for many patients, who find that denials by insurers leave them with larger out-of-pocket expenses.

"Utilization review is a growth industry and a very expensive and inefficient one," said Dr. Arnold S. Relman, former editor of *The New England Journal of Medicine*. "There are companies that are growing by reviewing insurance claims for insurance companies, and other companies getting rich by helping hospitals fill out forms so they are reimbursed."

Health-care experts credit the outside reviews with reducing the length of hospital stays, but because of a lack of scientific standards for treatments, even proponents admit that it is hard to know if it generally leads to better care. With a dash of science and a pinch of custom, each insurance company now decides what it considers appropriate. "The problem is there are no accepted scientific practice guidelines for most procedures, so utilization review is inevitably arbitrary," said Bruce Kelly, a business executive at the Mayo. For example, said Dr. David Wong, a Denver orthopedist, the largest review organization in Colorado required until recently that patients seeking a hip replacement had to be unable to tie their shoes, a standard that had no medical justification.

Even as it spreads, this method of oversight is coming under attack from a growing number of medical experts who say there are better ways to promote sensible care. Even some insurers are starting to back away from questioning every doctor and operation. "Micromanagement is at best workable and at its worst a nightmare," said Dr. Alan Hillman, director of the Center for Health Policy at the University of Pennsylvania. "It takes infrastructure, money, and it makes doctors very unhappy."

A few insurers, including the Travelers Insurance Company, no longer insist on reviewing every case; rather, they are beginning to focus on procedures that are often performed unnecessarily, such as hysterectomies and magnetic resonance imaging, or MRI scans, and on doctors whose patterns of practice deviate from the norm. Under that approach, surgeons who have a good history might be exempted from applying for each case. Many experts, echoing some prominent proposals for sweeping changes in the nation's health system, hope to develop national guidelines that could be applied at the hospital level and preempt the need for outside review.

Although people in the young review industry admit that they have some kinks to work out, they say their scrutiny has spared thousands of patients unneeded surgery and maintain that an outside review is the only way to keep doctors up-to-date and honest. "We have tried to set standards and reduce the hassle factor, and we can begin to be a bit smarter about how we monitor care," said Elizabeth Friberg, who has worked as a review nurse for an insurer and is now executive director of the Utilization Review Accreditation Commission, a nonprofit group that accredits utilization-review companies. "But the medical world has to understand that people are going to be held accountable, and this is not going to go away."

The backbone of utilization review is a telephone conversation between a doctor or his office staff and a clerk or a nurse working for the insurer. If the call's purpose is to request permission for gallbladder surgery, for example, the doctor might be asked whether the patient had nausea and how often, what the results of an ultrasound scan were, and whether he had abnormal liver-function test results. The insurer uses the responses to decide whether the procedure is necessary.

But how this determination is made varies greatly from company to company, and insurers are not required to reveal what guidelines they use. "Many reviewers won't tell you what standard they're using, and when they do it's unreasonable or ridiculous," said Dr. Wong, the Denver orthopedist who had to fight for permission to perform hip replacements.

At Aetna Life and Casualty in Hartford, one thousand nurses and fifty doctors form the core of the review department. To evaluate requests, the company uses a variety of guidelines, some developed internally and some purchased. The nurse feeds responses into a computer, which makes a recommendation. So far the company has computer guidelines for about forty procedures, including cardiac bypasses, MRI scans of the knee, and tonsillectomies, said Dr. Allen Meyer, Aetna's director of medical programs.

For some conditions the interview is brief. "If someone has an imaging procedure that shows multiple gallstones, that may be the only question, since we know that people with multiple gallstones need their gallbladders out," Dr. Meyer said. "In other cases the decision is much more complicated: A little of this and a lot of that might add up to a yes, while a little of that and a lot of this might be a no." Although initial denials can be appealed for a second review by a doctor, 3 percent to 10 percent of cases are ultimately turned down, Dr. Meyer said. Requests for cataract surgery and total joint replacements are rarely denied, he said, while 20 percent of carpal tunnel surgery and 25 percent of MRI scans of the knee are deemed unnecessary.

Travelers Insurance Company has bought computer software from Value Health Science, a California company that researches medical outcomes. The software measures the appropriateness of hospitalization for about three dozen diagnoses. Requests that are rejected by the computer are reviewed by a doctor, and 50 percent are reversed. The overall denial rate is 6 percent to 12 percent, said Dr. F. Warren Tingley, Travelers's medical director. Where no good guidelines have been developed, Dr. Tingley said, the company tends to grant approval. While Dr. Meyer said Aetna saved ten dollars for every dollar invested in utilization review, Dr. Tingley placed the savings at about half that. "It's very hard to measure what doesn't happen," he said.

Insurers say the review saves money in many ways. For one thing, they say, the reviewers help educate doctors in cost-effective care; for another, the prospect of being scrutinized makes doctors think twice before ordering tests and surgery. But critics say that if education is a goal, the system is poorly designed. Insurers often do not tell doctors specifically why their requests have been denied. Indeed, many insurers worry that sharing their criteria will make it too easy for doctors to cheat the system, giving all the "right" answers over the phone. "One of the big problems with the case-inspection method is that doctors don't learn anything from it; they're just told it's denied," said Tom Granatir of the American Hospital Association. "They don't learn about what insurers consider appropriate care, so practice habits can't change."

For hospital business offices scrambling to keep track of what Aetna deems appropriate and Travelers does not, the diversity can be maddening. The billing office at the Mayo deals with more than 2,400 insurers, each with its own standards. To ease the crunch, the 70 employees in the office have subspecialized—for example, with one in psychiatry and another in rehabilitation medicine. Together they make an average of almost 500 phone calls a day to insurers: 200 to get clearance for surgery and the rest to discuss patients who are already in the hospital.

"We have tried to keep track of the different requirements manually, but it's not working very well anymore," said Mark Koch, unit manager of the Mayo's billing office. "The complexity and the bureaucracy associated with this system is mind-boggling."

Doctors also complain that insurers sometimes use underhanded methods. Dr. Charles Sheldon, head of the surgery department at the University of North Carolina at Chapel Hill, said insurers had started calling clerks and nurses at his hospital, asking them to peek at the patient's chart if the patient's stay was running long. Many hospitals and doctors complain that the reviewers do not have adequate training. Although half of initial rejections are later overturned, the doctor or his office staff must repeat the case for the appeal. And sometimes when the insurer saves money, it is the patient who pays, especially when a test or procedure is reviewed and denied approval after the fact, which can happen with care provided outside the hospital.

Because of complaints from doctors and patients, in 1991 the insurance industry helped create the Utilization Review Accreditation Commission, which offers voluntary accreditation to the estimated three hundred utilization-review companies in the nation. So far ninety-one companies have applied, and about half have been approved, some after making changes demanded by the commission. Four have withdrawn, and the rest are being processed. No company has been denied accreditation.

To some people, the concept of creating a new bureaucracy to manage the abuses of an old one makes little sense. Instead, many experts believe that the process can be made better by decreasing the number of reviews and concentrating scrutiny where there is clear evidence it is needed. Dr. Robert Brook of the Rand Corporation would like to see more aggressive review within hospitals, so that a surgeon considering an operation would have to justify it to colleagues.

"Before you do a bypass that is going to cost fifty thousand dollars, you should have to go down a checklist and answer questions to justify the decision just like an airline pilot," said Dr. Brook. "And if you're planning to do something unusual, like taking off with only two engines, then you should have to explain why." Today all hospitals have an internal utilization-review division, but they generally concentrate on curtailing hospital stays that have outlasted insurance payments. Rarely, if ever, do they prohibit a doctor from performing a procedure.

Others believe that efforts should concentrate on doctors with histories of improper care and on procedures that are known to be overused. Travelers no longer requires preapproval for cystoscopy, in which a urologist inspects the bladder through a fiber-optic scope, since denial rates on this procedure tended to be low. "This lowers our costs, and the doctors love it," said Dr. Tingley, Travelers's medical director. "We feel ultimately we may get to a point where we could say this group of doctors always asks the right questions and cares for patients appropriately." [ER]

NEITHER RESPECT NOR
SATISFACTION

DR. Stanley J. Tyler is no longer practicing medicine. He is not exactly certain what the final straw was, but it may have been the day he learned that the simplest of laboratory tests —as basic as the pregnancy tests sold in any pharmacy—would now be subject to several layers of new government forms and fees if he were to perform them in his office. "If it weren't for the paperwork, I would never have retired," said Dr. Tyler, fifty-nine, who closed his Commack, Long Island, internal-medicine practice in 1992. "The handwriting was on the wall, and the encroaching government was more than I could take."

Dr. Tyler is not alone. Throughout the New York region and across the country, senior, seasoned doctors are choosing to retire early, cut back their hours, or switch to jobs that do not involve patient care because of what they see as a loss of control to insurance companies and government agencies. Although medical associations have not measured the extent of the trend, they say that doctors are leaving the profession earlier and more often than ever before—particularly those in primary practices, such as internal medicine and pediatrics, where earnings are less than in other specialties.

"This used to be a profession where people never really retired," said Dr. Nancy W. Dickey, a family practitioner in Richmond, Texas, and a trustee of the American Medical Association.

"Now we're finding a fair number of physicians leaving in their late fifties or early sixties. The trend in other business is for people to work longer and try to change the rules so they don't have to retire," said Dr. Dickey, forty-two, who on particularly stressful days has flirted with the idea of becoming a professor. "But in medicine it's the reverse. It's a terrible loss."

If that trend continues, experts say, the relationships between doctors and patients may be permanently changed. "In some areas that are already underserved, it will be even harder to find a doctor," said Dr. M. Roy Schwarz, senior vice president of the American Medical Association. "And everywhere else, it will be unlikely that you will stay with your same physician for your entire life."

Doctors have become steadily more frustrated over the past three decades, surveys show, and the most recent polls found that if given a second chance, about 40 percent would not enter medicine. The main reason they give is the "hassle factor"; the growing levels of paperwork and scrutiny by insurers that are now the norm in health care. A 1990 study by the American Medical Association found that of those who had soured on the profession, 42 percent cited outside interference and regulation as the major reason.

In fact, the hostility toward paperwork is so high that some doctors said they would be willing to accept less money if it would make the hassles go away. In a study by *Annals of Internal Medicine,* a medical journal, 30 percent of internists said they would forgo part of their income in exchange for the "assurance that there would be substantially fewer administrative requirements and less interference in clinical decision making."

Doctors leaving their practices concede that they get little sympathy. After all, they have the wherewithal to retire early, an option not available to most Americans. But they point out that one aspect of the profession that had appealed to them was the autonomy. Many now retiring are of a generation brought up on the lesson of the Great Depression: that doctors were always their own boss and were always in demand. Today, however, doctors are beholden to layers of oversight from the government and the insurance industry, a loss of independence that is likely to worsen under the forms of national health policy that appear to be under discussion in Washington.

"An awful lot of physicians have been calling and saying, 'I've had it, this isn't worth it,'" said Timothy Novak, a spokesman for the Connecticut State Medical Society. "They don't see it getting any better, so they're getting out." Much of that frustration is with the approach known as "managed care," under which insurance companies require doctors to clear all major treatment decisions in advance. The intent is to hold down medical costs, but doctors have long complained that care was in the hands of the insurer rather than the physician.

"When I'd call for approval, there was never a doctor on the other end of the telephone," Dr. Tyler said. "If you were lucky, there was a nurse. Most likely it was a clerk who had a checklist." In interviews, many doctors said that managed care had changed the relationship between doctors and patients. "The nature of medicine has changed to a corporate practice," said Dr. Leonard Weitzman, who practiced family medicine in Commack for thirty years before cutting his hours in half in 1992. "The medicine that I went into with such gusto, where a patient was served by his doctor—it's gone. Now you do what the insurance company wants you to do, or you get forced out."

Dr. Anne Harrison was a pediatrician in Scottsville, New York, for twenty-nine years before she retired in 1992 at sixty-two. By the time she retired, she said, 75 percent of her patients were part of a managed-care plan, and many came to her because she was on a list provided by the insurer, not because they expected a personal relationship. "It became a business," Dr. Harrison said. "I'd say, 'Mrs. Jones, why did you bring Betty in today?' The answer would be, 'Oh, I'm covered under the plan, and she had a runny nose, so I decided to come on in.'"

For each of those visits Dr. Harrison would get a small copayment and a rising feeling that she was just part of an assembly line. "Almost half the visits under the plan were unnecessary," she said. "Pediatrics should be putting out medical brush fires before they become big fires. But we were blowing out matches and filling out forms."

The feeling that they are working harder for less money and satisfaction is echoed by other doctors. In part, that is because there are more patients: The baby-boom generation is aging and in greater need of doctors. And, in part, it is because each visit requires more follow-up paperwork. Adding to the fatigue from the workload is resentment that it seems to go unappreciated. "All we read about is, 'Why do doctors charge so much?'" said Dr. A. Burton White, an orthopedic surgeon in Great Neck, Long Island, who stopped doing surgery in 1987, then cut his office hours in half five years later. At the hospital where he used to perform operations, he said, the oldest surgeon now is fifty-three.

"They burn out faster," he said of his colleagues. Patients, he said, view doctors as "the enemy. That gets tiresome. This used to be a highly respected profession that we wanted to be part of. Now we are the enemy." For many doctors the aggravation came to a peak in 1992 when two new sets of federal rules took effect, one covering even the smallest and simplest in-office labs and the other regulating office safety, going so far as to detail how employees' clothing was to be laundered.

Compliance with the rules was so complicated that state medical societies held dozens of courses to teach doctors what to do. Some, like Dr. Tyler, looked at the cost and effort and decided to retire early instead. Others, like Dr. Weitzman, decided to cut back their hours. He now works twenty hours a week as a family practitioner and the rest of the time as the in-house doctor for the Suffolk County Police Department.

Still others take a job that does not involve direct patient care. Dr. Warren Glaser was an internist in Rochester, New York, for nearly twenty years before he left private practice in 1991 and became the associate medical director of Preferred Care, a health-maintenance organization. He closed his office, he said, because he was constantly justifying his decisions to insurance companies and federal Medicare clerks. "It's terribly aggravating and annoying," he said. "It's an affront every single day. I like to think that I practice good medicine, and to have someone second-guess you all the time wears you down."

Now he defends the actions of others, namely the doctors in his new HMO. "If you can't lick 'em, join 'em," he said. It is much less stressful to answer questions about other people, he said, than about himself. He teaches at an area medical school to keep up his clinical skills but does not regret leaving daily, hands-on medicine. "Things are changing so rapidly, and there are going to be more changes coming down the line," he said. "Rather than let it hit me, I decided to jump out of the way."

As the oldest doctors act on their frustrations and retire, the profession is waiting to see what their successors, who know managed care as an established practice, will do. Dr. Vincent Parry cut his hours in half in July 1992, twenty-eight years after opening his family practice in Hauppauge, Long Island, and the same month that his son finished his own medical training. The younger Dr. Parry, his father said, sees opportunity where the older Dr. Parry sees only despair.

Rather than open a private practice of his own, Dr. Parry's son is working in an urgent-care center, a free-standing, twenty-four-hour clinic that is an increasingly popular alternative for those without a regular physician. "He'll see what Clinton has to offer," the elder Dr. Parry said. "He'll find a way." [LB]

THE ETHOS OF
CONSERVATIVE CARE

DR. James C. Blankenship, a cardiologist with a health-maintenance organization in central Pennsylvania, performs costly, risky procedures in which tubes are pushed to the heart to help find whether coronary vessels are clogged. In his catheterization laboratory, he studied X rays revealing a partly blocked artery in a fifty-five-year-old man. "What are the chances this will shut off, causing a heart attack, versus the risks of surgery?" he asked. "The studies differ.

"I'll advise him to watch and wait," said the doctor, whose salary would not be affected one way or the other. "I want to do everything that's necessary, but not too much."

As Americans consider a more frugal medical future, possibly dominated by competing HMOs or other forms of "managed care" that limit consumer choice, urgent questions are rising about the quality of care and how to protect it. Will people be pushed into health plans staffed by sullen, rushed doctors whose decisions are second-guessed and who are paid extra to scrimp on costly tests and operations? Or will they find sensitive doctors who have no financial incentive to do too much or too little, have ready access to the best technologies, and hold down costs by preventing illness and avoiding procedures with little benefit?

Medical experts are scrutinizing better health plans around the country to see how large savings might be gained through efficiency and prudence, not through shortchanging the sick. And the evidence suggests that institutions that foster physicians like Dr. Blankenship and allow them to exercise professional judgment may be in the best position to pursue that goal. At his organization, the Geisinger Foundation in Danville, Pennsylvania, the decision about how much is enough is left to the doctors. Their cautious style of medicine has held costs well below the national average. Increases have still averaged 8.6 percent in recent years, though, raising questions about whether the country will be able to tame medical inflation without cutting into the quality of care.

The 530 salaried doctors who work at Geisinger, and offer care through a prepaid insurance plan, do receive prodding from above. But it involves not constant second-guessing or rewards for scrimping, but rather a steady flow of research news and tips that helps suffuse the institution with an ethic of conservative care. "Here we don't police; we trust our doctors," said Dr. Howard G. Hughes, who directs the HMO, the Geisinger Health Plan. In the case of the fifty-five-year-old man, some doctors would have recommended immediate surgery, but Dr. Blankenship felt sure that a trial period of drug therapy was in his patient's best interest.

In Danville, a town of 6,000, Geisinger runs an advanced 577-bed hospital as well as a network of clinics over a wide area of central and northeastern Pennsylvania. Its growing HMO serves 142,000 members, while the same doctors and clinics also provide the same style of care to hundreds of thousands more people covered by the government or other insurance. The doctors insist that their brand of medicine improves on a system laden with incentives to overuse procedures.

And they are saving money. The HMO has the lowest rates in Pennsylvania, according to the state insurance department, with monthly premiums in 1993 of $109.70 for individuals and $285.22 for families for a plan covering nearly everything but prescriptions. But the numbers suggest too just how severe the challenge is. The health plan's charges have risen by an average of 8.6 percent a year since 1985, Dr. Hughes said. That is a good record compared with that of most insurers: Nationwide, HMO rates grew by an average of 11.7 percent per year from 1986 to 1992, and rates for traditional fee-for-service plans rose annually by 14.2 percent, according to A. Foster Higgins & Company, a consulting firm.

But these rates remain well above the national goal of steady real spending set by President Bill Clinton. Recent increases have mainly reflected the rising cost of nurses, technicians, and other personnel, the soaring price of new drugs, and other factors, officials said. Geisinger doctors and administrators, most of them practicing physicians, insist that through steady refinement they can save much more without compromising care. Just how much and how fast, though, no one is sure. "If this model can't hold down prices enough, then I'm not sure it can be done in a way that fulfills the medical expectations of society," said Dr. Stuart Heydt, president of the Geisinger Foundation.

While America's medical costs are increased by administrative waste, excess equipment, incentives to use procedures lavishly, and outright fraud, in the end spending mainly reflects the routine decisions of physicians. They decide when a patient needs a $70 electrocardiogram, when to order a $100 dollar antibiotic instead of a $10 one, and when $40,000 bypass surgery is truly likely to improve a patient's chances of survival or quality of life.

"The best way to control costs and preserve quality is to have the physicians do it," said Dr. Arnold S. Relman, the former editor of *The New England Journal of Medicine*. "The whole health-care system is built on the behavior of doctors, and that behavior is greatly influenced by the way health care is organized." Dr. Relman, who has been studying health plans around the country, praised Geisinger for high doctor morale and a system of mutual review that promotes excellent care.

While no organizational structure guarantees quality care, Geisinger has several traits that promote it. The bedrock, its officials say, is the careful selection of doctors who share the group philosophy and are happy to work for a salary. Since they are not paid piecework, they make decisions with no direct financial interest at stake. (Nationally, doctors are salaried in some but not all HMOs or other forms of managed care.)

The salaries are enough to support an affluent life in rural Pennsylvania, but for many doctors they are well below potential earnings in private practice. Primary-care doctors have starting salaries in the range of $75,000 to $90,000, while among the most experienced specialists who might earn several times as much elsewhere, "very few go beyond $300,000," said Dr. Laurence H. Beck, senior vice president charged with improving efficiency and quality. Morale rests on the pleasures of patient care, collaboration, teaching, and research, said Dr. Francis J. Menapace, the director of cardiology. "We look for a different type of physician, one who still looks at medicine as a profession, not a business."

As in most HMOs, all patients must choose a primary-care physician. Usually trained in family practice, internal medicine, or pediatrics, these doctors provide most care and refer sicker patients to specialists only when necessary. Now about 30 percent of the plan's doctors provide primary care, but studies suggest the proportion should rise to close to 50 percent, Dr. Beck said. This means cutting back on specialties, a painful and controversial topic among the medical staff.

Dr. Ernest W. Campbell, a primary-care physician and head of the Geisinger clinic in the nearby town of Bloomsburg, had been in independent practice for eighteen years before he and his partner decided to join the salaried group in 1985. "We looked at the HMO and liked what they were saying," he said. "It's more geared toward preventive medicine, keeping people healthy rather than just meeting the acute needs as they arise." He said the switch involved a significant loss in income, but offsetting this was a drop in work time to sixty to seventy hours a week. Since patients are in a prepaid plan, he said, "now we can tell them they have no excuse for not coming in when they are ill."

A large unified system such as Geisinger's can also avoid duplication of costly equipment and readily monitor its use. For example, all cardiac catheterizations, which are Dr. Blankenship's diagnostic specialty, are performed at the main hospital in Danville, as is open-heart surgery. This does mean, though, that some patients have to travel up to one hundred miles for major procedures.

With central control too can come imbalances in staffing, sometimes causing long waits. Currently, for example, because of a shortage of gynecologists in the group, an appointment for a routine pelvic checkup can take several months. Officials insist that is a temporary side effect. But in surveys of HMO patients that generally find high satisfaction with care and doctors, intermittent difficulty in getting quick appointments has been the most common complaint, said Dr. Duane Davis, medical director of the health plan.

For all its emphasis on efficiency, Geisinger does little of the routine oversight that is now so prevalent in the health-insurance industry and so annoying to doctors. Instead the doctors are expected to watch themselves. "We have a high awareness of what our colleagues are doing in the next room," Dr. Blankenship said. "There's lots of intercommunication, lots of informal second opinions."

However, peer review is increasingly backed up with research and suggestions from above. The HMO, for example, keeps track of prescribing patterns and sends out newsletters urging physicians to prescribe cheaper drugs or generic versions where they have been shown to be equally effective. In another example, officials studied whether patients who were put on an expensive cholesterol-lowering drug were first asked to experiment with dietary change.

By sharing the results with other physicians and stressing the recommended course, doctors found that the proportion of patients trying diet changes had risen. Some will end up needing the drug anyway, but some will avoid indefinite use of a drug that can have dangerous side effects. Dr. Campbell, the primary-care doctor, said he welcomed these "timely reminders" and stressed that he remained free, without any pressure, to pre-scribe a costly alternative when he felt it was indicated.

When a doctor's prescribing and referral patterns diverge sig-nificantly from the norm, a senior doctor might ask why. In one case, a doctor who has since left for private practice was found to be ordering twice as many tests and costly drugs as his col-leagues. Asked to explain, he said, " 'I'm a Cadillac; can you afford a Cadillac?' " recalled Dr. Robert M. Haddad, who over-sees seven primary-care clinics. "But I would say he overused tests," Dr. Haddad said. "A thirty-year-old man doesn't need an EKG every year."

The continuous search for "better" ways of doing things is not simply a code word for "less," Dr. Beck said. "What our physicians insist on is to look at the outcomes and make them as consistent and good as possible," he said. "If we do things the right way and reduce variation, we will end up with savings." The question is how far even the best-organized providers can trim without choking off tests and treatments of significant benefit.

Dr. Beck said he believes that Geisinger and other similar groups still have large opportunities to wring out expense. In-creasingly important, he said, will be reliance on clinical guide-lines that reflect research, done locally or nationally, on what sequences of tests and treatments work best. Still, Dr. Beck said, "At some point there will be trade-offs between cost and quality." If price controls are too severe, he said, society will have to openly face the issue of rationing. "Those are decisions the indi-vidual physician can't make in his office." [EE]

THE SEARCH FOR FAMILY
DOCTORS

A GROWING shortage of doctors willing to practice general medicine has left some hospitals and health-maintenance organizations desperate for qualified candidates and, in the long term, stands as a major obstacle to overhauling the nation's health-care system. Almost all changes under consideration include a central role for what used to be known as the family doctor—today generally an internist or family practitioner—who can save the system money by taking care of a wide variety of ailments on his or her own and referring patients for more costly specialty care or tests only when absolutely necessary. Although such primary-care doctors were once the cornerstone of American medicine, their numbers have dwindled as younger doctors have been drawn to specialty fields by money and the lure of new technology. So today, as more patients enroll in health-maintenance organizations or physician networks that rely heavily on general doctors to hold down costs, a rising demand is confronting a declining supply.

Health economists say that a medical system should have about 50 percent of its doctors practicing primary care, which includes family practice, internal medicine, and pediatrics, and that is the mix now favored by most large HMOs. But the current percentage of primary-care doctors in the country is only about 33 percent, and worse, it is falling. In 1992, only 14.6

percent of medical students decided to go into general medicine, an all-time low. At that rate, the proportion of primary-care doctors will drop to 28 percent or less by 2010. "We should try to achieve a fifty-fifty balance as soon as possible, but we have a long way to go," said Dr. Robert Harmon, administrator of the United States Health Resources and Services Administration. "Even if medical schools started graduating 50 percent primary-care specialists today, it could still take us to beyond the year 2000 to achieve a good mix."

Already, "patients are not getting the right kind of attention from the right kind of doctors, and specialists are not getting enough patients in their specialty to keep their skills up," said Professor Eli Ginzberg, a health economist at Columbia University. Health economists say it will take a mixture of market forces and policy changes to fill the gap. The marketplace is already at work in some parts of the country, where hospitals and HMOs fighting to attract coveted generalists are dangling bonuses and salaries that top those for some specialists. It is hoped that money will draw doctors back into the field. The government, too, is offering or considering various incentives like low-interest loans to such doctors as well as to the schools that train them. But few expect such enticements to fully staff primary-care clinics in the near future.

In the short term, health economists, including some of those advising President Clinton, have suggested various solutions, from relying on nonphysicians like nurse practitioners or physician's assistants to retraining underemployed specialists, like neurosurgeons or cardiologists, to do front-line medicine. In the long term, they say, medical schools and hospitals must be prodded to encourage more doctors to go into primary care, a field that has slipped to second-class status in a medical world increasingly focused on procedures and new technologies. "Everything in the current system conspires toward" an uneven division, Professor Ginzberg said. "Why shouldn't someone want to go into a specialty? You're admired by your peers. You can control your time and life better, and then, not unimportant, you make more money."

If there is a shortage of primary-care doctors, there are still plenty of young men and women who want to be some kind of doctor: the Association of American Medical Colleges in Washington reported last week that applications for the 1993–94 school year will be at an all-time high, surpassing the record of 42,621 set in 1974–75. Many of the applicants said they thought the health-care changes proposed by the Clinton administration would benefit society, but it remains to be seen whether those sentiments will mean more medical school graduates going into primary care. As of this year, federally sponsored low-interest loans previously available to all medical students will be restricted to those who commit to practicing primary care. Some economists say the government must go further, cutting off money to specialty training programs altogether. "The federal government has to redirect subsidies to fields that people need rather than the fields that the teaching hospitals want," said Dr. Alain Enthoven, a Stanford University economist who is a principal architect of the health plan said to be favored by President Clinton.

Of the 600,000 doctors in the country, fewer than 200,000 are in primary care, and of those some 40,000 are "general practitioners" who never completed residencies after medical school, widely considered an important precursor to good general practice. (General practitioners do one year of practical training after medical schools, compared with three or four for internists, family practitioners, or pediatricians. Most specialists receive five to seven years' training after medical school.) Faced with this shortage, health-maintenance organizations and hospitals around the country are offering internal-medicine and family-practice doctors bonuses and salaries almost double those paid five years ago. Harvard Community Health Plan is looking for forty general internists, said Dr. Thomas Inui, chairman of the new Department of Ambulatory Care and Preventive Medicine at Harvard University. "If forty people who were qualified walked in the door today, they would be hired on the spot," he added.

The tight market has forced FHP, a large health-maintenance organization in the Southwest, to pay its generalists an annual salary of more than $100,000, more than it pays pulmonary specialists or rheumatologists. Dr. Frank Marino, a family-practice doctor who now works for FHP, said that when he finished his residency two years ago he had more than a hundred job offers, from virtually every part of the country.

Where HMOs have become common, as in Minnesota and Southern California, "they are having trouble finding primary-care providers, and you're experiencing what could be the future, right now," said Dr. William Straub, a senior policy analyst with the Jackson Hole Group, a research organization whose members have close ties to the Clinton administration. Kay W. Slayden, president of Jackson & Coker, a large medical-placement firm based in Atlanta, said that in addition to offering higher salaries for primary-care doctors, areas with the greatest unmet primary-care needs had begun requesting physician's assistants or nurse practitioners. Jackson & Coker this year started a placement service for these professionals in response to the growing demand.

Estimates differ about exactly how many primary-care doctors are needed in the United States, but the general sentiment is: more, and a lot more in rural areas and the inner cities where there are virtually no general doctors left. In 1989, the Community Service Society of New York found that of the 701 doctors who claimed to provide primary care in New York's nine poorest neighborhoods only 28 met minimum standards for an effective primary-care practice; this included being affiliated with a hospital and having after-hour coverage. "Not only was the picture real bleak, but there weren't signs that there was going to be a fresh infusion, there are no new doctors coming into the area," said David R. Jones, president of the society. "New York and other cities will have a particular problem in instituting managed care because of the absence of decent primary care in these neighborhoods." Jones estimated that 500 primary-care doctors would be needed to care for the people who live in the nine survey areas alone.

In practice, the shortage of primary-care doctors is often masked in areas with large numbers of sub-specialists because they tend to round out their office hours by doing primary care. In some of the smaller specialties, like infectious diseases and endocrinology, doctors tend to maintain interest and expertise in general practice for years. But this is often not true in procedure-oriented fields, like cardiology and gastroenterology. And studies have shown that primary care dispensed by doctors who are mainly specialists is unnecessarily expensive since these doctors tend to order more tests and must refer patients to other doctors when their problems fall outside their relatively narrow range of knowledge. "Many people who trained in cardiology or pulmonary medicine begrudgingly do this general stuff," said Dr. Jack Resnick, president of Managed Health, Inc., an HMO on Long Island. "But many of those people are not adequately trained and do things the wrong way." Dr. Resnick said that most health-maintenance organizations specifically prohibited specialists from doing general practice since "the two groups play very different roles."

As more patients enroll in managed care, experts predict that more and more specialists will find themselves unable to fill their time. And they hope that at least some will be interested in switching to primary care. "We are going to need specialists to dedifferentiate, and I think we can create incentives, financial and otherwise, to encourage them to do so," said Dr. Inui of Harvard, adding that some transitions, like neurosurgeon to pediatrician, were "improbable." But Dr. Harmon said that as salaries for generalists rose and specialty salaries fell because of oversupply, even unlikely switches would become at least thinkable: "I guarantee you that once the incomes of sub-specialists drop below general internists, these doctors will be quite happy to do general medicine." Such switches are most plausible for doctors in the medical specialties like cardiology or pulmonary medicine, since they completed general medical training before narrowing their focus. Switching fields is more problematic for some surgical specialists, like neurosurgeons or ophthalmologists, who have highly specialized knowledge and little general training.

Health planners are also looking for ways to reverse the nose dive in the number of medical students who are interested in primary care. While educators say higher salaries will help somewhat, they say the values of the medical world will have to change. Fifteen years ago, relatively few medical school graduates went into fields like radiology and anesthesiology since medical school deans actively discouraged these "no patient contact" specialties. But in recent years, the balance has flipped, so that these and other specialties have been the rule. Dr. Larsen of FHP said that when his daughter, a fourth-year medical student at the University of California at Irvine, decided to go into family practice, an oncology professor said to her: "What a waste; you're too sharp."

With a bit of government urging, many medical schools are now offering students more exposure to front-line medicine and offering a more positive image of primary care. As at Harvard, they are creating departments specifically devoted to outpatient medicine, affiliating with outpatient clinics in the community, and urging students to spend time with practicing doctors treating sore throats and sprained knees as well as learning how magnetic resonance imaging works or doing genetic research in the laboratory. Still, this is not always easy in the huge referral hospitals generally connected with medical schools, where rare tumors often outnumber sore throats and sprains. In such hospitals, "you're much more likely to hear a dissertation about what cement to use in hip replacements than about how to diagnose a hurting shoulder," Dr. Resnick said.

The government, long reluctant to intervene in academia, now seems poised to use its financial muscle to force teaching hospitals to respond. Medicare contributes $5.5 billion to hospitals to subsidize medical education, the Department of Veterans

Affairs spends $600 million, and the Department of Defense, $280 million. Some health economists, like Dr. Enthoven, have suggested that this money should be withheld not only from specialty training programs but also from academic hospitals that do not produce at least a fifty-fifty split in training slots. "So far, there has been no significant weighting toward primary care in directing funding," Dr. Harmon said. "But now that is certainly under consideration." [ER]

LESSONS FROM
A CORPORATE GIANT

MARIE T. LYONS, a twenty-eight-year-old computer operations troubleshooter at the Xerox Corporation headquarters in Stamford, Connecticut, joined a health-maintenance
organization for the first time in late 1991, largely because the
price seemed right. As a single person, she pays $6.33 in
monthly premiums, while her employer contributes the balance
of the $183.43 a month that her HMO charges. The big office-
machine manufacturer provides the subsidy to encourage workers to join HMOs that have met Xerox's standards for quality of
care and service and, even more important, have held down
costs.

Xerox, a $17 billion company with 55,000 employees in 47
states, has been one of the most aggressive and innovative large
companies in the pursuit of lower health costs. It has given its
employees strong incentives to join HMOs, in which care is offered for a prepaid price and patients are limited in their choice
of doctors, and the company has fostered competition among
HMOs for its contracts. In its stress on "managed care" and
competition, the Xerox method includes several elements of an
approach known as managed competition that has gained the
interest of many economists and President Bill Clinton.

Yet Xerox, which has been refining its strategy since the mid-
1980s, still faces jumps in health costs that it considers unaccept-

able. Although one company with employees spread around the country cannot make the sweeping changes in the health system that many experts think are needed, its experience offers lessons about both the potential rewards and limits of managed care within the current system. More than 60 of the 190 HMOs that serve Xerox employees are limiting their 1993 price increases for Xerox workers to an average of only 5.5 percent, well below the rise in health costs most companies face. But most of the HMOs have not held down cost increases as extensively. And 16,500 Xerox employees—30 percent of the company's work force—still choose to remain in traditional insurance plans despite the extra cost.

Like many Americans, including Xerox's chairman, Paul A. Allaire, they want to be able to choose any family doctor or medical specialist rather than being limited to a list of HMO-approved physicians who would control the patients' access to specialists. "I love my doctor; he's the best," said Nancy-Jean Bono, a twenty-nine-year-old administrative assistant. To keep him she pays $137.83 a month to cover her family. She could get similar coverage in an HMO for less than $20 a month. But then she would need a new doctor. She said that her current physician prefers to remain independent.

So while nearly two-thirds of the company's employees have selected the prepaid health plans (and about 7 percent are covered by their spouse's benefits), Xerox's overall medical costs were expected to rise by a burdensome 12.7 percent in 1993, quadruple the projected national inflation rate. Projected costs per active employee jumped to $4,324 in 1993 from $3,154 in 1990, the first year of the company's current system.

Even a company as large and profitable as Xerox blanches at the prospect of facing 12 percent annual increases, doubling its expenses every six years. If this continues, Mr. Allaire, the chairman, said, "it would clearly make us less competitive internationally." His main competitors are Japanese companies that spend far less than their American counterparts for employee health care.

The company uses many of the country's most admired health-maintenance organizations, including the Kaiser Foundation's national network and two in Rochester, where the largest cluster of Xerox employees live. Health-maintenance organizations are the cornerstones of most proposals to address the nation's growing medical problems. But most have yet to demonstrate significant, steady savings. "HMOs are not the magic bullet," said Dr. Robert H. Brook, health-sciences director at the Rand Corporation, an independent research center in Santa Monica, California.

Following a practice called shadow pricing, HMO charges usually rise steadily at a rate that is just a bit lower than traditional health plans. Kaiser, for example, has increased its rates by an average of 12.8 percent a year since 1990, while national rates for traditional fee-for-service medicine were rising about 16 percent annually. And too often, economists and other experts add, HMOs attract the younger and healthier members of a group who need relatively little care, but this is not reflected in lower rates. The fee-for-service plans, meanwhile, get more than their share of people who believe they have medical needs, said Helen Darling, Xerox's health-care strategy manager.

Kaiser, which is under pressure from large customers such as the California Public Employees Retirement System and employers hit by the recession in its California stronghold, raised its 1993 rates only 6.8 percent, on average, across the country. In several regions, Kaiser wooed Xerox employees with 5.5-percent increases. In Rochester, where Xerox has joined with other large employers to restrain medical spending, prices are 25 percent to 35 percent below national averages. But Rochester Blue Cross has also posted HMO rate increases averaging about 12 percent for the last four years. In the same period, its fee-for-service increases averaged 17 percent a year. Contrary to the common perception of health-maintenance organizations as the lower-cost choice, Xerox said HMO rates for its Rochester employees were currently higher than fee-for-service charges there.

Traditional medicine is expensive for Xerox and getting more so. It was expected to cost $6,322 per active employee in 1993, up 15.4 percent from the year before. Xerox projected $3,846 per employee for HMOs in 1993. And even though participants in the traditional health plans face steep deductibles before the company starts picking up most of the costs (they have to pay all charges until they reach 1 percent of their income), Xerox estimated it would spend nearly half of its $235 million health-care budget to cover these employees.

Xerox promotes enrollment in its lowest-cost HMOs by paying more than 90 percent of the charges. These HMO members pay only $239 a year for full family coverage, which includes expensive items such as fertility therapy as well as free checkups and other preventive care. To steer people away from HMOs that charge more, the employees' share of the costs is increased. Employees pay the most, $1,654 a year for family coverage, for the company fee-for-service plan, which covers 80 percent of physician fees but only after the employee has paid 100 percent of the deductible.

Patricia M. Nazemetz, Xerox's benefits director, chose six HMOs, including some of the nation's largest, to direct the network. The goal, she said, was to concentrate the company's buying clout, which had been dispersed across 250 Xerox offices and 180 HMOs. "It struck me that I wasn't able to have a relationship with two hundred HMOs," she said. With the smaller group of HMOs, Xerox was able to insist on improvements in quality of care as measured by surveys that asked employees to assess their health plans' performance. "Some are doing a very good job," she said, "but it doesn't mean they couldn't get better. Can they say to a member, for example, 'You've just passed your fortieth birthday; it's time for your mammogram?' " she asked. "Are they saying, 'The last time you had your blood pressure checked was twelve months ago; it's time to come back in'?"

Employees at Xerox headquarters in Stamford have a choice of three of the six HMOs in the company system: Kaiser Foundation Health Plans; U.S. Healthcare, whose home office is in Blue Bell, Pennsylvania; or Prucare, which is owned by the Prudential

Life Insurance Company in Newark. The other HMO contractors are Blue Cross and Blue Shield of Rochester, where Xerox has 13,000 workers; FHP International, based in Fountain Valley, California; and the HMO Group in New Brunswick, New Jersey, an association of several nonprofit plans. Besides their own enrollees, these six also supervise the scores of independent Xerox-approved HMOs around the country, so employees usually have a choice.

Xerox is ready to "share our ideas with the Clinton administration, if they're interested," Mr. Allaire said. But he avoided making specific recommendations. "I'm not sure we could say that what Xerox did is right for the country," Mr. Allaire said. "It sure isn't perfect." [MF]

WRESTLING COSTS TO THE MAT

FROM his third-floor office in a sleek Sacramento building near the domed capitol of California, Tom J. Elkin is a commander in the war against the ever-rising costs of health care. "I know what is a reasonable price for a compact disk or a refrigerator," he said. "But what is accessible health care worth? I don't know yet what a fair price is for the product we're buying. That's what we're after."

Mr. Elkin has plenty of ammunition in this crusade to drive costs to rock bottom. Each year he buys $1.3 billion worth of health care as associate executive director of the California Public Employees' Retirement System, or CALPERS, which represents more than 875,000 state and local government employees and their families across California. He has taken up the banner of "managed competition," a hotly debated approach for reorganizing the nation's medical care that has attracted support in Washington. In essence the approach holds that costs can be controlled by forcing health providers to compete with one another under government supervision.

CALPERS is a prototype for insurance-purchasing cooperatives, a concept that lies at the heart of managed competition. The cooperatives are envisioned as giant pools that smaller companies and individuals would join to gain leverage in buying coverage from competing health plans. But CALPERS has already shown promise, even without the benefit of the sweeping national changes in insurance, tax incentives, and delivery of care called for by proponents of managed competition. Exercising the power of its numbers, CALPERS shocked the California health industry in 1992 by freezing new enrollments for the state's largest insurer, Kaiser Permanente, because it refused to restrain its rate increases. Apart from Kaiser, CALPERS was able to hold twenty other insurers it deals with to average premium increases of 3.1 percent in 1992, when the state industry average was 13.2 percent. In another success, average premium increases for 1993 were in the low single digits.

Promoting such competition has been endorsed by President Bill Clinton and has drawn support in both liberal and conservative circles. But the full-blown proposal for managed competition includes other major changes that are more contentious, and it is not clear how many the nation will embrace.

Managed competition, as envisioned by the informal group of health economists who originated the concept, would require employers to help pay for a standard package of benefits for full-time workers. Tax incentives would push most people into health-maintenance organizations or similar groups that offer comprehensive care for a prepaid annual fee but limit choice of doctors and hospitals. On the other side, most doctors, hospitals, and insurers would join together in HMOs or similar arrangements that operate within fixed budgets. To promote comparison shopping the government would study and publicize each HMO's quality and cost of care, while a national board would decide what coverage should be mandatory and which medical procedures were wasteful.

Skeptics say managed competition, with its combination of regulation and free-market innovation, is untested. In fact, it is already being tried in California to some degree, although these efforts cannot be fully effective in the absence of a comprehensive national scheme. Pressure from CALPERS, an early example of the kind of giant insurance-purchasing cooperatives called for in managed-competition plans, is forcing Kaiser, Health Net, and other insurers there to root out wasteful administrative costs, reduce unnecessary care, and squeeze hospitals and doctor groups to lower their rates.

"The experience of CALPERS is a preview of what the nation will encounter, given President Clinton's commitment to hold down health-care costs," said Gray Davis, the state controller, who sits on the thirteen-member CALPERS board. "Ultimately something has to give: speed of access to elective surgery, the right to choose a doctor, the range of procedures that will be covered. Everybody wants the best care."

But Mr. Elkin maintains that far more fat can be trimmed away before consumers notice such effects. "You'd be amazed how low some of these plans will go with their rates before it goes to the quick," he said. "There is an astronomical amount of unnecessary administration and unnecessary procedures. We have not gotten fully into it yet." Yet one person's unneeded procedure—a hip replacement, for example—may be what another doctor and patient feel is necessary, illustrating how divisive any uniform national standards may become.

CALPERS administers health-care plans not only for the state government but also for 784 other public employers, including local school districts, cities, and even tiny entities such as the California Prune Board, which has eight employees. Joining the cooperative gives each employer bargaining power it would otherwise lack. CALPERS offers its members a choice among nineteen HMOs, with which it negotiates rates and services; it offers a traditional health-insurance plan for members in remote areas not served by HMOs.

The agency was galvanized into creating an ambitious program to eliminate waste when fast-climbing premium increases peaked at 21 percent in 1990. With the advice of Alain C. Enthoven of the Stanford University Business School, an architect of the managed-competition concept, CALPERS took a tough new stance starting in 1991 and began to standardize benefits among plans to make comparisons easier. It demanded detailed data from each provider so that the costs of services could be compared, then used that information to encourage carriers to cut waste.

For 1992 it set a zero increase as its initial negotiating position. When Kaiser, an HMO that cares for about 345,000 CALPERS members, insisted on increases of more than 10 percent, CALPERS barred new enrollments in it. "That served as an example that CALPERS meant business," said Scott R. Kelly, vice president of major accounts at another major carrier, Foundation Health, a California Health Plan, which is a profit-making company based in Sacramento that serves about 78,000 CALPERS members. Foundation settled for a 2.9 percent increase. (Kaiser said it was unable to go so low because it offered richer benefits.)

For the most part the CALPERS system appears to be well accepted by patients, although some younger, healthier workers have complained about rising premiums. Under the system, a member chooses among participating HMOs and may then pick a personal physician within the HMO selected. If the patient seeks care outside the HMO, he must pay himself. For all the new pressures, leaders of Kaiser and the other HMOs in California say they prefer managed competition to alternative proposals because it maintains a measure of consumer choice and avoids the kind of government-run plan used in Canada, which leaves insurers with little role.

Indeed, any system that pressures more people to join HMOs stands to benefit large, efficient operators like Kaiser, which has 4.7 million members and 6,500 doctors in California. "We are a strong exponent of managed competition," said Robert J. Erickson, senior vice president for government relations for Kaiser in California. He added that Kaiser expected to ask CALPERS for "little or no rate increase" for the coming year.

HMO-type medicine has long been more accepted by patients and doctors in California than in New York City and other areas, and it remains to be seen whether CALPERS's success could be matched in communities that resist HMOs. But even in California, patients may soon find their care more closely managed in ways such as these:

• Health Net began an experiment in February 1993 in which neonatal nurses made six monthly telephone calls to certain pregnant CALPERS members to give them advice and encourage them to seek early maternal care. The results will later be compared to other pregnancies in which such calls were not made.

• The eighty-doctor Bay Shores Medical Group in Torrance has installed a new computer system meant to thwart patients who visit different doctors within the group to get excessive prescription pain killers and other drugs or to seek redundant care. The system is also used to detect when doctors prescribe excessive diagnostic tests.

• Southern California Permanente Medical Group, which contracts with Kaiser to care for 2.3 million people, is developing strict guidelines for its 3,200 doctors to bring consistent care to its network of hospitals and clinics. For example, its medical director, Dr. Frank E. Murray, said the guidelines would probably eliminate routine mammography for women before age fifty because research had found no benefit in early testing.

Such tight management has forced a new reality on doctors. After eight years of private practice, Dr. Mark P. Schwartz, an internist, found his work dwindling as his patients joined HMOs. So he left his practice in 1990 and became a salaried employee of Bay Shores. "The handwriting was on the wall," Dr. Schwartz said.

The change was something of a shock. "In a setting like this, there's a great deal of attention to the dollar figure," he said. "So I had to reorient my thinking in terms of what can I spend for a test. The consensus is there has not been any suffering in patient outcome. But my big fear is how far this will be taken." [RR]

The Politics
of Reform

AN AMERICAN-STYLE ANSWER?

ONCE just another proposal, the "managed competition" strategy for revamping health care has now been endorsed by many health experts as an ingenious, American-style answer to runaway costs. More important, elements of the approach, which seek to prune waste with a combination of market forces and government oversight, were embraced by President Bill Clinton as he developed proposals for national reform. But critics have emerged from left, right, and center to question everything from the morality to the practicality of the approach.

If it works the way proponents say, the strategy could make Americans happier, healthier, and richer. "Everyone would have health insurance and you could move from place to place without worrying," said Dr. Paul M. Ellwood, a physician and health economist who is a chief designer of managed competition. "There would be higher quality care and it would be cheaper."

But critics call this a pipe dream. Managed competition would rob patients of choice and doctors of autonomy, worsen inequality, and fail to curb costs to boot, said Dr. Steffie Woolhandler of the Harvard Medical School, a leader of a group of 5,500 liberal doctors who want a Canadian-style system in which government pays for all health care. "It's basically an effort to preserve a role for the private insurance companies," she charged.

Conservatives praise the emphasis on market forces but lament the infringements on patient choice and the new regulatory bodies that the approach requires. They also question whether it can reduce costs. "If they end up with an even bigger bureaucracy than today, then the very reasons why they proposed competition will be lost," said Robert E. Moffit, a health expert at the Heritage Foundation in Washington. Dr. Moffit and other free-market advocates propose using tax credits or other measures to help individuals buy their own health insurance, without all the intermediaries and regulators called for in managed competition.

The debate is clouded by the daunting complexity of the issues and public unfamiliarity with key concepts—not least the phrase "managed competition" itself, which the president's advisors now shun. However the nation proceeds, transforming an overbuilt health system into a sleek machine will involve painful change. What some call waste, whether excess hospital beds, unnecessary operations, or redundant insurance brokers, others consider their livelihood. "We have an extremely wasteful and inefficient system that has been bathed in cost-increasing incentives for over fifty years," said Alain C. Enthoven, a Stanford University business professor and main theorist of managed competition. "We badly need a radically more efficient system. That will mean closing hospitals and putting surgeons out of work."

The strategy: Under managed competition, most people in a region, including those now buying insurance on their own, those employed by smaller companies, and the uninsured, would be clustered in large, state-organized purchasing groups, or "health alliances" as the president's advisors now call them. These pools, and large employers that made their own health arrangements, would bargain with health plans for good prices on a standard set of benefits. Group members would then be offered a choice of several plans.

Tax incentives would encourage people to choose lower-priced plans, but they could pay extra for plans that offered extra coverage or more freedom to choose nonplan doctors. For their part, doctors, hospitals, and insurers would join together to offer such plans, most of them similar to health maintenance organizations in which all care, from vaccinations to cardiac surgery, is given for a preset annual fee. As the designers foresee it, these plans would compete for patients on the basis of price and quality, forcing them to continually search for ways to trim waste. Government agencies would supervise the process, protecting the quality of care and helping the poor join in. Everyone would have access to at least the same basic insurance whether young or old, healthy or sick.

In essence, managed competition seeks to transform the way most Americans buy health insurance, making them more conscious of the price of their coverage, and to change the way care is delivered, making doctors more aware of the costs and benefits of medical decisions. This is not a simple structure, and even many experts who favor the approach are worried about how aspects may work in practice. Would price competition force plans to scrimp on care? Would the savings be as large as the nation needs? The president, while adopting elements of managed competition, has developed his own blend of measures, adding on other measures to control spending.

Hundreds of important specific details have to be worked out. How will the system work in rural areas where there are too few doctors and patients to create competition? How should plans that attract a surplus of older or sicker patients be compensated? No one can predict exactly how all the interacting forces would play out. Proponents say they have built in corrective measures to steer things in the right direction. Critics, mindful of how the health system has eluded controls so far, are skeptical.

Freedom to choose doctors: Mindful of the sensitivity of the issue, the president's advisors are calling theirs a prochoice plan. Many people, though, will unquestionably have less freedom to select their doctors if strong financial pressures are used to push them into HMOs. Some people may feel they have been torn from a trusted physician.

But the issue is not simple. Some forty-one million people already belong to HMOs. Tens of millions more have little choice anyway because they are uninsured, have Medicaid benefits that are scorned by many doctors, or live in rural areas where they have few choices. The thirty-five million elderly people on Medicare may not be pressured to switch, at least in the near term. There is a chicken-and-egg aspect. If most patients join prepaid plans, most doctors will have to join them too, so many people may be able to follow their current doctor, though problems may arise when family members want doctors from different plans.

In the strategy, people would be offered a choice of several health plans, including some that allow patients to go outside the approved roster at extra cost and, perhaps for an extra premium, an old-fashioned fee-for-service plan allowing use of any doctor. The point is not to curb choice, according to Dr. Enthoven, but to make individuals bear the economic consequences of their choices. Within an HMO, patients are generally free to choose a primary doctor from among many. Dr. Arnold S. Relman, the former editor of *The New England Journal of Medicine*, who supports greater reliance on HMOs, said he felt the choice issue was overblown. What most people really mean when they speak about choice, he said, is the freedom to change doctors when they are not satisfied, something they could still do within limits. "I think we have to disabuse the average American of the idea that you can't get good care unless you have a large menu of doctors out there, look at their qualifications, and pick one," he said. "That's not what most people do anyway."

At a different level, some people fear restrictions on their ability to consult outside specialists when confronting serious diseases like cancer. The medical groups under managed competition should be large enough to allow for second opinions, but patients may have to use their own money for consultations or therapy elsewhere. For desperate patients this may seem important—but discouraging costly shopping-around for hopeful diagnoses or marginal therapies is also a key to cost control.

The quality of care: Perhaps the most alarming charge is that medical groups, forced to cut prices in a fierce competition for patients, will shortchange patients—pressuring doctors to avoid needed tests, for example, or to prescribe a cheaper drug when a more expensive one would help the patient more. Proponents say they have built-in safeguards so that the competition would turn on quality as much as price. They envisage fostering medical groups that would behave like the best of current HMOs around the country, which tend to leave doctors rather than insurance officials in charge of medical decisions and try to save by improving care.

Beyond setting minimum standards for benefits, the government would require plans to collect new data on their medical performance, health outcomes, and patient satisfaction. Published in easily digestible form, this information would help people compare the quality of care as they shop among offered plans. New research would also provide doctors with feedback on their own performance, promoting steady improvements. These various measures, Dr. Ellwood said, would be a vast improvement over the present, where opinions about proper treatment vary wildly and neither patient nor physician has any way to judge the quality of care.

But critics question whether tools are yet available for accurately distinguishing good care from mediocre, and for, in effect, standardizing medical decisions. "If we don't have a serious attempt to develop measures of quality, we'll compete on price and drive care down," said Dr. Robert H. Brook of the Rand Corporation. Some, such as Dr. Relman, think that nonprofit medical groups would be more likely to protect quality than the investor-owned groups they fear will prevail. But others, including Dr. Ellwood, say they find no evidence from past experience that this is necessarily so.

Dr. Ellwood also stresses that HMOs promoting a prudent medical style can avoid the overuse of tests and surgical procedures that not only drive up costs but often do more harm than good. "Most consumers think more is better in medical care, but it isn't," he said. "You hear about Cadillac medical care. I think that's crazy. The best medical care in the U.S. right now is costing less."

Controlling costs: In fee-for-service medicine, with insurers simply paying what they are billed, doctors and hospitals have incentives to perform more rather than fewer services. But in plans with preset budgets, providers instead have incentives to save—hopefully, to concentrate resources where they can do the most good, weeding out useless or marginal care. In managed competition, more prudent medical practice would also be encouraged by new national standards for appropriate uses of medical technology. Dr. Ellwood said he believed that within four or five years the strategy would bring health costs in line with the general inflation rate, ending the surge that has created the current crisis. Dr. Enthoven has gone further, suggesting that total health spending, now at 14 percent of the gross domestic product, might even be driven back to 9 percent or 10 percent of the economy.

But many experts, pointing to the march of technology, the inertia in medical habits, and the limited success of managed care in holding down costs so far, fear the savings would not be as steep and fast as the country needs. "They are asking the nation to take a high-stakes gamble," said Henry Aaron, an economist at the Brookings Institution who favors devising additional ways to limit spending. Advocates of a Canadian-style system say managed competition and its continuing role for private insurance companies would only add to paperwork, wasting large sums that could be devoted to care. A government takeover would limit high administrative costs, they say, and could be combined with annual spending ceilings.

Dr. Enthoven has been reluctant to endorse budget caps and opposes price controls. He argues that arbitrary ceilings or price controls may cause hardship without wringing out the worst inefficiencies, something the guided but impersonal hand of the market can best achieve. Given political realities, he argues, governmental controls are more apt to freeze existing arrangements in place.

From the other side, conservatives like Moffit charge that the government boards and mandates called for in managed competition would lead to over-regulation, stifling innovation and needed restructuring of the health economy, and would invite costly political meddling with the free market. But defenders say the new institutions are needed to help individuals accurately compare health plans, avoid the costs of administering multitudes of conflicting plans and approaches, and promote quality and fairness.

Equality of care: Dr. Woolhandler predicted that affluent people would pay extra for plans offering better coverage and freedom to choose the best doctors, while others would be left in cutrate HMOs. "You'll see a rigid class stratification in health care," she said. Some critics also fear that as large companies make their own deals with medical providers, the regional purchasing pools through which others obtain coverage might become second-class.

Several measures in the strategy are aimed at preventing serious inequities, mainly by promoting a high level of care for the majority who accept the lower-cost plans. Proponents of managed competition say the basic benefits required of all plans should be generous, offering insurance most would find ample. Government-sponsored research should uncover plans providing substandard medicine, forcing them to improve or lose access to major insurance purchasers. And approved plans would be required to accept all applicants without screening. Already, Dr. Ellwood said as an example, a growing share of patients at the Mayo Clinic in Rochester, Minnesota, are in prepaid plans like those called for in managed competition. Under the new system, these would presumably become available to anyone in the region. "If you can buy better care than that, go ahead," he said. [EE]

THE RESTIVE LEFT FLANK

T HEY are the guerrilla fighters of the health-care debate: outfinanced by the industry groups, outmuscled by the policy gurus in the White House, viewed by most of the pundits as hopeless idealists. But supporters of a Canadian-style health-care system have a simple message: They are not dead yet. The only true reform, they argue, is a system of national health insurance, in which the government uses tax money to pay for all medical care. Contrary to conventional wisdom, which considers this concept too radical for American politics to digest, they believe that the public, over the long run, will rally to their side.

In the meantime they are presenting a withering critique of the approach President Bill Clinton favors on health-care reform: the blend of market forces and government regulation known as "managed competition." And like any good guerrillas, they are organizing the provinces. As a result, the advocates of a single-payer system—in the tortured language of health policy it means there is one entity, the government, paying the bills—are a force to be reckoned with in the coming struggle on Capitol Hill. They are President Clinton's restive left flank.

The Clinton administration cannot afford to ignore them, reason many analysts, because the battle to enact a major overhaul of the health-care system will be hard enough without losing a constituency committed to reform. "If I were worried about who

I was going to have to compromise with, I think I'd play to my strength," said Rep. Pete Stark, the chairman of the Ways and Means Subcommittee on health and himself an advocate of single-payer systems.

As the administration was completing its proposals, the single-payer advocates, in the best lobbying tradition, were pushing for what they could get, such as a guarantee that any health-care revamping will extend coverage to all Americans as quickly as possible. The willingness to compromise varies widely within the single-payer movement, but many said they hoped to be able to support Mr. Clinton's final package.

It is an eclectic group, with much more of an edge than the dryly intellectual defenders of the Clinton task force. There is Dr. David Himmelstein, a forty-two-year-old associate professor at Harvard, a doctor, a former Vietnam War protester, and a spokesman for Physicians for a National Health Plan. In a recent speech Dr. Himmelstein noted that just 3 percent of the Canadians in one Harris Poll said that they would prefer a health-care system like that in the United States. "To put that in perspective, 16 percent of Canadians believe that Elvis Presley is still alive," he said.

There is Sen. Paul Wellstone of Minnesota, a chief sponsor of single-payer legislation in the Senate and a former professor of political science. Reflecting on the theory of managed competition: "It always seemed to me to be an A-plus discussion paper in an advanced public policy class. But go out and try to explain it to people." There is Rep. Jim McDermott, a psychiatrist and chief sponsor of a single-payer bill in the House. McDermott warned his colleagues that the votes they cast on health care might be the most important in their careers—and they had better be able to explain them.

There is Citizen Action, an advocacy group that earnestly organizes 900 numbers and petition drives on behalf of a Canadian-style system. And Consumers Union, which publishes *Consumer Reports* and *Mother Jones* magazine, which included preaddressed postcards to Congress endorsing a single-payer system in this month's issue.

The single-payer movement is hardly monolithic, but its advocates strike a few basic themes. They argue that the Canadian health-care system, in which the federal and provincial governments share costs, is a proven and largely successful way of delivering quality care to all. They argue that taxpayers will be willing to pay for such a system once they understand that it replaces all other health-insurance costs. Or, as Dr. Himmelstein puts it, "Instead of writing a check to the insurance companies, you write a check to the government." And they assert that managed competition, while presented as a less radical alternative, will in fact prove far more burdensome to consumers. Mr. McDermott presents that argument in a nutshell: "You think the *insurance industry* is going to do right by you?" he asks.

Mr. Clinton, in keeping with the theory of managed competition, would encourage most consumers and employers to band together into regional cooperatives to purchase insurance, thus maximizing their bargaining clout. On the other end, the system would force doctors, hospitals, and insurance companies into networks—like health-maintenance organizations—that would compete for the cooperative's business, trying to offer the best quality health plan at the lowest cost.

Unlike a single-payer system, which in many versions would largely replace the private health-insurance industry, managed competition would preserve a role for insurance companies in health care. It would almost certainly further the trend toward "managed care," in which insurance companies or other administrators play an important role in monitoring the treatment given to patients with an eye toward preventing unnecessary services and holding down costs. Many single-payer advocates present this as extremely ominous, asserting that it pushes the insurance companies further into the doctor-patient relationship and inevitably erodes the right of patients to choose their own physicians. Spokesmen for the Clinton administration said again and again that they would preserve the patient's freedom of choice, but that did not deter this argument, which is widely seen as one of the most potent lines of attack against a managed-competition system.

If the advocates of a Canadian-style system seem combative, there are reasons. Most of the savants in Washington tend to write them off, arguing that their proposals are utterly unrealistic, particularly at a time when public distrust of government is high. "In focus groups, they don't trust insurance companies, but they don't trust the government either," said Robert J. Blendon, an expert on public opinion and health care at Harvard. "They say, 'Don't tell me how it works in Canada, I don't believe it will work that way in this country.' " Adding to the argument against a single-payer system are the numerous new taxes it would require, even though its advocates argue that the system would pay off in administrative savings and greater efficiency and obviously replace private insurance costs. Critics also say that government control of medical spending could slow the pace of technological progress and produce long lines for expensive procedures.

In general, single-payer supporters assert that the public is far more open to this idea than the political professionals think they are. "It's one of those disconnects," said Mr. Wellstone. "At the very moment that the public is in a bold mood, calling for sweeping change, everyone here has turned incremental." Mr. Clinton seemed to close down debate on the issue when he directed his health-care task force to produce some form of managed competition with spending limits. But the single-payer advocates have been pushing hard ever since. If they cannot get their preferred system in its entirety, they say, they hope to push for as many of its features as they can get.

Some of the goals are similar to the administration's. Among them, supporters say, are extending health insurance to all, as quickly as possible; making the basic benefits guaranteed under the plan as generous as possible; building in strong cost controls; and assuring enough flexibility so that individual states have the option to adopt a single-payer system if they choose. Single-payer advocates say they are doing extensive grassroots organizing, rallying much of their support around the McDermott/Wellstone bill, which has more than sixty cosponsors in the House. Most of them say they hope to be able to push Mr. Clinton's plan their way as legislation makes its way through Congress.

One Senate staffer, a Democrat who has strong misgivings about a single-payer approach, nevertheless said its supporters' influence could not be discounted. "If we wind up with universal coverage, the single-payer people will deserve a lot of the credit for that," the staffer said. "They'll have been the ones who kept up the pressure to cover everyone." Still, others worry that these activists will hold out too long for too much and thus jeopardize a real chance at health-care reform under a sympathetic president.

The single-payer people say they are confident that history is on their side. But they also say they do not underestimate the fight. Dr. Himmelstein closed a recent slide presentation at a "managed care" convention with this: "I just show this slide to let you know I'm not completely out of touch with reality, that I'm not a dreamer. This is a picture of the Boston skyline. Our two tallest buildings there—John Hancock on your left, and Prudential on your right." [RT]

THE POTENT PLEAS OF SMALL
BUSINESS

SMALL businesses are making an emotional appeal to head off proposals to require all companies to pay for health insurance for their workers—a mandate that some say could bankrupt thousands of companies and cause massive layoffs. Small business is squaring off not only against President Bill Clinton, who needs employers to help finance the huge cost of extending coverage to uninsured Americans, but also large companies, which already provide health coverage and say small companies are not doing their share.

The resistance of small businesses could be the political Achilles' heel of the president's health plan. If small business blocks the requirement, the president will have a devilish time groping for other ways to pay for his ambitious changes in the health-care system. The debate has pitted an array of small-business organizations, like the National Federation of Independent Business, the National Restaurant Association, and the National Retail Federation—all of whom say many of their members cannot afford to contribute to health benefits—against the United States Chamber of Commerce and many of the nation's industrial giants. "There's a huge division here," said Stephen Elmont, chairman of the National Restaurant Association. "For large companies, this is a nonissue, because they are already providing

278

insurance, but for small business, it's a huge issue—not because we don't want to do it, but because it's unbelievably expensive."

The Urban Institute estimates that it would cost American companies at least $30 billion more a year if the government required them to cover employees working eighteen hours or more a week, and some other estimates run even higher. Of the 37 million uninsured Americans, 28.5 million are workers or their families.

To cushion the impact on small businesses, the president has considered placing a ceiling on a business's health-care payments at some set percentage of its payroll. If a ceiling were applied, some businesses would pay only a part of the cost of insuring minimum-wage employees; the federal government would pay the rest. Some small businesses can live with such a ceiling but are pressing for it to be as low as possible. But many businesses oppose any requirement to provide coverage, arguing that workers can buy their own insurance, perhaps with the help of tax breaks or government subsidies. How, they ask, can a small retailer or restaurant owner who relies on minimum-wage workers afford thousands—perhaps tens of thousands—of dollars in health-care insurance or taxes each year?

In the view of large businesses many small companies are trying to shirk their responsibilities. It is unfair, big-business executives argue, that many small companies do not provide coverage because the rest of society ends up paying the medical bills for their workers—with big businesses picking up much of the tab. The Big Three auto makers and other large manufacturers are particularly galled that many small businesses routinely hire the spouses of workers at large manufacturing companies without providing health coverage, knowing the manufacturers will foot their health insurance bills by providing family coverage. "As a nation in a global economy, we can no longer continue having our manufacturers carrying the health-insurance costs not only of their own workers but of the workers' spouses who are employed elsewhere," said Walter Maher, director of federal relations for the Chrysler Corporation. He cited one estimate that all of this cost shifting has socked American manufacturers with $11.5 billion a year in extra health-care costs. This represents a fourth of their health-care bills.

Mandated coverage would fall disproportionately on businesses with fewer than fifty employees, because so many of them do not provide coverage. About 10.5 million of their 40.2 million workers lack health insurance, according to the Employee Benefit Research Institute. By contrast, among businesses with more than 500 employees, only 5 million of the 54 million workers lack coverage. By one estimate, about 75 percent of businesses with less than 100 employees provide coverage; far more than 90 percent of those with more than 100 workers provide insurance.

Although big business appears to be carrying the day so far, small business is optimistic that it can persuade its friends in Congress to block any mandate requiring employers to pay for health insurance. Some Republicans, especially conservatives in the House, are expected to pounce on the issue. "I think this will have a lot of trouble on the Hill," said Mr. Elmont of the National Restaurant Association. "Workers' compensation costs are already out of control. We pay through the teeth in payroll taxes. The administration has just added a parental leave requirement, and they're talking about raising the minimum wage. To say we're going to pull out the stops over health insurance is an understatement."

For some small businesses, the prospect of mandated health coverage or new health taxes is downright scary. Typically it costs small business $1,800 to cover an unmarried employee and $4,000 to $5,000 for a worker with dependents. Jack Faris, president of the National Federation of Independent Businesses, gave the example of a business owner earning $35,000 with five employees who earn $15,000 each. "If the small-business owner has to pay three thousand dollars a year in health insurance for each one, that's fifteen thousand dollars," he said. "This lowers his earnings to twenty thousand dollars, and it could mean he has to lay off workers or go out of business."

Supporters of mandatory health coverage insist that requiring companies to help pay for insurance for all employees could ultimately lower health insurance costs. They argue that only when every employer provides coverage will the administration be able to fully set up its managed competition plan to squeeze down health costs. Under the administration's plan, individuals and small businesses would pool their resources and buy health-insurance coverage through cooperatives. These powerful cooperatives would be able to bargain for much lower rates than small businesses now receive. "If small business got off its knee-jerk opposition to a mandate and analyzed these proposals, they'd say it is extremely fair to small business," said Henry E. Simmons, president of the National Leadership Coalition for Health-Care Reform, which represents large corporations. "It would control their costs and enable them to do something most of them are already doing—providing health coverage—without having their health costs double every six years."

Among the states, only Hawaii requires employers to provide health-care coverage, a mandate that took effect in 1974. Jack Lewin, the state's health director, says the system has helped to hold down health costs without imposing huge burdens on small business. Oregon and Washington are now phasing in such a requirement. But illustrating the political difficulties of such mandates, a Massachusetts plan to require employer coverage in 1992 has been delayed by the heated opposition of small business.

Small businesses also fear that they would be required to make health-insurance payments for part-time workers. But if companies are not required to pay for any coverage for part-time workers, as small-business lobbyists are demanding, that would be a substantial incentive for them to hire two part-time workers rather than one full-time worker. [SG]

THE DANGERS OF DECLARING
WAR ON DOCTORS

WILL Washington soon be in the business of telling doctors and hospitals how much they can charge? In the spring of 1993, as President Bill Clinton's advisors were assembling his proposals for overhauling health care, there was much talk of "interim cost-containment measures." The president faced a dilemma: Even if his long-term strategy for bringing down costs through greater competition was adopted, costs would continue to soar for several years at least, putting almost unbearable pressures on the federal budget and an unravelling system of health insurance. And for the long term, there was talk of imposing overall budget limits on health spending to prevent it from gobbling an ever greater share of the national economy.

While they recognize the political temptation to clamp down on runaway health costs, most economists are extremely skeptical that price controls will do more good than harm. They worry that the immediate financial gains from squeezing health care providers could be more than offset by the additional worthless procedures and bad will elicited in treating physicians and hospitals as enemies.

The point has not been lost on the medical lobbies. "Price controls are a simple quick fix that will alienate the medical profession," said Dr. James Todd, senior vice president of the American Medical Association. Economists also fear that a focus on

prices would distract from the core issue driving medical inflation: the failure to ration ever more expensive technology.
"Once you have controls, you won't be able to muster political
support for tough structural changes," argued Barry Bosworth,
an economist at the Brookings Institution.

Up to now there has not been a competitive market in health
care to lose. Consumers of medical services barely understand
what they are buying in the best of times, and the bulk of services are consumed in the worst of times, when people are
hardly capable of rational choices about who should dissect their
innards or how much they should pay. Even if patients were up
to the task of comparison shopping, they rarely would have the
incentive because most bills are paid by insurance companies or
the government.

The distortions created by these third-party payments are
probably large. A classic experiment run by the Rand Corporation in the 1970s showed that requiring patients to write checks
when they went to the doctor sharply reduced the demand for
routine health care. It should not be surprising, then, that
Henry Aaron of the Brookings Institution thinks the fees currently paid by private insurers "are essentially arbitrary"—virtually unrelated to actual costs.

To help inject market forces into the health system, Mr. Clinton has endorsed a form of "managed competition." He wants to
encourage consumers to join large health-insurance purchasing
groups that would bargain for low prices with prepaid health
plans, which provide all care for an annual fee. This should save
money over time, but no one knows how much or how soon, and
there is an outcry for quick relief.

If the country does embark on medical price controls—and
"voluntary" price restraints would amount to much the same
thing, since they would be enforced by the threat of mandatory
controls—there are a number of options. The simplest is a
freeze, with prices locked in place on the date of announcement.
But "even thirty to sixty days is a long time" for a freeze, said

John Dunlop, the Harvard economist who administered the general price controls imposed in 1971 by President Nixon.

At some point Washington would have to allow providers to pass through increased costs, a process that could quickly become unworkable unless the government was also prepared to dictate wages, employment levels, and capital spending. Such micromanagement of medical-care providers would not be very different from nationalization. This is what happened during the Nixon era. Wage increases were limited economywide to 5.5 percent and price increases to 2.5 percent. If a company—or, in this case, a hospital—wanted more, it had to justify each item in its budget to the regulators.

This task was never easy for services, like medical care, where there is no clear measure of total output and therefore no straightforward way to measure cost per unit of output. And Mr. Bosworth noted that the difficult became close to impossible after the big jump in oil prices affected the economy a million different ways. To the relief of almost everybody, the system was phased out in 1974. "Administered price controls sound tempting," said Mr. Bosworth, who worked on the price regulators' staff. "But the details drive you nuts." Uwe Reinhardt, an economist at Princeton University, is not even tempted. "It's like lending the car to teen-agers and telling them not to make love: How do you police it?"

The more preferable alternative, economists say, is one that builds on efforts to curb the costs of Medicare, the government insurance program for the elderly and disabled. Washington, struggling to contain double-digit cost increases in Medicare since the early 1970s, came up with a comprehensive program for hospitals in 1983. Since then hospitals have been required to classify each Medicare patient's illness into one of 487 Diagnosis-Related Groups, or DRGs in the alphabet soup of health care. They are paid a flat fee for each DRG admission, which is calculated to cover the average cost of treatment—provided the hospitals are running efficiently.

A parallel system is now being phased in for physicians. Called the Resource-Based Relative Value Scale (RBRVS), it divides Medicare treatment into some seven thousand procedures graded according to the time and expertise needed. For example, a colonoscopy rates as 8.43 times as valuable as an ordinary office visit for an established patient, so Medicare will pay 8.43 times as much for it. The idea would be to extend the DRG and RBRVS scales to the treatment of all patients, not just those insured by the government. Adjustments might be made to reflect lower rents and wages in, say, Alabama than in California.

Would it work? Care providers have beaten the Medicare caps by shifting overhead expenses to bills paid by unregulated private insurers. Medicare now covers just 90 percent of the average cost of care, while private patients pay more than 120 percent. But if all payments were regulated, there would be no place to shift.

Well, not quite. Economists worry about what health planners euphemistically refer to as the behavioral response. "The services provided by doctors are infinitely expandable" as they struggle to make up income lost to price controls, said Dr. Jack Resnick, the president of Managed Care, Inc., a health-maintenance organization on Long Island. Physicians and hospitals could also fight back by "upcoding" (billing for procedures that receive higher reimbursement rates) and by "unbundling" (billing for one procedure as two or three parts that cost more than the whole). Indeed, these practices are apparently so acceptable to the medical community that software makers sell programs to help physicians and hospitals maximize Medicare billing. Today, Medicare administrators assume that every dollar saved by binding fee limits is offset by a fifty-cent increase through volume, upcoding, and unbundling.

One solution is to put a cap on total payments to health plans —a form of what the cognoscenti call global budgeting. Insurers might, for example, hold back a portion of the payments due physicians and hospitals and then cut reimbursements for individual services if the total bills exceed the allotted expenditure for the insured group.

This is guaranteed to work, if the philosopher-kings in charge of budgeting are resolute. But it might not work in a way that satisfied patients or providers. For one thing, global budgeting is an accounting exercise, not a way to determine how much medical care is enough. It would not, for example, address which new procedures would be covered, and at what rates. This is no small matter. Joseph Newhouse, an economist at Harvard, estimates that half of the increase in the national bill for medical care now goes to pay for new technology. For another, unless they were working on salary in a medical group, individual doctors would have a strong incentive to order every test and procedure they could. The alternative would be to lose income to less scrupulous practitioners.

Then there is the issue of regional equity. Alabamans spend less per medical procedure and undergo fewer procedures than Californians. Would global budgets lock these differences in place, or would they be used to equalize the quality of care? If the latter, would Californians be asked, in effect, to sacrifice to make Alabama a healthier place to live? Kenneth Raske, the president of the Greater New York Hospital Association, points out that this issue is further complicated by the fact that some states have already begun to squeeze hospitals. In New York City, regulated reimbursement rates for private insurers kept hospital operating margins to 0.3 percent in 1991, compared with the national average of 3.9 percent. Curbs on capital spending pushed occupancy rates to 88 percent, compared with 66 percent nationally. Would states that have already pared the cost of hospital care be asked to cut back proportionately?

Despite these problems, some economists support capping overall medical payments as the only way to insure an end to runaway inflation of health costs. If most physician and hospital services were offered through prepaid plans, spending caps could be imposed without a need for price controls on particular procedures. The providers would in effect be forced to regulate themselves to stay within their budgets.

Experts are divided, then, about the merits of price controls and global budgeting. What comes through loud and clear, however, is that tough regulation aimed at saving money during the transition to universal care and competition would carry heavy penalties. Dr. Reinhardt of Princeton University points out that countries that have arguably done a better job at containing medical costs while delivering high-quality care—notably Germany and Canada—have managed it by emphasizing cooperation with providers. The prospects for creating such a social contract here are bound to be diminished by a declaration of war on the industry.

Mr. Bosworth worries that controls could undermine what comes after. The experience of the Nixon controls, he says, suggests that an effective squeeze on medical bills would generate a burst of inflation when controls were lifted. And hardly anything could do more to discredit reforms in health care. [PP]

WHEN CUTS START TO HURT

THEY don't like the word even in Oregon, the state that thrust it into the news. "I certainly don't use the term 'rationing' unless someone forces me to," says Jean I. Thorne, director of Oregon's Medicaid program, which in March 1993 received federal permission for a plan in which poor people will not be covered for low-priority treatments while basic health benefits are extended to everyone.

Americans are worried about health costs, which now soak up 14 percent of the gross national product, surveys show, and want the government to do something about them. But one thing Americans emphatically do not want, these same surveys find, is rationing of medical care. The idea that someone might be denied, say, an organ transplant that might save his life just because it costs so much is abhorrent.

Nor is it part of American medical tradition. "Twenty years ago, when making ward rounds with my students, I'd say that we'll go on trying the next test or treatment and the next one until there is no hope of helping the patient," said Dr. William B. Schwartz of the University of Southern California. That approach—do anything that might help whatever the cost—still prevails today, though it often does not benefit the uninsured. It is implicit in laws that, for example, require the government to license new drugs that promise the slightest benefit, without regard for their sometimes astronomical prices. "If we want to continue to teach that philosophy, it's going to be incredibly costly," said Dr. Schwartz, who has for years argued that rationing is inevitable if the country wants health spending to level off. "That is a societal decision."

But do not expect any politician, this year or next, to use the dreaded word in the debate over health costs. Instead, watch for the phrase "cost-effective" and read the fine print telling how it will be applied. In those two words lie the seeds of wrenching change. Already medical researchers are trying to reduce ineffective or harmful procedures by developing guidelines on, for example, which patients will benefit from operations such as coronary bypass. Insurers, through "managed care," have also tried to weed out procedures and hospital days that are not medically necessary. Pruning out inappropriate care is only sensible—but it is not rationing. Refusing to pay for something, not because it is ineffective but because its costs greatly outweigh potential benefits, would be the great departure.

Not every expert agrees that rationing is needed in the forseeable future, even if the country adopts a ceiling on spending. After studying the results of many procedures, including coronary bypass, angioplasty, hysterectomy, and gallbladder operations, Dr. Robert H. Brook and his colleagues at the Rand Corporation concluded that one-quarter to one-third of all medical care in the country is either inappropriate or carries risks that equal potential benefits. "We have to get rid of all that before we talk about rationing," Dr. Brook said. "We have at least ten years before we have to think about rationing."

Another optimist is Dr. Paul M. Ellwood, a physician and health economist in Jackson Hole, Wyoming, and a father of the "managed competition" model favored by President Clinton. "The health system has overshot," Dr. Ellwood said. "It's doing more with patients than will benefit them." Under managed competition, most doctors and hospitals would join prepaid plans such as health-maintenance organizations that would compete for the business of large consumer groups. By rewarding doctors for prudent care and publicizing comparative medical results, he said, the approach should help "move medical care back to where most things that are done to patients actually improve their health." By drastically reducing waste, he said, "we can avoid or at least delay rationing."

Dr. Schwartz counters with harsh mathematics. The inescapable truth, he said, is the relentless upward trend in medical costs, compounded annually and driven mainly by new technology and the aging of the population. He is all for stopping useless care, but once those savings are achieved, then the upward trend resumes, scarcely dented. "Maybe for five years real costs increase by 4.5 percent instead of 6 percent," he said. "That's wonderful, but then you're back to the full trend of 6 percent."

While some advances, like vaccines, cut medical costs, many more add to them, Dr. Schwartz said. Many wonder drugs control rather than cure disease. AZT is not just expensive in itself; in keeping AIDS patients alive it encourages extra treatment at huge expense for infections and anemia. Other advances bring incremental gains for a high price. An example: injected contrast mediums, used in diagnostic imaging about ten million times a year. The commonly used medium is inexpensive but causes death in a tiny percentage of those cases, about three hundred fatalities a year. A new, safer medium being adopted, Dr. Schwartz said, will save those three hundred lives at a cost of $1 billion a year.

In March 1993 a federal advisory panel, prohibited by law from considering cost, recommended the licensing of tacrine, a drug that may lead to modest improvements in cognition for one in five Alzheimer's patients who take it. But there is no way to identify those who will benefit or to easily measure the benefits, so many of the country's four million Alzheimer's patients may take it, and insurers will pay. Costs for the drug and required monitoring of side effects may be several billion dollars a year.

Dr. Schwartz says medical resources must somehow be directed to where they give the best returns. He cited the use of $1,000 magnetic resonance imaging scans for patients with head injuries. High priority would go to patients in a stupor or confused state suggesting a fifty-fifty chance of a life-threatening but treatable blood clot. The cost would be $2,000 per life saved. But in patients who merely complain of a few bad headaches and some dizziness—many of whom today are receiving scans just in case—the chance of finding a dangerous, treatable condition like a clot may be one in two thousand, Dr. Schwartz said, which means the expenditure of $2 million for each life saved. "As a physician I hate this idea, but we can't afford to spend two million dollars per case," Dr. Schwartz said. "When that one fatal case is missed there will be pain and misery. It's a social trade-off. We lost that one in two thousand, but what about environmental pollution, or education?"

If the day of reckoning does come, how should rationing be done? Uwe Reinhardt, a health economist at Princeton University, said there are basically two approaches. One is the "civics textbook" approach, in which government makes open and formally stated choices. The second is to "muddle through elegantly," decentralizing rationing with "ad hoc decisions in the trenches." The latter approach may not satisfy the civics books, he said, but it may be the more realistic route.

Oregon's plan of "prioritization," as officials there prefer to call it, which has involved exhaustive public hearings and the creation of a formal ranking of diseases and treatments, is the epitome of approach No. 1. Its evolution also suggests that Dr. Reinhardt may be right about the difficulty. As finally approved, the plan hardly deserves to be called rationing; almost all the excluded treatments involve self-limiting conditions, cosmetic procedures, and therapy of unproven value. By drawing the cut-off so low, the state gained wide support and federal approval, but it expects to save only about 3 percent of its Medicaid costs over time, Ms. Thorne said.

Oregon officials "did not get into serious consideration of cost-effectiveness," she said; they lacked data and "did not want to be in the position of attaching dollars to a person's life." A few things clearly of slight benefit and extreme cost, like aggressive care for advanced, terminal cancer patients, were ranked near the bottom. But expensive organ transplants of proven value will be paid for. Some of the hardest decisions with huge financial impact—when to put critically ill patients into intensive care and on artificial life support—were largely left where they are now, in the hands of doctors and patients.

In what could become a forum for overtly balancing costs and benefits, advocates of managed competition are calling for a national board that would set guidelines for appropriate care, based on research. But for now, at least, such guidelines should not bar beneficial care, Dr. Ellwood said. "I'd like to delay that as long as we possibly can." Dr. Reinhardt doubts, in any case, that a public body could ever articulate and enforce such explosive trade-offs. "Do you think there is a political body strong enough to say we are not going to do hip replacement surgery on a ninety-year-old man or woman?"

The messier, more realistic way to ration, Dr. Reinhardt said, involves capping the funds available for care and limiting expensive investments like MRI machines and intensive-care beds. Doctors would have to make new judgments, sometimes subconsciously, in seeking to provide the best care in a setting of limited resources. If there was a waiting list for the MRI, the patient with mere headaches would be given reassurance rather than a referral for a scan. If the intensive care unit was overflowing, the cancer patient with a few weeks to live anyway would not receive cardiac resuscitation.

Something like this already happens in Canada and Europe, where costly equipment is more restricted. How deeply the rationing would cut into care would be determined by the level of spending, which is higher by far in the United States than in any other country. In the United States no one envisions a system that would prevent wealthier individuals from buying extra care with their own money, even if insurers refused to pay.

Dr. Reinhardt's invisible rationing would work best if doctors and patients were in HMOs, which must work within annual budgets, he said. In fee-for-service medicine, perversely, doctor and hospital both make more money by keeping a doomed patient alive an extra week or two. "No physician in America would ever say that money even vaguely affected his decisions," Dr. Reinhardt said. "They may never even admit it to themselves." But eliminating perverse incentives and forcing medicine to operate within clear limits would make a difference, he is sure. "They'll tell the family, 'Look, this just doesn't make sense.' " [EE]

BUT WILL THE PATIENT AGREE?

E VERY politician learned the lesson in 1991 and 1992: Health care has become a source of great anxiety for the middle class. Every politician learned to use the issue—as Democratic poll takers and strategists constantly urged—to show their empathy for the middle class.

But on health care, more than on any other issue, election-year politics is easy, policy is hard, and the details can be downright killing. The Clinton administration's official working groups on health care have confronted the biggest challenge in domestic policy since the Great Society, and arguably since the New Deal. The difficulties begin with the very basics: What does the public really want?

"Health-care reform" is the easy answer on the campaign trail. But as many experts note, what that means to policymakers and what it means to average taxpayers can be quite different. Policymakers worry about covering thirty-seven million uninsured Americans, about establishing some kind of national limit on health-care spending, about getting health costs under control in the federal budget. They talk about building a system that encourages competition among health-care providers and informed decision making among purchasers.

But Celinda Lake, a Democrat who has polled extensively on the issue, says that middle-class voters want three simple things:

controls on the costs they pay for health care, some guarantee that their health insurance will remain secure (if, for example, they change jobs), and assurances that the quality of their health care will remain high. They worry about rationing, waits, less innovation, and less freedom of choice as potential by-products of many "reforms," Ms. Lake said. According to a recent Harris Poll, Americans are more likely to support government cost controls than a system of managed competition, in which employers and individuals band together in large cooperatives to shop around for the best health-care plan.

Robert J. Blendon, an expert at Harvard University on public opinion about health care, noted the obvious but easily overlooked truth in an essay he coauthored: "Because health care is seen as a family, not a national problem, people will judge the proposed reform plan on the basis of what it will do for them." In an interview, he added, "If what you do looks like it's going to make costs higher and disrupt their care, they're going to get scared very quickly."

What this means in policy terms, analysts say, is that the benefits of a health-care reform program must be readily apparent before the tab for it is presented. It means that price controls, which are anathema to many economists, have an appealing political rationale, at least in the short term. And it also means that all the talk about managed competition and cost-conscious choices by consumers needs to recognize the special relationship many Americans have with their doctors and local hospitals. Mr. Blendon, who has briefed the Clintons and members of the health-care task force, argues that government stepping in and "deliberately disrupting the pattern of care that families have" could strike the same angry chords that court-ordered busing did.

The Clintons have studied a recent example of an utterly failed health-care program begun with the best of intentions: legislation signed by President Ronald Reagan in 1988 to protect the elderly from the cost of catastrophic illness. Interest groups mounted a ruthless campaign against the "seniors only" surtax that was levied on the most affluent 40 percent of the beneficiaries to pay for it. The program's benefits were overwhelmed by the perceived costs, and legions of angry—and frightened—retirees demanded that it be repealed. It died an ignoble death.

Advisers in the White House said they were well aware of these dangers as they moved toward their self-imposed 1993 deadline for a massive new health care plan. At the Democratic National Committee, strategists were already preparing a campaign to sell whatever was produced by the Clinton task force, which was headed by First Lady Hillary Rodham Clinton. A political aide to the president said, "One of the things we're counting on is that the bad guys will overplay their argument and overstate their case." Recalling the backfiring attacks on Mrs. Clinton at the 1992 Republican convention in Houston, the aide added, "If they say, 'Look at lefty Hillary trying to bring socialized medicine to the country,' that's great."

The greatest danger, the White House was convinced, was in doing nothing. The pressure on the nation's economy and the federal budget has been unrelenting. And the expectations from the public have been extraordinary. While many Americans have been unusually understanding of Mr. Clinton's broken promises, 88 percent in a 1993 Harris survey said it would be a "serious failure" for the Clinton presidency if he failed to control health costs.

On Capitol Hill, Democratic leaders generally cheered Mrs. Clinton on, although Rep. Dan Rostenkowski, chairman of the House Ways and Means Committee, expressed doubts that a bill could make its way through Congress in 1993. "I just think there's a lot of skepticism about how fast this thing can move," said an aide to the Democratic leadership.

In a hard-wired radio-call-in democracy, a bill as complicated as comprehensive health-care reform stirs many fears. Rep. Jim McDermott, the Washington Democrat who is sponsoring a bill backing a single-payer system, like Canada's, appeared on a C-Span call-in show and found himself answering questions about rationing. "All the mythology is really scaring people," said McDermott, a psychiatrist in his former life.

Blendon agrees. "The president and Mrs. Clinton are going to have to be teachers," he said. "They're going to have to bring the country along with them." Rep. Richard A. Gephardt, House Majority Leader, said of the process: "It is fast, but we are in a crisis. It's just unsatisfactory for someone to be saying, 'It's too complicated, we need more time.' Time's up." [RT]

The
Clinton
Proposals

THE PRESIDENT'S
PRESCRIPTION

President Clinton's September 22, 1993, address on his health proposal to a joint session of Congress and a prime-time television audience was widely hailed as masterful, laying out the moral and economic case for change. Here is the prepared text, from which he spoke without significant departure.

MR. Speaker, Mr. President, Members of Congress, distinguished guests, my fellow Americans:

Tonight, we come together to write a new chapter in the American story.

Our forebears enshrined the American dream—life, liberty, and the pursuit of happiness. Every generation of Americans has worked to strengthen that legacy to make America a place of freedom and opportunity, where people who work hard could rise to their full potential, and where their children could live a better life than they did.

From the settling of the frontier to the landing on the Moon, ours has been a story of challenges defined, obstacles overcome, new horizons secured. This is what makes America what it is and Americans who we are.

Now we are in a time of profound change and opportunity: the end of the Cold War, the information age, the global economy that have brought us both opportunity and hope, and dislocation and uncertainty. Our goal in this dynamic age is to make change our friend and not our enemy. To achieve that goal, we must face our challenges with confidence, faith and discipline—whether it's reducing the deficit, increasing investment, creating jobs and expanding trade, converting from a high-tech defense to a high-tech peacetime economy, making our streets safe or rewarding work over idleness. All these challenges require change.

If Americans are to have the courage to change we must be secure in our most basic needs. Tonight I want to talk with you about one of the most essential things we can do to build that security: It is time for America to fix a health care system that is badly broken.

Despite the dedication of millions of talented health care professionals, our health care is too uncertain and too expensive; too bureaucratic and too wasteful. It has too much fraud and too much greed.

At long last, after decades of false starts, we must make this our most urgent priority: giving every American health security—health care that's always there, health care that can never be taken away.

On this journey, as on all others of consequence, there will be rough stretches and honest disagreements about how to reach our destination. After all, this is a complicated issue.

But every successful journey is guided by fixed stars. And if we can agree on some basic values and principles, we will reach that destination together. So tonight I want to talk with you about the principles that must guide our reform of America's health care system: security, simplicity, and savings; choice, quality, and responsibility.

When I launched our nation on the journey to reform the health care system, I knew we needed a talented navigator, someone with a rigorous mind, a steady compass, and a caring heart. Luckily for me and for our nation, I didn't have to search very far. Because I could turn to the First Lady. I think she has done a brilliant job.

Over the past eight months, Hillary and those working with

her talked to literally thousands of Americans to understand the strengths and frailties of our health care system.

They met with over 1,100 health care organizations. They talked with doctors, nurses, pharmacists, hospital administrators, insurance and drug company executives, and small and large business owners. They talked with the uninsured and the self-insured, with union members, older Americans and advocates for children.

The First Lady consulted extensively with government leaders of both political parties, across the states of our country, and especially here on Capitol Hill.

Hillary and the Task Force received and read 700,000 letters from ordinary citizens. And what they wrote—and how bravely they spoke about their struggle—is what calls us all to action.

Every one of us knows someone who has worked hard and played by the rules but has been hurt by this system that just doesn't work. Let me tell you about just one.

Kerry Kennedy owns a small furniture franchise that employs seven people in Titusville, Florida. Like most small business owners, Kerry has poured his sweat and blood into that company. But over the last few years, the cost of insuring his seven workers has skyrocketed, as did the cost of the coverage for himself, his wife, and his daughter. Last year, however, Kerry could no longer afford to provide coverage for all his workers because the insurance companies had labeled two of them high risk simply because of their age. But you know what? Those two people are Kerry's mother and father, who built the family business and now work in the store.

That story speaks for millions of others. And from them, we have learned a powerful truth: we have to preserve and strengthen what is right with our health care system and fix what is wrong with it.

This is what is right: We are blessed with the best health care professionals, the finest health care institutions, the most advanced research, and the most sophisticated medical technology on the face of the earth. My mother is a nurse, and I grew up around hospitals. The first professional people I ever knew and looked up to were doctors and nurses. They represent what is right with our health care system.

But we cannot ignore what is wrong. Millions of Americans are just a pink slip away from losing their health coverage, and one serious illness away from losing their life savings. Millions more are locked in the wrong jobs because they'd lose their coverage if they left their companies. And on any given day over 37 million of our fellow citizens, the vast majority of them children or hard-working adults, have no health insurance at all. And despite all of this, our medical bills are growing at more than twice the rate of inflation.

Our health care system takes 35 percent more of our income than any other country, insures fewer people, requires more Americans to pay more and more for less and less, and gives them fewer choices. There is no excuse for that kind of system, and it's time to fix it.

The proposal I will describe tonight will reform the costliest and most wasteful health care system on earth without any new broad-based taxes.

Many of the principles in my plan have already been embraced by Republicans as well as Democrats. For the first time in this century, leaders of both political parties have committed themselves irrevocably to providing universal, comprehensive health care for every American.

I have been deeply moved by the spirit of this debate. We now have both Republicans and Democrats willing to say, yes, let us listen to the people, and let us act. Both sides understand the ethical imperative of solving this problem; both sides know it will define who we are as a people. Let me ask all of you every Member of the House, every member of the Senate, every Democrat and every Republican—let us keep this spirit and keep this commitment until our work is done.

* * *

The first principle of health care reform—the most important—must be security. This principle speaks to the human misery and costs that we hear about every day when Americans lack or lose health care coverage.

Security means that those who do not have health care coverage will have it, and for those who have coverage, it will never be taken away. We must achieve that security as soon as possible.

Under our plan, every American will receive a health security card that will guarantee you a comprehensive package of benefits over the course of your lifetime that will equal benefits provided by most Fortune 500 corporations.

This card will guarantee you a comprehensive package of benefits that can never be taken away. And let us pledge tonight: Before this Congress adjourns next year, you will pass and I will sign a new law to create health security for every American.

With this card, if you lose your job or switch jobs, you're covered.

If you leave your job to start a small business, you're covered.

If you are an early retiree, you're covered.

If you or someone in your family has a preexisting medical condition, you're covered.

If you get sick or a member of your family gets sick, even if it's a life-threatening illness, you're covered.

And if an insurance company tries to drop you for any reason, you'll still be covered—because that will be illegal.

This card will give you comprehensive coverage. You will be covered for hospital care, doctors' visits, emergency and laboratory services, diagnostic services like Pap smears and mammograms, substance abuse and mental health treatment.

And our proposal will pay for regular checkups, well-baby visits and other preventive care. It's just common sense.

People will stay healthier and at affordable costs. You know how your mother told you that an ounce of prevention is worth a pound of cure? Well, your mother was right. And we've ignored that lesson for too long.

Security must also apply to older Americans. This is something I feel very strongly about: We will maintain the Medicare program. And for the first time, Medicare will cover the cost of prescription drugs. And over time our proposal will provide assistance in the home for the elderly and disabled who need long term care. As we proceed with health care, we must not break faith with our older Americans.

The second principle is simplicity. Our health care system must be simpler for the patients and simpler for those who actually deliver health care: our physicians, our nurses, and our other medical professionals.

Today, we have more than fifteen hundred insurers with hundreds and hundreds of different forms. They are time consuming for health care providers, expensive for health care consumers, and exasperating for anyone who has ever tried to sit down at the kitchen table and wade through the paperwork.

The medical care industry is drowning in paperwork. In recent years, the number of administrators has grown four times as fast as the number of doctors. A hospital should be a house of healing, not a monument to bureaucracy.

A few days ago, the Vice President and I visited Children's Hospital in Washington, where they do wonderful, often miraculous things for very sick children.

Nurse Debbie Freiberg in the cancer and bone marrow unit told us that the other day a little boy asked her to stay at his side during his chemotherapy. But she had to tell him no.

She had to go to yet another meeting to learn how to fill out yet another form. That's wrong.

Dr. Lillian Beard, a pediatrician in that same hospital, said she did not get into her profession to spend hours every week filling out forms. She became a doctor to help save lives. If we can relieve them of that burden, they believe that each doctor in her hospital could see 500 additional children each year.

Under our proposal, there will be one standard insurance form, not hundreds. We will simplify government rules and regulations so that a doctor doesn't have to check with a bureaucrat in an office thousands of miles away before ordering a simple blood test. And you won't have to worry about the fine print, because there won't be any fine print.

The third principle is that reform must produce savings in our health care system.

Today, rampant medical inflation is eating away at our wages, our savings, our investment capital, and our public treasury. It undermines America's economy, competitiveness, confidence, and living standards.

Unless we curb health care inflation, American workers will lose $655 in income each year by the end of the decade. Small businesses will continue to face skyrocketing premiums, and a full third say they will be forced to drop insurance. Large employers will have to pay as much as $20,000 a year for each employee. And health care costs will devour more and more of the federal budget.

Every state government and every local government will continue to cut back on everything else they must do—from police protection to education—to pay more for the same health care.

These rising costs are a special nightmare for America's small businesses—the engine of entrepreneurship and job creation. Health care premiums for small businesses are 35 percent higher than those of large corporations, and they will keep rising at double-digit rates unless we act.

How will we achieve savings? Rather than looking away as the price spiral continues, and rather than using government to set health care prices, our proposal relies on a third way. We want to give groups of consumers and small businesses the same bargaining clout that the biggest corporations now have. We will force plans to compete on the basis of price and quality, rather than making money by turning away people who are sick or by performing unnecessary procedures. And we will back the system up with limits on how much plans can raise their premiums. We will create what has been missing for too long: a combination of private market forces and sound policy to support that competition.

Unless every one is covered, we can never put the brakes on health care inflation. Because when people don't have insurance, they wait to see a doctor until their illness is more severe and more costly, and they often seek treatment in the most expensive settings—like emergency rooms. And when they can't pay their bills because they aren't insured—who do you think picks up the tab? The rest of us do: through higher hospital bills and higher insurance premiums.

We will also save money by simplifying the system and freeing health care providers from costly and unnecessary paperwork and administrative overload that now costs $100 billion a year. We will crack down on the fraud and abuse that drains billions per year.

This system will work. You don't have to take my word for it. Ask Dr. C. Everett Koop. He says we could spend $200 billion less every year without sacrificing the high quality of American medicine. Ask the public employees in California, who have held their own premiums down by adopting this very same approach. Ask Xerox, which saved an estimated $1,000 per worker.

Ask the staff of the Mayo Clinic, who provide some of the finest care in the world, while holding their cost increases to less than half the national average. Ask the people of Hawaii, the only state that covers virtually all of their citizens, and whose costs are well below the national average.

People may disagree over the best way to fix the system. But no one can disagree that we can find billions of dollars of savings in the most costly and bureaucratic system in the world, and we ought to be doing something about it now.

*   *   *

The fourth principle is choice. Americans believe they should be able to choose their own health care plans and their own doctor. And under our plan they will have that right.

But today, under our broken health care system, that power to choose is slipping away. Now it is usually the employer and not the employee who makes the choice of what health care plan will be provided. If your employer only offers one plan, as do nearly three-quarters of small and medium-sized businesses, you're stuck with that plan and the doctors it covers.

We propose to give every American a choice among high quality plans. You can stay with your current doctor, join a network of doctors and hospitals, or join a health maintenance organization. If you don't like your plan, every year you'll have the chance to choose a new one.

The choice will be left to you—not your boss, and not some bureaucrat.

And we also believe that doctors should have a choice as to what plans they practice in. We want to end the discrimination that is now growing against doctors and permit them to practice in several different plans. Choice is important for doctors, and critical for consumers.

The fifth principle is quality. If we reformed everything else in health care but failed to preserve and enhance the high quality of our medical care, we would have taken a step backward, not forward.

Quality is something that cannot be left to chance. When you board an airplane, you feel better knowing that plane had meet standards designed to protect your safety. We must ask no less of our health care system.

We don't propose a government-run health care system. We propose that government sets standards to ensure health care quality. Our proposal will create report cards on health plans so that consumers can choose the highest quality providers and reward them with their business. At the same time, our plan will track quality indicators, so that doctors can make better and smarter choices about the kind of care they provide.

We have evidence that more efficient delivery of health care does not decrease quality, and may even enhance it. Let me give you an example of one commonly performed procedure, the coronary bypass operation.

Pennsylvania discovered that patients who were charged $21,000 for this surgery received as good or better quality care as patients who were charged up to $84,000. High prices don't always equal good quality.

Our plan will guarantee that quality health care is available in even the most remote areas of our nation, linking rural doctors and hospitals with high-tech urban medical centers. And our plan will ensure quality by speeding research on effective prevention and treatment measures for cancer, for AIDS, for Alzheimer's, for heart disease, and for other chronic diseases. Our plan safeguards the finest medical research establishment in the world, and makes it even better.

The sixth and final principle is responsibility. We need to restore a sense that we are all in this together, and we all have a responsibility to be a part of the solution.

Responsibility must start with those who have profited from the current health care system. Responsibility means insurance companies will no longer be allowed to cast people aside when they get sick. It must also apply to laboratories that submit fraudulent bills; to lawyers who abuse the malpractice system; to doctors who order unnecessary procedures. It means drug companies will no longer be allowed to charge three times more for prescription drugs here in the United States than they charge overseas. Responsibility must apply to anyone who abuses our system and drives up costs for honest, hard-working citizens and health care providers.

Responsibility also means changing the behavior in this country that drives up our health care costs and cause untold suffering. It's the outrageous costs of violence from far too many handguns, especially among the young. It's high rates of AIDS, smoking and excessive drinking; it's teenage pregnancy, low-birth-weight babies, and not enough vaccinations for the most vulnerable.

But let me also say this. And I hope you will listen, because it is a hard thing to hear. Responsibility in our health care system isn't about "them." It's about you. It's about me. It's about each of us.

Too many Americans have not taken responsibility for their health. Too many Americans use this health care system but don't pay a penny for their health care. I believe those who do not have health insurance should be responsible for paying something. There can be no more something for nothing.

Your contribution may be as small as a ten dollar copayment when you visit the doctor. But all of us must have insurance. Why should the rest of us pick up the tab when a guy who doesn't think he needs insurance gets in an accident and winds up in the emergency room?

Reform is going to produce a better health care system for every one of us. But no one should think it's going to be a free ride. We have to pay for it. Tonight I want to tell you very plainly how we plan to do that.

Most of the money will come, as it does today, from premiums paid by employers and individuals. But under our Health Security Plan, every employer and every individual will be asked to contribute to health care. This concept was first conveyed to the Congress by President Nixon. And today a lot of people agree that the concept of shared responsibility between employers and employees is the best way to go, from the U.S. Chamber of Commerce to the American Medical Association.

Some people call it an employer mandate, but I think it is the fairest way to achieve responsibility in the health care system. It builds on what we already have and what already works. It is the reform that is easiest for consumers to understand. It includes a discount to help struggling small businesses meet the cost of covering their employees. It requires the least bureaucracy or disruption and creates the cooperation we need to make the system cost-conscious even as we expand health coverage.

Every employer should provide coverage. Three-quarters do it now. Those that pay are picking up the tab for those that do not. And it's just not right.

To finance the rest of reform, we'll achieve new savings in both the federal government and the private sector through better decision making and increased competition, and we will impose new taxes on tobacco.

These sources will cover the costs of the proposal I have described to you tonight. We have subjected our numbers to the scrutiny of the major agencies in our government as well as some of the most respected actuaries from private accounting firms and Fortune 500 companies.

What does all this mean for you as individuals?

Some will be asked to pay more. If you are an employer, and you are not insuring your workers, you will have to pay more.

If you are a firm that provides only limited coverage, you may have to pay more.

If you are a young single person in your twenties and you are already insured, your rates may go up somewhat. But someday you will get older. And then under this proposal, you will be guaranteed affordable coverage.

But the vast majority of you watching tonight will pay the same or less for your health care coverage and, at the same time, get the same or better coverage than you have today.

If you currently get your health insurance through your job, under our plan you still will. And for the first time, all of you will get to choose what plan you belong to.

If you're a small business owner who wants to provide health insurance to your family and your employees but can't afford to because the system is stacked against you, this plan will give you a discount that will finally make insurance affordable. And if you are already providing insurance, your rates will drop because we'll help you join with thousands of other small firms to get the same benefits big corporations get.

If you are self-employed, you will pay less, and you will get to deduct from your taxes 100 percent of your health care premiums.

If you are a large employer, your health care costs will stop increasing at double digit rates, so that you will have more money to put into higher wages and new jobs.

These are the principles on which we must base our efforts—security, simplicity, and savings; choice, quality, and responsibility. These are the guiding stars that we must follow on our journey toward health care reform.

Over the coming months, you are going to be bombarded with scare tactics by those who profit enormously from the current health care system. Some of the arguments you hear will be sincere. Others will be motivated by self-interest. And when they tell you that we cannot afford to change the current system, I want you to stop and think: Who are they trying to protect, you or themselves? And can we afford to stay with the current system?

As representatives in Congress, you have a special duty to look beyond such arguments. I ask you to look into the eyes of a sick child who needs care. Look at the face of a woman who has been told not only that it is malignant but also that it's not covered by her insurance. Look at the bottom lines of the businesses driven to bankruptcy by health care costs and at the forest of FOR SALE signs in front of homes of families who have lost their health insurance. Then look in your heart and tell me that the greatest nation in the history of the world is powerless to confront this crisis. Our history and our heritage tell us we can meet this challenge and we shall meet this challenge.

Let us write that new chapter in America's story, and guarantee every American comprehensive health benefits that can never be taken away.

Some people have said that it would be a miracle if we passed health care reform. But, my fellow Americans, I believe we live in a time of great change when miracles do happen.

Just a few days ago, we saw a simple handshake shatter decades of deadlock in the Middle East. We have seen walls crumble from Berlin to South Africa. Now it is our turn to strike a blow for freedom—the freedom for Americans to live without fear of their own nation's health care system.

It's hard to believe that once there was a time—even in this century—when retirement was nearly synonymous with poverty, and older Americans died in our streets. That is unthinkable today because over a half century ago Americans had the courage to change—to create a Social Security system that ensures that no Americans will be forgotten in their later years.

I believe that forty years from now our grandchildren will also find it unthinkable that there was a time in our country when hard-working families lost their homes and savings simply because their child fell ill, or lost their health coverage when they changed jobs. Yet our grandchildren will only find such things unthinkable tomorrow if we have the courage to change today.

This is our change. This is our journey. And when our work is done, we will know that we have answered the call of history and met the challange of our times.

Thank you. And God bless America.

STREETWISE POLITICS

T HE civics books suggest that the real wheeling and dealing over restructuring the health care system began on September 22, 1993, when President Clinton formally presented his proposals to a joint session of Congress. But in fact, for seven months, in a marathon series of meetings within the Government and with 1,100 outside groups, the administration's health planners had already agreed to a complex series of political trade-offs. One way of comprehending the intricacy of this plan, which is a challenge even to those who have spent their careers in health policy, is to understand the basic political strategy behind it.

As outlined by administration officials and those close to the policy-making process, these strategic principles are recognizable to any self-respecting precinct captain:

• Solidify your base. In this case, that meant trying to take care of the elderly, organized labor, and the liberals whose hearts are really across the border with the Canadian system, in which the government pays all medical bills and guarantees coverage to all.

• Defuse the most dangerous potential opponents. That meant subsidies for small businesses to help them meet the new requirement of contributing to health insurance; preserving the existing fee-for-service system for doctors, and backing off direct price controls on hospitals, doctors, and other providers.

• Remember the middle class. Unless the health care over-haul is seen as a new benefit for the middle class, the administration's political advisers believe, it is doomed. This goes to the heart of the decision to reject a broad-based tax and the decision to make the guaranteed benefits package as comprehensive as it is.

• Remember your campaign promises. That meant covering the 37 million Americans who are uninsured, controlling health costs, and somehow doing all this without major new taxes—just through greater efficiencies in the system, as Mr. Clinton had promised so expansively and repeatedly.

Just how well all this careful politics will work is, of course, still a question. Even experts friendly to the administration voice qualms about its financing system, which, while still being re-fined, appears to be heavily based on projected cuts in the rate of growth of Medicare and Medicaid. "I think how to pay for it is a leap of faith," said Stuart Altman, an expert on health policy at Brandeis University who advised the administration during the transition.

Theoreticians on the left and right already object to the blend of market forces and government regulation that characterizes the preliminary draft of the Clinton plan. Some suggest that the Clinton penchant for splitting the difference and hugging the center may have produced a Rube Goldberg–like system, a mar-vel to look at but with questionable efficiency. An administration official, speaking on condition that he not be identified, acknowl-edged the situation: "The risk is that we're kind of in the middle. The regulators want more regulation, and the pure managed-competition buffs are saying more competition. But we're also in the only place where we can win."

It is also far from clear how well the administration has suc-ceeded in muting the opposition. Small businesses so far have hardly been mollified, and most groups continue to express reservations of one kind or another, althought this is also part of the bargaining process. But there seems to be more wariness than outrage in many of these quarters. Moreover, the administration at times seems to be trying to finesse that which cannot be finessed—like its avoidance of the word abortion in the draft of the plan, in lieu of the more opaque promise to cover "pregnancy-related services." Kate Michelman, president of the National Abortion Rights Action League, said, "If the administration is trying to finesse this and get it through with a wink and a nod, it's impossible."

Still, the plan reflects some arduous efforts at building a coalition to do what has never been done before: reorganize the American health care system. From the start, health planners were solicitous toward the elderly, the natural constituency for new health care benefits and one of the best organized and most powerful at the grass roots. The prescription drug benefits in the plan have long been sought by advocates for the elderly, who make up 13 percent of the population but 34 percent of all spending for outpatient prescription drugs. They had, but lost, some prescription drug benefits in the short-lived program to protect the elderly from the cost of catastrophic illnesses, abolished after a backlash from older Americans, who had to pay a surtax to finance it.

Health planners were unable to deliver on the other priority of advocates for the elderly: a comprehensive new long-term nursing care program. But the plan does offer a start along those lines, with new benefits for care for the disabled at home. The draft also caused some jitters among advocates for the elderly because of the projected cuts in the growth of Medicare spending.

Administration officials met early and often with leaders of the AFL–CIO, another longtime advocate of restructuring the health care system with the ability to mobilize troops. This helps explain why the taxation of benefits in excess of the basic package, a cherished precept of some of the gurus of managed competition, would be watered down and very gently phased in under the Clinton plan. Organized labor bitterly opposes the concept of taxing employee benefits.

At the same time, the administration clearly hopes that the promise of universal coverage is enough, over the long haul, to hold another important chunk of the base: those who support a system of national health insurance run by the government and financed with taxes, like Canada's. (About a third of the House Democrats signed on to a bill that would establish such a system.) The Clinton draft also says individual states may establish state-run systems if they so choose.

Efforts to defuse the most dangerous potential opponents have accounted for some of the plan's most intricate politics. For example, assuring doctors that a fee-for-service option—the traditional system of allowing people to see any doctor and pay on the basis of each service rendered—would be an explicit part of the plan "made it possible to have a serious dialogue with the AMA," said one of the President's political advisers. Dr. James Todd, executive vice president of the American Medical Association, said that the plan being circulated in September 1993 was a good first draft, although "it has some things that we're going to be very stubborn about." Among them, Dr. Todd said, are the controls on insurance premiums and other efforts to cap health spending.

For all the careful interest group maneuvering, though, the administration's political advisers tried to keep the middle-class audience in mind. A broad-based tax increase was floated early on by some administration officials, but ultimately abandoned especially because of the budget debate, in which the Republicans succeeded in presenting the Democrats as back to their old habits of taxing and spending. Keeping the benefits package as generous as possible was also a crucial part of this strategy. "If this was not comprehensive, the middle class would ultimately not see its interests tied up with this reform," said Stan Greenberg, the President's pollster.

All of this, of course, will rest on the administration's financing projections, on its ability to control spending and to make all these individual trade-offs add up. It will also depend on people getting beyond the sheer magnitude of the plan and figuring out what is in it for them. "It's a politically smart plan if you can get people to understand the specifics, if you can get each audience to really bear down and understand the details," said a Democratic strategist in the Senate. "It's a politically tough plan from the standpoint that, on the surface, it's dense and complex and hard to figure out." [RT]

CONSUMER CONCERNS

FOR the 37 million Americans who now lack health insurance, and the tens of millions more who may find themselves without it in the next few years when they lose or change jobs, the appeal of the Clinton proposal is obvious: guaranteed coverage regardless of employment status, age, or illness. But the majority of Americans who are already decently insured and happy with their own doctors may have a harder time deciding about their own prospects.

The administration's goal is to reorganize the way health care is paid for and delivered so that nearly everyone would be better off. Officials say most people would pay little, if any, more than they do now in return for generous benefits and lifelong peace of mind. By bringing order and efficiency to a chaotic system, officials say, the new system would enhance the quality of care despite stringent new limits on the growth of medical spending. Americans would continue to have a wide choice of doctors and health plans, they insist.

But the heart of the Clinton strategy for holding down medical spending is to make people acutely aware of the true cost of their health care. And that may be jarring for many Americans who have long received generous benefits at work. In the structure outlined by the White House, many people may find themselves choosing among unfamiliar new health plans and accepting new limits on their freedom to choose doctors or hospitals, or paying extra to use the system as freely as they are accustomed to. The question remains whether the lower-cost health maintenance organizations into which many people might be pushed will offer long lines and second-class medical care, as some critics fear, or efficient, prudent, top-flight care, as officials predict.

Under the Clinton proposal, everyone would be required to have health insurance and to contribute to its cost. All companies would be required to contribute for workers and their families, with the employers paying at least 80 percent of the average cost of premiums in their region and workers the remaining 20 percent. Officials estimate that the average premium would be $1,800 a year for individuals and $4,200 for families; so an employee would pay an average of $360 for individual coverage and $840 for family coverage. The self-employed and unemployed would be responsible for the entire amount, but depending on income, could be eligible for subsidies.

Individuals and most companies would no longer directly buy their own health insurance. Instead, they would sign up with large cooperatives, or regional health alliances, which would present their members with a choice of health plans that have the same basic set of benefits. These plans would be made up of groups of doctors and hospitals, often organized by insurers. A company employing at least 5,000 people could function as its own alliance or join the regional alliance.

The proposal envisions three basic kinds of plans. They are: "low cost-sharing" plans, HMOs in which patients pay $10 per office visit to affiliated doctors; "high cost-sharing" plans, which allow patients the familiar freedom to visit any doctors and health centers on a fee-for-service basis, but require families to pay a deductible of $400 and 20 percent of all subsequent bills, to a maximum of $3,000 per family per year; and "combination" plans, in which patients pay little to use affiliated doctors and more to use others.

In more populated areas, an alliance might offer several plans with varying premiums. Any patient could choose any plan; the idea is to force plans to compete for customers by offering the best price and quality. In turn, financial incentives would be used to nudge more people into the most cost-effective HMOs. Consumers choosing higher-priced plans, whether HMOs or otherwise, would have to make much larger contributions to the initial premiums than those who chose low-cost plans. And, through stiffer deductibles and co-payments, consumers would pay heavily for the ability to choose any doctor—an amount, officials say, that fairly represents the extra cost of unmanaged care. Thus, while many Americans might be able to choose plans that cost them little more than they have paid in the past for comparable or better benefits, others might find themselves spending much more to keep the same freedoms they have enjoyed.

One of the hottest issues raised by the Clinton proposal is freedom to choose one's doctor. Critics attack the plan as restricting choice, while the White House says it will be opening more choices to Americans. Both are right. More than 41 million Americans are already in HMOs. But to the extent that more Americans feel pushed against their preference into HMOs, they will face new limits. These groups usually allow a choice of primary physician among affiliated doctors, but patients must go through this "gatekeeper" to visit specialists, who must also be in the group.

Critics raise the specter of chronically ill patients ripped from a trusted doctor. This might happen, but the chances would be reduced if virtually all doctors sign up with health plans, as the proposal envisages. Administration officials also point out that large numbers of Americans do not now enjoy the hallowed freedom of choice. Some 37 million are uninsured and the 30 million people of Medicaid, the program for the poor, often have trouble finding decent care. Many residents of rural areas and inner cities have few choices already. And a growing number of workers are offered only a single HMO by their employers.

Health maintenance organizations save money not only by negotiating lower fees with doctors, hospitals, and other suppliers but also by scrutinizing medical decisions and discouraging wasteful, costly services. At best, this could produce fine care and weed out useless and harmful procedures. At worst, doctors' groups and HMOs would be tempted to scrimp on costly but useful care, jeopardizing health, and on personnel and equipment, producing long waits. Administration officials say their proposal would insure high-quality care. As they make their annual selection of health plans, consumers would vote with their feet, shunning plans that perform poorly. Equally important, according to the proposal, a national program would develop ways to measure the quality of care offered by health plans. Annual performance reports, covering both consumer satisfaction and medical indicators for all health plans, would be made available to consumers, which officials say would create a higher level of public knowledge and accountability than now exists in the health system. But critics question how consumers can adequately compare medical performance.

A crucial longer term issue of medical quality is ignored in the White House draft proposal. Over time, the system would set sharp limits on the growth in medical spending, holding by fiat, if the marketplace does not do it, the average premium increases around the country to the general inflation rate, adjusted for population growth. In contrast, medical costs have recently risen at more than three times the inflation rate.

The theory is that the current system carries so much waste—in duplicated technology and facilities, in unneeded medical procedures, in use of unnecessarily costly drugs or procedures, in profiteering and fraud—that huge amounts of spending can be wrung out over time without impairing care. But some new costs also reflect advances in medical technology that reduce suffering and disease, advances that will continue at a furious pace.

At some point, many experts believe, the demand for useful forms of care could press against cost controls, forcing a kind of rationing that few Americans support. Others think that efficiency gains could stave off such bitter choices for many years at least, but agree that at some point the nation may have to come to grips with divisive issues of medical limits. This is not a debate the White House wants to foster. [EE]

THE WARY STATE PARTNERS

PRESIDENT Clinton's health plan creates a mind-boggling array of new duties for the fifty states, which would be responsible for carrying out Mr. Clinton's promise to guarantee insurance coverage for all Americans. Health care experts say a handful of states, like New York, New Jersey, Hawaii, Minnesota, Vermont, and Washington, have established innovative programs to control costs and expand insurance coverage. But, they say, it is unclear whether other states have the political commitment or technical expertise to arrange insurance for all their residents by July 1997, as Mr. Clinton would require. Under the President's plan, all Americans would be entitled to a comprehensive package of health benefits, one that states could not reduce.

Toby S. Edelman, a lawyer at the National Senior Citizens Law Center, said, "Our experience is that states are not eager to be in the forefront of any health program that costs them money. They will kick and scream about federal regulation, but many do not act until forced to do so by the federal government." While states would take on much responsibility and be given many new powers over medicine and business, state officials say they will not have all the authority or flexibility they need. States could provide benefits beyond those in the standard package, but state officials say most states will stay with this package. As a result, there would be much more uniformity in the nation than in the current patchwork of private health insurance and Medicaid programs, which vary widely.

James D. Bentley, senior vice president of the American Hospital Association, said that hospital executives were worried about some of the new powers Mr. Clinton's plan would give to the states. For example, he said, only state-certified health plans could care for large numbers of patients. States would set the criteria that health plans must meet to be certified, and the states would appear to have enormous freedom in setting these criteria. Under the Clinton plan, Mr. Bentley said, "there is no constraint on what a state can require" of health plans.

Stan Dorn, who has represented poor people as a lawyer at the National Health Law Program, said he feared that "under the President's plan, states may be given freedom to terminate Medicaid benefits beyond those covered in the standard package." For example, he said, many states now cover dental care and eyeglasses for adults and would apparently not be required to continue doing so.

Specifically, the Clinton plan, as described by administration officials and White House documents, would give states these expanded responsibilities:

• To establish one or more regional health alliances, which could be state agencies or private nonprofit corporations, to buy insurance coverage for their residents. The states would draw the boundaries of the alliances and would have to make sure that "all eligible individuals," including homeless people, drug addicts, and residents of remote areas, enroll in a regional alliance. Mr. Clinton does not say how states are to accomplish this.

• To certify health plans, the networks of doctors, hospitals and insurance companies that care for most Americans. Only state-certified health plans would be allowed to provide insurance and benefits to members of the regional alliances. States must guarantee that at least one health plan is available in every part of every state, even where no health plan applies for this privilege.

• To set and enforce financial standards for health plans to make sure they do not run out of money. If a health plan goes bankrupt, the state would take control of its assets, provide continuous coverage for consumers, and pay claims with money from a state guaranty fund. The federal government would enforce a national budget for all health spending, but states would bear the financial risk if the limits are so tight that health plans fail.

• To regulate private health insurance premiums "when necessary to meet budget requirements" or to guarantee the solvency of a health plan.

• To pay subsidies to help poor people and small businesses buy health insurance. Federal and state money would be used for this purpose.

• To collect huge amounts of data needed to measure and compare the quality of care provided by health plans within their borders.

• To run a new program providing long-term home care to people with severe disabilities. States would pay 5 percent to 25 percent of the total cost, estimated at $68 billion over five years.

Governors say Congress will probably not grant states all the discretion proposed by Mr. Clinton. Members of Congress responsible for health policy, like Representatives Henry A. Waxman and Pete Stark, both Democrats from California, tend to distrust the states and have, in recent years, written highly detailed federal laws specifying what states must do to care for low-income people, nursing home residents, pregnant women and children.

Lawmakers from both parties predict that Congress will, by the end of next year, pass a scaled-down version of the plan Mr. Clinton presented. But the legislation is only the first step. The federal government will have to issue dozens of regulations translating any new law into terms that can be applied to doctors, hospitals, clinics, and insurance companies. And every state will need to pass legislation filling in details of the federal framework.

Many elements of the Clinton plan are already being tried by states. In Washington state, a new law provides that all residents shall have access to a uniform package of health benefits by 1998. Minnesota is setting statewide and regional limits on health spending. New Jersey is requiring insurers to offer coverage to small groups. New York has been a leader in regulating insurance premiums to prohibit discrimination against people with medical problems. In Florida, a new law creates eleven community health purchasing alliances to provide coverage to small employers.

Mr. Clinton's proposal would open a new chapter in the history of federal-state relations, placing huge new obligations upon the states to run a social welfare program that would dwarf Social Security in terms of money. While poor people worry that their needs may be neglected, state officials, for their part, fear that the Clinton plan may duplicate a fundamental problem of Medicaid: the proliferation of federal mandates without enough federal money to pay for them.

Mr. Clinton, a former governor of Arkansas, proposes to give states a large degree of flexibility. A state could, if it chose, set uniform rates for all doctors and hospitals. Nevertheless, many governors say they fear that the health care system would be too highly centralized. Some of the new state powers envisioned by Mr. Clinton are politically explosive. For example, states, with permission from the federal government, could require elderly Medicare beneficiaries to join the regional health alliances. States could also tax big corporations that run their own health plans outside the alliances. Mr. Clinton would also require states to "maintain current levels of financial support for the Medicaid program." But the administration has not decided exactly how to define and enforce this requirement.

Even though states would get sweeping new powers under Mr. Clinton's plan, the latest version of the proposal does not explicitly require public participation in state decision-making. Mr. Bentley of the American Hospital Association said, "We want to be sure there is a public process that allows hospitals to comment as states take action. We worry that these decisions may become back-room deals." For example, he said, states could conceivably require that health plans have a minimum enrollment, have certain types of people on their governing boards, or have large financial reserves. These requirements, he said, could put some hospitals or doctors out of business. [RP]

RESHAPING THE MEDICAL BUSINESS

I F the health care proposals of the Clinton Administration become law, they would throw into fast forward trends that are already reshaping the fates of doctors, hospitals, and the insurance companies that pay them. Doctors would win a victory that leading medical organizations like the American Medical Association have long sought: guaranteed insurance coverage for tens of millions of the uninsured. But physicians would find that, under the plan, they would have even less autonomy than they do now. The market, under the plan, could be expected to force doctors to find patients by signing up with health care networks run by insurance companies and health maintenance organizations. Even when they treat patients who are not members of such networks, they would be required to charge them according to a schedule of fees approved by regulators for every service, the type of arrangement that has applied to Medicare and Medicaid.

The impact of the plan would probably be just as great on the hospital industry. As hospitals and treatment centers are drawn into managed care networks, they, too, would be put under ever-growing pressure to cut costs. Experts say the Clinton program would probably speed the pace at which such institutions are already shutting down wards, merging with other hospitals, or closing their doors. In addition, the plan says teaching hospitals would be forced to stop turning out so many highly paid specialists and to redirect their efforts to training lower-paid primary-care physicians. And the plan is expected to bring changes in the medical marketplace that would force a significant number of specialists to retrain.

Some of the most drastic changes, however, would be seen in the health insurance industry. Most of the nation's five hundred or so health insurers are expected to be driven out of the field, and among the likely beneficiaries would be the five giants of industry—Prudential, Cigna, Aetna, Travelers, and Metropolitan Life—as well as the more than seventy Blue Cross and Blue Shield plans. The draft proposal offers a bit of relief to insurance companies that sell workers' compensation and automobile insurance. The Clinton plan would merge the $40 billion in medical coverage now offered by workers' compensation and automobile policies into standard health-care plans. But it assures property-casualty insurance companies that now sell such coverage that they will be allowed to stay in those lines of business by providing their coverage through the alliances.

What ties together the future of all sorts of medical providers, doctors, hospitals, health maintenance organizations, pharmacies, and laboratories is the requirement under the Clinton plan that Americans receive their health coverage through the yet-to-be-created purchasing groups. These health alliances, region by region, perhaps metropolitan area by metropolitan area, will tell insurers and health maintenance organizations what minimum requirements they must meet before they will be allowed to offer coverage to the public.

By assuring that all Americans have complete medical insurance coverage, the government is guaranteeing that millions more patients and tens of billions more dollars will flow into doctors' offices. In addition, by permitting the 30 million people who are now covered by Medicaid to be covered by the alliances, the Clinton administration would create legions of patients who are suddenly more lucrative to treat. But the plan also spells out major constraints on doctors. Insurers could still offer the traditional type of insurance that lets a doctor bill for each procedure performed. Since such plans are expected to be by far the most expensive, however, experts predict that the vast majority of consumers will choose managed-care plans. As a result, doctors searching for patients will find themselves joining managed-care plans as well, as many already have even without national reforms.

Such plans vary greatly, but one common element for doctors is that they have to agree to work under the rules of an insurance company or a health maintenance organization that closely supervises how much care and what kind of procedures should be given. In addition, they are often paid by a system designed to motivate doctors to think twice before they go ahead with expensive and time-consuming procedures. Under this "capitation" system, an insurer might offer a doctor a fixed fee for treating a hundred patients. If the patients need less care than the average for such a group, the doctor makes more profit, but if the group needs more care than the average, the expense comes from the doctor's pocket. Doctors may decide to join one of many such networks, but executives in some of the nation's largest health insurance companies say that over time, they expect more and more doctors to affiliate with a single plan.

In some specialized fields that now have many practitioners in a given area, like cardiologists or neurosurgeons, there may not be enough spaces in networks for all the doctors. The result may be that many such highly trained and well-paid physicians will have to retrain in a lower-paying field of primary-care medicine to be able to join a network and get patients.

Much of the nation's hospital industry has already been shaken in the past five years by the need to get rid of excess beds and lower their costs. As hospitals, too, find that they have to affiliate with managed-care networks, the process will certainly speed up. The administration suggests easing regulations in an effort to encourage hospitals to merge.

The Clinton plan also suggests a five-year phase-in period in which academic hospitals would try to decrease the number of specialists they train. The goal would be to increase the proportion of primary-care physicians they train to 50 percent of the new doctors. The plan suggests achieving that goal by reducing the financing of specialty training programs.

But Dr. William T. Speck, the president and chief executive officer of Columbia Presbyterian Medical Center in New York City, said that changing the financing of residency programs alone would not be enough. He said the average medical student graduates with tens of thousands of dollars of debt and would not be attracted to lower-paying fields. "There is now not enough incentive to bring doctors into primary care," he said.

For the nation's $300 billion health insurance industry the future is one of transformation. The vast majority of the hundreds of health insurance companies in the United States offer the old-fashioned fee-for-service plans. Those plans are already losing customers to managed care networks, and under the alliance system, economists say, most would have to leave the business entirely. What would remain, health economists predict, would be a smaller number of HMOs, insurance health plans, and similar networks run by doctors and hospitals in every medical market supervised by an alliance. In urban areas, experts say, it could be as many as fifteen or more, in more rural areas, perhaps one or two.

Those most likely to survive and flourish are networks that signed up physicians, hospitals, and other providers early. In dozens of markets many local HMOs and groups of hospitals or physicians have banded together to form networks of their own and many of these smaller players may grow in their individual markets under the Clinton plan. In addition, analysts say some multistate HMOs like Kaiser Permanente and U.S. Healthcare are well positioned to grow.

But experts say that among insurance companies the five biggest players, led by Cigna and Prudential, are most likely to flourish nationally. Each of them, along with Blue Cross and Blue Shield plans, have made large capital investments and already signed up large numbers of doctors and hospitals in dozens of regions around the country. Their market share, analysts say, appears destined to grow if the Clinton plan passes. Not surprisingly, the five biggest insurers have broken away from their smaller competitors to form an insurance lobbying group in Washington that is working for the administration's proposals. [PK]

SHIFTING THE CORPORATE
BURDENS

P RESIDENT Clinton's plan for reshaping the health care
system would cause a vast shift in financial burdens among
American corporations. Health costs would ease for companies,
most of them manufacturers, that now offer generous benefits,
and rise for those that do not, among them not only small neighborhood shops but also corporate giants like Wal-Mart, Sears,
and Wendy's. How those burdens would be reapportioned
emerges from a look at insurance costs and prospects at four
companies representing the variety of corporate experiences:
Ford Motor Company, an older manufacturer; Apple Computer,
a young high-tech company; Lehigh Valley Racquet and Fitness
Centers, a small Pennsylvania business that uses part-time in-
structors; and Manpower Inc., the nation's biggest supplier of
temporary workers.

Once the President's plan is in place, "the variation in burdens
among firms is going to be much less," said Paul Starr, a senior
White House adviser and an architect of the plan. For Ford, the
Clinton plan holds out great promise of slowing the steady rise
in the company's health care expenses. At last, Ford says, it will
not have to pay a disproportionate share of the nation's medical
bills, in effect picking up payments to treat the indigent and the
uninsured. What the company really wants, though, is to shift to

the government its huge outlay for retirees' health care, and the White House has not yet said how it would handle that issue.

Apple, another big manufacturer, also looks favorably on the Clinton plan, which would set a national standard for health insurance that would cost the company less than it now pays for the same, or better, coverage. But Manpower and Lehigh Valley Racquet are worried. Lehigh Valley Racquet pays nothing for its part-time employees' health coverage, and Manpower pays very little for its temporary workers. Under the Clinton plan, each company would have to contribute for each of those employees. Lehigh Valley Racquet, among other companies, is strongly lobbying against any health plan that would give the government a larger role.

The uninsured employees at Lehigh Valley Racquet and at Manpower are among the nearly 48 million workers—nearly 40 percent of all employed Americans—who hold jobs at companies that do not offer them health insurance, according to the Employee Benefit Research Institute in Washington. While some of those workers are at small companies that say they cannot afford to give benefits to anyone, the majority are part-time employees, temporary workers, and contract workers at giant corporations as well as neighborhood businesses.

A great majority of these workers are in fact insured, under a spouse's or parent's policy or a personal policy. The Clinton plan would have all employers share the cost of insuring their workers and their families, no matter what other arrangements an employee might have. At present, Ford often pays for health insurance for the family of a worker, although the worker's spouse might have a job at a Wal-Mart or a Manpower. Under the Clinton plan, Ford's obligation would be reduced, while the spouse's employer would have to help pay for the family's coverage.

To hold down rising costs, Ford is slowly drawing its workers to plans that are less expensive than the company's traditional fee-for-service coverage, in which a worker goes to a doctor of his choice and the Ford health plan pays the bill, whatever it might be. The less expensive plans, preferred provider networks or health maintenance organizations, in effect require workers to use groups of doctors and hospitals with whom the company has negotiated set fees. Even with the migration to networks, Ford is paying more for health care—$5,000 on average for each active and retired worker in 1992—than the Clinton plan would require for its standardized coverage, which is less comprehensive than Ford's. What's more, while the Clinton plan would require an employer to pay at least 80 percent of the insurance premiums of its workers, Ford now picks up the entire bill, using a standard negotiated with the United Auto Workers. But the Clinton plan sets only a minimum employer obligation, and such negotiated company benefits would continue.

When it comes to retirees, Ford has a problem. Apple Computer and many other nonunion companies founded in recent decades have no retirees yet, and no intention of giving them health insurance when they materialize. Ford, on the other hand, has 125,000 retirees, a number almost as large as the company's active work force of 145,000. And all have the same coverage as the active workers. Nothing seems to strike Robert L. Ozment, Ford's director of corporate and employee insurance, as more important than lowering, or eliminating, the cost of retiree health care, which is currently more than $600 million a year, or 40 percent of Ford's total health cost. "Any company that is successful for many years and provides health care for its growing corps of retirees is at a competitive disadvantage," Mr. Ozment said. And then he expressed a fervent hope: "We think that Clinton should do what other countries do: anyone unemployed or uninsured, including retirees, should get health coverage fully paid from general tax revenues."

Such an arrangement would hold not only for retirees under sixty-five, who now are fully covered by a company-paid medical plan at Ford, but also those sixty-five and older who qualify for Medicare and also receive a company-sponsored supplemental policy. The Clinton plan offers some relief, offering to help pay insurance costs for retirees under sixty-five and ineligible for

Medicare, covering 38,000 of Ford's retirees. For older retirees on Medicare, it would add a new prescription drug benefit, relieving Ford of a big current cost, as it provides supplemental insurance to its retirees on Medicare. "We would favor that, absolutely," Mr. Ozment said. But a full takeover of all retiree health costs has not been proposed.

Ford is also happy with Clinton proposals to reduce the cost of health care generally. Mr. Ozment endorses provisions that would limit malpractice claims and set national standards for treating specific ailments to help eliminate excess care and overcharging. "We think Ford has done well in controlling costs," Mr. Ozment said, "but our rate of cost increase is still 8 percent a year, and that is more than double the inflation rate."

One way to cut this growth rate further, Mr. Ozment said, is to reduce the cost of hospital construction, an outlay that ends up in Ford's health bill. Mr. Ozment, for example, would like to prevent construction of a new hospital in Pontiac, Michigan, which already has three hospitals and not enough patients to fill them. Nevertheless, one hospital, occupying an old building, is planning a new structure, despite the efforts of Ford and other companies to stop the project. "The construction cost will show up as higher hospital charges to care for Ford workers, and eventually, higher costs for our health insurance," Mr. Ozment said.

The big effort at Apple has been to reduce the cost of company-sponsored health insurance for its 8,000 American workers. With the cost of premiums rising 18 percent a year, the computer company announced in 1987 that instead of having only one form of insurance, its employees would be able to choose from four types of plans, each involving a different cost to the employees themselves and different levels of coverage.

"We proceeded gradually," said Sally Gottlieb, benefits manager at Apple. "We did not jack up charges overnight. By 1989, the difference between the most expensive and least expensive plans was only $300 in annual premium cost to the employee.

That was not enough, so we have changed the pricing to represent different values. Now the difference is $800."

Like most companies, Apple had relied for years on a fee-for-service health plan that paid 80 percent or more of medical costs after the employee and his or her family covered an annual deductible. The company now also offers two preferred provider networks in which employees are charged only small amounts for care, once an annual deductible is covered, as long as they stay within their networks. Apple also does business with three health maintenance organizations, or HMOs, which in effect provide full medical and hospital care at a fixed annual premium per employee.

HMOs offer the best opportunity for Apple to control costs. But the company, like most of corporate America, has been reluctant to force its employees into the cheapest plan. While 19 percent of Apple workers have joined an HMO, 49 percent have chosen once of the preferred provider plans. Partly as a result, the increase in Apple's annual health care costs fell to 12 percent in 1992 and 10 percent so far in 1993, Ms. Gottlieb said. While that represents an improvement over past years, it remains a much steeper rise than the President's plan calls for.

The Clinton plan might also help Apple lower costs. A number of Apple employees—the company will not say how many—have working spouses but get their entire family coverage through Apple, driving up the company's total costs. In the formula the White House proposes for handling two-earner families, a spouse's employer would also have to pay, with each employer contributing something less than the 80 percent of a premium. The family pays its share of the premium, 20 percent of the total if they choose and average-priced plan, only once.

Apple now pays $3,600 a year, on average, for each worker's coverage, more than the Clinton approach would require. The Apple plan is somewhat more generous in doctor and hospital coverage than the Clinton minimum standard, and that raises the possibility that Apple could gradually adjust its health coverage to the federal standard. Or the company could keep paying for extras, to maintain health insurance as a recruiting lure. "These options are too speculative to consider now," Ms. Gottlieb said.

For John F. Brinson, president of Lehigh Valley Racquet, costs would rise by what he considered an unbearable amount if Mr. Clinton's plan was adopted. He distinguished between voluntarily deciding to let his 121 part-time employees participate in the company's plan at their expense—a step he said he would consider—and being ordered to do so by the government and at rates mandated by the government. "I would not mind if the government said, 'All right, we think employers have to make health coverage available to their employees,'" Mr. Brinson said. "I can live with that. But they can't come in and tell me how much I have to pay for it."

Forty people work full-time at the company's fitness centers in Allentown and Bethlehem; they are the administrators, clerks, and maintenance workers. For each, Mr. Brinson pays $1,200 a year toward the cost of his company's group policies, either fee for service or HMO. Each of the forty pays the rest of the premium, which averages $415 a year for single coverage and $3,882 for a family.

The company's plan offers more coverage to his core staff, Mr. Brinson said, than the Clinton plan does. But at government-mandated premiums of $2,300 for family coverage, Mr. Brinson would almost double his cost for employees with families, while adding $600 a year for those who are single. "It would not be fair to pay more for a married person than a single person," he said. "Most companies disagree with me on that point; they think married people are better employees. I don't think that is true." Only ten of his full-time staff members are married.

Many of his full-time employees earn less than $24,000 a year, and below that level the government, under the Clinton plan, would subsidize part of the premium expense. Such subsidies would also apply to the part-time employees, since their average pay is only $7 an hour. A part-time employee would have to earn $15 an hour to disqualify the company for the subsidy. Without the subsidy, Mr. Brinson would find himself paying an extra 50¢ an hour to cover employees earning $7 an hour; with it, the government would pick up half of that amount. This would help, he said, but the subsidy is also an incentive to hold down wages to qualify for the government aid.

Mr. Brinson insisted that any additional company expense for health insurance—subsidized or not—could not be offset by charging his customers more. "In this weak economy, our members are very sensitive to price," he said. "I don't mind being required to make coverage available to part-timers. But they should pay the entire cost."

Mr. Brinson's first reaction to published details of the Clinton plan was to declare that he would dismiss all of his part-time employees and replace them with forty or fifty full-time workers, even though he said that would be less efficient than the present system. But a few days later, he suggested he would keep the part-time workers. Mr. Brinson is speculating about ways to absorb the cost. Perhaps, he suggested, he can cancel raises, which have averaged 3 percent a year. "The marketplace will figure out a way to make this as painless as possible," he said. "But I can't raise my prices."

No one would benefit more from the Clinton plan than the nation's nearly two million temporary workers, people who sign up with agencies like Manpower, which in turn rents them to work for a day or for weeks as secretaries, clerks, administrators, and factory workers. The rate covers the wage for the temp— averaging $8.50 an hour—plus a sum paid to the government for workers' compensation, in case the employee is injured, plus an amount to cover Manpower's costs and profit. The temporary agencies will now have to add another sum for health insurance.

"It is devastating economics," said Douglas Long, director of compensation and benefits at Norrell Services, an Atlanta-based temp agency. "Ultimately it will force us to raise our rates by 7 to 9 percent." Mitchell Fromstein, Manpower's chairman, is more sanguine, saying, "We are supporting the reform effort, as we know it so far."

Like Lehigh Valley Racquet, Manpower pays all or most of the cost of the health insurance that it makes available to its 6,000 permanent employees. But the temps get no help, except for a small percentage of them who work 400 hours over ten weeks. If they continue after that, Manpower will pay half the premium of a company policy.

Mr. Fromstein bases his optimism on three points. First, he said, all the temporary-help companies faced roughly the same new costs, so their rental rates would rise by similar amounts. In addition, under the Clinton plan, some of the cost of health insurance for low-wage temps will be subsidized by the government, even at profitable companies like Manpower. Finally, Mr. Fromstein said he hoped that hoped the administration would reduce his cost for workers' compensation. While the Clinton plan would not take over the costs of treating workplace injuries, it would bring the treatment provided under workers' compensation into the system of managed care.

But Mr. Fromstein is lobbying for folding all costs of medical treatment under workers' compensation into the federal health insurance program. "It does not make any sense to have a health care plan and not cover in it the medical portion of workers' compensation," he said. [LU]

HOW MUCH IS ENOUGH?

PRESIDENT Clinton's proposed ceiling on the future growth in medical spending has emerged as one of the most hotly contested aspects, prompting warnings of a degradation in the quality of care or even rationing. To brake medical spending as sharply the President proposes—cutting annual growth to less than half its recent rate—could force strapped medical groups to shortchange patients, denying them useful tests and treatments, maintain some doctors and insurance executives. These are groups that also fear for their own incomes and profits under the plan, but their warnings are echoed by many economists too.

Nonsense, reply administration officials and many medical experts who portray an American system so replete with inefficiency, duplication, overcharging, and overuse of procedures that huge sums can safely be squeezed out for many years to come. Right now, health care consumes 14 percent of the gross national product, up from 10 percent in 1981. In the Clinton plan, spending would be allowed to bulge in the next three years as the uninsured were covered, reaching 17 percent of the economy, then would remain at that share for years to come. Without the Clinton reforms, government experts predict, spending in the year 2000 would reach 19 percent of the national product—with tens of millions still uncovered—and would keep climbing.

"When an American physician tells you that at 17 percent of the GNP we'll have to ration, that seems bizarre on its face," said Uwe E. Reinhardt, a health economist at Princeton University and an expert on European health systems that spend far less than the American one. But he added: "The issue is the speed of the slowdown in spending, not the ultimate level." If the desired transition to a system dominated by lean, efficient health maintenance organizations is too rocky in some regions or does not incorporate proper safeguards for consumers, he said, he can foresee "bad outcomes here and there, rationing in effect."

Even as some critics warn about pressures to scrimp on needed care, others fault the President for avoiding more explicit discussion of medical priorities, of the need to start making hard choices amid an unending flow of new, costly technologies that could drain society's resources. Advocates of planned rationing like Daniel Callahan, director of the nonprofit Hastings Center in Briarcliff Manor, New York, which studies medical ethics, even say the President's plan may be too generous. "I feel that 17 percent of the economy is absolutely excessive," he said, and would rob other important social needs such as education and investment in jobs for trivial gains in health.

Even many doctors say that the country should find a way to curb hugely expensive intensive care for patients with slight chance of survival. But White House officials, facing a tortuous political fight on health care already, do not want to provoke debate on such divisive questions. The medical structure they have proposed for the country—with doctor and hospital groups providing care under fixed annual budgets—is designed to help weed out senseless treatment. But officials insist that talk of overt rationing of helpful care is premature.

Mr. Clinton seeks to halt the spiral in medical spending by encouraging stiffer market competition and, if that fails, imposing mandatory controls that would keep health costs in line with expansion of the economy. Under the President's proposals, American medical spending would continue to dwarf that of other industrial countries with high medical standards. In 1991, the latest year for which international data are available, health spending accounted for more than 13 percent of the American economy. It accounted for 10 percent in Canada, for 9 percent in France and Germany and for 7 percent in Japan and the United Kingdom. Most other countries have controls in place that will keep spending from rising much above the 10 percent range, if that.

Paul Starr, a senior White House advisor and an architect of the Clinton proposal, said large savings would come through reduced administrative costs and a large-scale shift of consumers, prodded by the new financial incentives, toward health plans that provide good care for less. Starr predicted that competition among medical groups, something already happening in parts of the country, will keep spending in most regions below the proposed caps anyway, but that "it's also important to create certain expectations about spending." He added: "I don't think that 17 percent of the GNP is all that tight. We have been through a period of enormous growth in health costs, and I think we have built up a huge cushion of inefficiency."

The White House view is supported by Dr. David M. Lawrence, chief executive of Kaiser Permanente in Oakland, California, the nation's largest and oldest HMO and a model for the medical groups that would be encouraged by the Clinton plan. "Our position is that the way to live under the proposed constraints is through improving the quality of care," said Dr. Lawrence, whose nonprofit company serves 6.6 million patients in sixteen states. "You can only do that so long before you finally reach the limits," he said, "but I'd suggest that the American health care system isn't even close."

The best HMOs are trimming costs while if anything improving care, experts say, by negotiating lower prices for goods and even organ transplants, by stressing preventive measures and by carefully studying how their doctors make decisions. For example, when studies show a cheaper drug is just as effective as a costlier one, the group informs its doctors and asks those who prescribe the expensive one to justify it.

HMOs use more primary care doctors who provide most care and serve as "gatekeeper" to costly specialists, which not only holds down bills but also reduces the level of unneeded surgery and other procedures. As an indication of the potential savings, Dr. Lawrence of Kaiser and other executives point to research like that of Dr. John E. Wennberg of Dartmouth Medical School, which has found huge variations in surgery rates around the country with little impact on patient welfare.

Applying these methods aggressively since 1990, a year when its costs jumped by 15 percent, Kaiser had premium increases in 1992 of 9.6 percent and in 1993 of 6.8 percent, well below the double-digit numbers still seen in fee-for-service plans. "We're on a very steep learning curve in terms of understanding where all the levers are to keep improving the costs," Dr. Lawrence said. However, while managed groups like his and others are poised for rapid gains in efficiency, he said that "it is an open question" how quickly the rest of the medical system can reorganize.

David F. Simon, executive vice president of U.S. Healthcare, a for-profit HMO based in Bluebell, Pennsylvania, that serves 1.5 million patients in the Northeast, said that a broad transition to managed care, using methods like those described by Dr. Lawrence, could reduce total medical spending quickly and dramatically—"We'd estimate in the 15 to 20 percent range, perhaps even more." But Simon said his company was concerned about "an overlay of bureaucratic and regulatory controls" in the proposal that would hamper competition. "I don't think you'll see the kind of savings they are projecting," he said, and "if the budget caps kick in, a by-product could be the need to ration care, or cut back on benefits."

If traditional fee-for-service medicine offers financial incentives to do too much, prepaid plans have an incentive to minimize treatment, raising fears that patients could be shortchanged. Leaders like Dr. Lawrence and Simon insist that their companies would lose over time only if they allowed small problems in their patients to grow into big ones. But some groups reward individual doctors directly for ordering fewer tests and referrals, and a financially troubled for-profit organization could take a short-term view of patient welfare, warns Dr. Arnold S. Relman, editor emeritus of *The New England Journal of Medicine*. The White House thinks that publication of data about the performance of each health plan and about the incentives each offers its doctors will help consumers protect themselves; plans that scrimp will lose customers. Dr. Relman would go further, strongly encouraging not-for-profit HMOs run by salaried doctors and patients rather than the investor-owned medical plans that are proliferating.

Economists like Joseph Newhouse of Harvard University argue that given the steady march of useful, expensive medical technologies, any spending limit will necessarily involve sacrifices over time, which should be admitted and discussed. But Dr. Relman counters that "no one has any idea what would happen to the forces causing costs to rise if we had a better system." Currently, he noted, all the financial incentives for development and use of new technologies encourage high prices and overuse. The argument that progress will inevitably drive up costs, he said, "makes an unwarranted assumption that there is a blind, uncritical introduction of new technology with no savings as a result."

Whether they would actually reduce the nation's medical spending, as Callahan proposes, or simply call for future planning, many ethicists say the country must decide when to withhold expensive care or technologies. Some of the most dramatic examples experts point to involve expenditures in the hundreds of thousands of dollars during the earliest or latest days of life: saving extremely premature babies who have high chance of severe disability even if they survive, or putting patients with advanced cancer, for example, on life-support systems to gain months of extra life at best.

But some experts, including Reinhardt of Princeton, think it is unlikely that a national political body could ever resolve such wrenching life-and-death issues. To some degree, the medical structure offered by the White House may take care of these issues implicitly, he observes. "That's the beauty" of a system of medical groups working within fixed budgets, he said. "It hides the rationing, makes it ad hoc, keeps in the obscurity of the HMO." Provided the right guidelines and ethical controls were in place and doctors were not being rewarded directly for cheating patients, he said, "it could be a good thing." [EE]

CLINTON'S GAMBLE

T HE Clinton administration's health care plan is imposing, not just in its intricacy and command of detail but also in its political audacity, which history may judge as courageous or reckless. The program would stir up and reorganize the medical business and shake up imperfect but familiar relationships, from those in family doctors' waiting rooms to those in the corridors of Congress. It would also promise security for individuals and deficit control for the country. It would try to do all this when the public's trust in the government is near a low point and when Congress is divided by partisanship.

It is an enormous political undertaking. No President in decades has bet so much on a single issue. As a political gamble, it ranks with Woodrow Wilson's advocacy of the League of Nations. But Clinton is risking not only his own capital but also that of Congress. By defining health care as the most important task of his Presidency, he is making the issue a crucial test for Congress, already the least-loved branch of the government. Congress, after all, blocked the efforts of two earlier presidents, Harry S Truman and Richard M. Nixon, to institute national health insurance.

There is no way to predict how Congress will deal with this President's proposals. They reflect a number of Republican ideas, or at least ideas Republicans have found appealing. One is the attempt to control fees less by detailed government directive than by limiting insurance premiums, and thus making private enterprise do the price fixing. But there is also some significant hesitance on the Democratic side. Representative Dan Rostenkowski of Illinois, the chairman of the House Ways and Means Committee, worried in September 1993, as the President's plan was unveiled, that the administration was overconfident about the Democrats. "They are in a fog with regards to how much enthusiasm there is for health care," he said. "They are very enthusiastic and I don't see it among the members."

House Speaker Thomas S. Foley said at that time that there was a consensus "that it will be done in this Congress" by the end of 1994. Mr. Rostenkowski was less confident, saying, "Doing the job right is more important than doing the job. I don't know that we're going to finish the job" by next year.

There are plenty of obstacles, aside from important but purely local constituent concerns, like the Congressional district with an insurance company headquarters, or one with very few doctors. Republicans worry about requiring small businesses to buy their workers insurance and about excessive controls. So do conservative Democrats. Some liberal Democrats regard the plan's reliance on competing medical groups as untested, needlessly complex, and inefficient compared with a government-paid system, and they are also concerned that Medicare and Medicaid will be shorted to help pay for the system. Whether or not to pay for abortions, a word that did not appear in the 246 pages of the draft plan but was subsumed under "pregnancy-related services," promises to incite a fierce fight that will cost a final bill votes however it turns out.

Senator Edward M. Kennedy, one of the handful of veterans of earlier congressional battles on the issue, is hopeful that debate can produce "a formulation that is acceptable, or tolerable, to all the groups." He contends that "not since Medicare was enacted in 1965 have the political constellations been so clearly in the right place for fundamental health reform." The Massachusetts Democrat, the leading congressional advocate of universal health care over the last quarter century, said Mr. Clinton faced a "once-in-a-generation opportunity."

His own efforts and those of President Nixon failed in the 1970s because neither labor nor the medical industry felt the urgency that compels compromise. At that time, he said, health care cost only 6 percent of the gross national product, and private insurers were expanding coverage. Today, health care consumes 14 percent of the economy and much insurance coverage seems uncertain. Kennedy said, "You have the health business as the fastest failing business in America. Its burden on families is out of sight, measured in the cost of doctors and the cost of hospitals. And its cost to American business is out of sight. Its bureaucratic nightmare to the providers is out of sight. So the major interests in health care all demand change."

There is one very important difference in the political lineup between 1993 and the Truman administration's effort in 1949 to combat what Mr. Truman called the real costs of inadequate health care: "the shattering of family budgets, the disruption of family life, the suffering and disabilities, the permanent physical impairments left by crippling diseases and the deaths each year of tens of thousands of persons who might have lived." As Professor Richard E. Neustadt, the retired Harvard scholar of the presidency, recalled from his days working on health care in the Truman White House, "Not one single scintilla of support did we get from the big business community in 1949." Big business, whose health costs are soaring, is one of the biggest boosters of the President's approach today.

Professor Neustadt said the President would still have a hard time winning passage and argued that the emphasis on the plan as a way to reduce the deficit might just produce popular disbelief. "The man's in an awful box," he said. "But at least he's not just sitting in it." At any rate, he added: "It's an appropriate issue for the Democratic administration. Nobody should be left out in this country."

Clinton campaigned on health care legislation as essential to reducing the nation's deficit and making individuals feel secure.

In his inaugural address he lamented that "the cost of health care devastates families and threatens to bankrupt our enterprises, great and small." Among all his campaign promises, it stood out as one the public thought he could, and would, keep. And the program has been structured with a serious eye on political realities, avoiding serious new taxes, stressing competition as a way to curb costs, even skirting large trouble spots by assuring labor that workers retired before sixty-five would not lose the coverage their union contracts now provide.

Stephen E. Ambrose, the Nixon biographer at the University of New Orleans, recalled President Wilson's failure as a comparable big issue. He said there were major political risks in the Great Society program of Lyndon B. Johnson and the variety of domestic programs Mr. Nixon planned for his second term before Watergate sank him. But each involved a variety of subjects, not just one like health care. Wilson and Nixon, moreover, were taking risks in second terms, chancing history, not re-election, as Mr. Clinton is. And Mr. Johnson had an immense congressional majority that Mr. Clinton lacks. As Mr. Ambrose said of the President, "He is gambling everything on it, even his wife's reputation." [AC]

INDEX